The Gray Raiders
Volume 2

The Gray Raiders
Volume 2
Accounts of Mosby & His Raiders During the American Civil War

Reminiscences of a Mosby Guerrilla

John Munson

Mosby's Men

John H. Alexander

The Gray Raiders Volume 2
Accounts of Mosby & His Raiders During the American Civil War
Reminiscences of a Mosby Guerrilla
by John Munson
Mosby's Men
by John H. Alexander

FIRST EDITION

First published under the titles
Reminiscences of a Mosby Guerrilla
and
Mosby's Men

Leonaur is an imprint
of Oakpast Ltd

Copyright in this form © 2014 Oakpast Ltd

ISBN: 978-1-78282-351-3 (hardcover)
ISBN: 978-1-78282-352-0 (softcover)

http://www.leonaur.com

Publisher's Notes

The views expressed in this book are not necessarily those of the publisher.

Contents

Reminiscences of a Mosby Guerrilla   7
Mosby's Men   163

Reminiscences of a Mosby Guerrilla

John S. Mosby, 1906

Contents

Preface	13
The Birth of the Rangers	17
Joining the Rangers	25
How We Lived	33
The Capture of General Stoughton	45
The Fight at Miskell's Barn	56
Warrenton Junction and Catlett's Station	62
Dranesville and Elsewhere	71
A Narrow Escape	82
The Berryville Fight	88
Turning the Tables	97
A Chapter of Personalities	105
An Unpleasant Episode	117
Incidents	123
I am Captured	131
I Escape	143
Trying for Big Game	151
The Sutler	158

The Celebrated Greenback Raid	165
Glimpses of Guerrilla Life	175
"The Chief"	183
The Colonel's Serious Wounding	188
The Guerrillas' Last Fight	191
The Beginning of the End	197
The Rangers Disband	202

To My Wife
Who For Thirty Years
Has Been
My most patient and Appreciative Listener
These Stories of
Mosby's Guerrillas
Are Affectionately Dedicated

Preface

Every man in Mosby's Command had ample material of which to make an interesting story of his experiences. Some of them have contributed portions of their recollections to the writer, who has unblushingly adopted them as his own, much in the spirit in which he was wont to appropriate whatever was contributed to him by the Yankees during the war. He is positive, however, that he is welcome to use whatever matter they have sent him, for the same spirit prevails among the survivors today as when all were welcome to whatever each had in the days when they stood together to acquire it. In fact in war times the ancient doctrine of the Scottish clan prevailed in all things:

For why? Because the good old rule
Sufficeth them; the simple plan.
That they should take who have the power,
And they should keep who can.

If only a whisper could be got from some of the closed lips, or the stiffened fingers of the dead be relaxed, these pages would be enriched beyond compare with now forgotten deeds; but those gallant spirits have long ago told their stories to a Higher Critic, and I believe have met His approval. They will not be forgotten, however, in these chronicles, for there were few incidents worth recording in any story of Mosby's Command that did not include acts of uncommon bravery and valour.

In the following pages Mosby's men will sometimes be spoken of as guerrillas, and their enemies as Yankees, in the same spirit in which these terms were used during the war. Mosby's men made the word guerrilla honourable from 1863 to 1865, and no fair-minded Southerner can deny that the Union Army has made the world respect the word Yankee.

With a pardonable over-sensitiveness some of the old comrades have objected to the use of the word guerrilla, but they need not be offended nor fear disparagement; their fame is established for all time. The men who fought them know what they were; and, after all, history is built upon facts. It is enough to know their old commander never has objected to the use of the word guerrilla, for he once wrote to the author asking to have an article written for the *New York Herald* which should deal with his old negro body-servant, Aaron, and to head it, "The Nestor of Mosby's Guerrillas."

It would sound odd to a Mosby man if he habitually referred to his friends, the enemy, as the Federals or the United States troops or even the Union soldiers. He knew them in the old days as Yankees, and as such he still remembers them; and moreover they are good enough Yankees for him, and it was not his good fortune to find many cowards among them.

As far as possible I have arranged in chronological order the incidents making up the story of our career. As they have come back to me, or have been communicated to me by my comrades, I have recorded them as nearly as possible in historical sequence; and if by chance the events are not always set down in the exact order of occurrence, the essential accuracy, nevertheless, has been preserved.

No claim to historical adequacy is made for what is contained in this volume. It is the desire of the author to be just and accurate in all statements; the truth about Mosby's Command is always as interesting as fiction. Eventually a complete history of the Command will be written, and its author will be the only man capable of doing it justice; the only man who saw everything and remembers everything is John S. Mosby himself. The purpose of the author is to write the interesting reminiscence of the Command; something that will crystallise the atmosphere of patriotism and romance that enveloped these men and their deeds during the period of their action, not only for the time being, but for all future; something that will make the younger generation of men, and the boys who love to read about fighting, wish they might have lived in those stirring times to have been a part of such a daring and a merry crowd; something that may contribute to the records of the Civil War certain facts that might not otherwise be preserved.

It is to be hoped that this volume will give to future generations a glimpse of the character that made it possible for John S. Mosby, the greatest and most daring "Raider" this country has ever known, to organise, command, and lead to innumerable victories, the men and boys who became world-famous as "Mosby's Guerrillas."

Acknowledgment is hereby made to the editors of *Munsey's Magazine* for their courtesy in allowing the author to use, as a small portion of the present work, and in another form, the substance of a brief series of articles published in that periodical in 1904.

Washington D.C.
June 28 - 1904.

Mr. Jno: W. Manson:
 Dear Manson
  I have your letter saying that you had engaged to write some War reminiscences. From your intimate relations with my battalion to wh. you belonged & your experience as a soldier from its organization to the close of the war you ought to be able to write some valuable & interesting history. As an actor in the scenes you will describe you can as truthfully say as Æneas did when he related to Dido the story of Troy — Quorum pars magna fui.
    Very Truly
    Jno. S. Mosby

Chapter 1

The Birth of the Rangers

There were many regiments and brigades and divisions in the Confederate armies known only by their respective commanders' names; rarely by their numbers. Our little body of men was called Mosby's Men, and Mosby's Command, and this was largely due to Mosby himself. He took great pride in speaking of us as "my men" and "my Command," but never as "my battalion," or "my troops," or "my soldiers." The Yankees referred to us, as did also the Northern papers, as guerrillas, in an opprobrious manner, of course, but the term was not applied to us in the South in any general way until after the war, when we had made the name glorious, and in time we became as indifferent to it as did the whole South to the word Rebel.

My story will cover, partially, our movements during the entire years 1863 and 1864, and that part of 1865 extending to the close of the war. I use the word, partially, because I could not hope to record all of the adventures that befell our Command in a work of much less dimensions than the *Encyclopaedia Britannica*; and then only if all the old fellows would contribute all their recollections. These were the years when the Northern and Southern armies were most industriously occupied in the conflict that seemed to grow fiercest just before it ceased.

I will endeavour to bring the reader as close to Mosby as I was during the struggle, and to relate, with as careful regard for details as is possible, the most stirring and interesting incidents which I can recall, referring but rarely to the ponderous documents that have been accumulating in Washington ever since Grant said "*Let us have Peace.*"

John S. Mosby, around whom these recollections will be woven, was born in Powhatan County, Virginia, in 1833, graduated from the University of Virginia in 1852, was admitted to the bar in 1855, and practised law in Bristol, Va., until 1861. At the breaking out of the Civil War he joined the First Virginia Regiment of Cavalry as a private and later became its adjutant, holding a lieutenant's commission. He participated in constant and strenuous service before his connection with the Partisan Rangers began. That organisation came into existence early in 1863, under a statute passed by the Confederate Congress as the Partisan Ranger Law, a statute said to have been framed by Major John Scott of Virginia, who tried unsuccessfully to put it into operation. Other commands were organised under the same act, but Mosby's was the only one, with a single exception, that survived during the entire course of the war.

In 1862 a reorganisation and consolidation of many regiments in the Southern Army took place, as graveyard gaps had to be filled up, and a number of commissioned officers were thrown out as a consequence. When Fitzhugh Lee was made colonel of the First Virginia Cavalry Regiment, Mosby resigned his commission as lieutenant and adjutant, and Lee accepted it. Finding himself once more in the ranks, he became attached to the headquarters of General J. E. B. Stuart, for whom he acted as a scout. His hour had arrived; opportunity knocked at his door and he grasped it. He knew he had found his proper sphere, and General Stuart was soon made aware of it. It was not very long before the Northern army also made the discovery.

Mosby's first notable scouting expedition—one without a parallel in the history of the war—consisted in making a circuit, entirely unaided, in the rear of General McClellan's army, which was lying in front of Richmond, in the early days of June, 1862. When Mosby proposed the daring feat to Stuart, the general at once gave it his hearty approval, for he seemed to know his man; but others made side remarks about the risk of one man's attempting such a feat and its almost certain failure.

When he returned from his expedition, during which he found it necessary to exercise all his energy and courage and ingenuity, he brought back a knowledge of the country and of the position of the enemy which enabled him safely to escort Stuart and his cavalry command over the same route. Thus it transpired that up to that time Stuart made the first and only recorded cavalry raid completely around an enemy's army; and Mosby rode in front of the column.

Mosby had no previous knowledge of the ground over which he made his first scouting expedition, and much of the route was covered in the night Federal soldiers were swarming around him in every direction and danger lurked in every step of his way. The exploit pointed out the way to his military future, and General Stuart realised, perhaps as soon as did Mosby himself, that the route of the Raider was stretching before the young Virginian who mapped out the way around McClellan's forces.

There was no more picturesque, romantic nor gallant cavalry leader; no more typical, courageous soldier on horseback in either army, than "Jeb" Stuart; but I question if he could have duplicated or even originated Mosby's scouting expedition. Mosby was not only fitted for scouting, but he developed into a remarkable leader also, a statement which I shall try to do my best to demonstrate.

Mosby's first actual Command of the Partisan Rangers began early in February, 1863, when General Stuart gave him a detail of fifteen men from his old regiment, the First Virginia Cavalry. His instructions were to take his little band into Northern Virginia and "operate inside the enemy's lines," as Stuart put it. A captain's commission was given him soon after.

The step was an irrevocable goodbye to regular army life and to camps, bugle calls, drills and picket duty. It meant the abolition of winter-quarters and the end of idleness. There were to be no more rations, clothing, boots, nor equipment from the government. Not a single round of ammunition nor a weapon for self defence. To "operate inside the enemy's lines" meant if necessary to cut off all communication with the lines that were friendly. It meant being in closer touch with Washington than Richmond, and not a man in Mosby's little band misunderstood the terrors that loomed before him. There was the earth for a couch, only the equipment with which each man started for protection, and the right to fight the enemy and, by sheer force, wrest from him the requisites with which to maintain the Command as a fighting force.

Few who saw this first handful of men move into the wilderness, singing the songs of war, ever expected any part of it to return.

It is perhaps justifiable and reasonable, at this juncture, to state that Mosby's Guerrillas were not highwaymen, bushwhackers or ruffians, and that they did not war upon any element other than that commonly recognised as the enemy. A very large percentage of them were well-bred, refined gentlemen and some of them had travelled widely; they regarded Mosby's Command as the proper channel through which to express their feelings on a subject that made action of some sort necessary. They were men of firm convictions, for which they

COLONEL MOSBY
In the uniform of a major in the Confederate States Army, to which rank he was promoted in April, 1863, after the fight at Miskell's Barn

were anxious to fight and willing to make sacrifices.

One may derive a fair impression of them by looking over the roster of those who survived the war. They will be found in the various professions in all parts of the Union; many of them leaders in social, political and commercial life. That there were a few adventurers among them there is no doubt, but as a whole they will compare favourably with any other body of men North or South. Since the war not one of them has been known to do anything to bring discredit upon the old Command.

Dr. A. Monteiro, a very prominent physician and surgeon, of Richmond, Va., who was a surgeon of Mosby's Command during the last few months of the war, says in his published memoirs:[1]

> I am enabled to say, after three years of active field service in the regular army, that I have never witnessed more true courage and chivalry, or a higher sense of honour, blended with less vice, selfishness and meanness, than I found during my official intercourse with the Partisan Rangers.

Mosby's original detail of a few men from the First Virginia Cavalry was the nucleus around which he built up the Forty-third Virginia Battalion of Cavalry, composed of eight companies at the close of the war, and at the last numbering, perhaps, six hundred men, of whom, owing to the large number constantly in prison or disabled, never more than about three hundred and fifty were available for any raid. The battalion was regularly enrolled in the Confederate Army, and was subject to the same regulations, and protected by the same laws, that applied to the army of Northern Virginia, of which it was a part. Mosby made his reports to Generals Lee and Stuart and worked in harmony with them. The particular mission of the Partisan Rangers was to keep the Confederate generals informed of the enemy's movements while "worrying and harassing" the Federal forces as much as possible.

Every man in Mosby's Command understood that he was expected to follow his commander without question, and the result was a blind unwavering faith in their leader. Mosby never asked a trooper under him to go where he would not go himself. This example spread itself and made its influence felt throughout the entire Command, and I recall an occasion where Lieutenant Ben Palmer, of Richmond,

---

1. *The Gray Raiders*—Volume 1 published by Leonaur contains *Reminiscences by the Surgeon of Mosby's Command* by Aristedes Monteiro along with *Mosby's War Reminiscences* by John S. Mosby.

Va., who was only a boy, during a fight, ordered one of the men, Bob Jarman, to get down and open a gate so we might dash through it at the enemy. The man was shot down as he touched the gate. A second man, Ben Iden, was ordered to open it, and he also suffered a similar fate. Then it was time to show, by example, what it meant to Command and to obey, and Lieutenant Palmer jumped down and opened the gate and, remounting his little grey thoroughbred, led the charge to a brilliant victory.

In after years I commented to the colonel on our invariable willingness to go where he directed, without being in any way informed of the work to be done, or the purpose or the reason for it.

"Munson," he replied, "only three men in the Confederate Army knew what I was doing or intended to do; they were Lee and Stuart and myself; so don't feel lonesome about it."

Very soon after Mosby entered upon his career as a Partisan Ranger the fame of his exploits began to spread through both the South and the North. Each day the newspapers told of this daredevil Southerner. Sutler's trains and wagon trains were raided; bridges were burned; ammunition and arms and supplies were taken; pickets disappeared as if swallowed up by the earth; scouts and stragglers from the Northern Army were plucked from the landscape by invisible hands and camps were raided and broken up. From a radius of fifty miles we began to hear of short, sharp and bloody engagements, and throughout Northern Virginia the cry echoed that "Mosby's men had been raiding" at this, and at that point. They seemed to have the power of striking at a half dozen places simultaneously.

In every Confederate regiment enlisted men began to display an interest in Mosby's movements. To be transferred to his Command from any other force in the field was almost an impossibility. Desertion from the army to him he would not permit. He recognised every claim that the regular army had on its soldiers, and punished deserters with a quick return to their regiments, if needs be under special guard. The discipline of the regular army was a law unto Mosby that was never broken.

These restrictions opened opportunities to civilians and ex-officers, so that Mosby soon found himself surrounded by the pick and bloom of the South. His recruits were some of the very best blood the Confederacy had to offer on the altar of faith. There were young fellows just coming into manhood, some of them mere boys; retired army officers anxious to return to the field; an occasional foreign soldier of fortune; a titled adventurer here and there, a hot-headed patriot just turning the shady side of life and ready as any *dervish* that ever invited Maxim bullets in the name of Mohammed to kneel down and receive death for his beliefs.

What Mosby liked best was youth. He agreed with Napoleon that boys make the best soldiers. There was in his Command a young fellow from Richmond, one John Puryear, handsome, daring, reckless, and actually frantic for fight all the time. Puryear had no admiration for cautious people, no sense of fear in his composition and not the slightest judgment in a crisis. All that he knew about war was what he gathered in each mad dash though the ranks of the enemy, with his long black hair flying in the wind and his revolver hot with action. He rode his horse like a Centaur, and no enemy ever existed that this boy would not engage hand to hand, hip and thigh. Nevertheless John Puryear lacked judgment, and the prospect of his acquiring it was extremely remote. After one of his most daring and brilliant rushes Mosby once said to him,

"Puryear, I am going to make you a lieutenant for gallantry."

Puryear swept his plumed hat in a bow that was royal in its grace.

"But," said the colonel, "I don't want you to ever command any of my men."

Puryear, not the least abashed, but evidently conscious of the compliment, repeated his courtly salutation as if the leadership of Mosby's Command was being conferred on him. It was the Partisan Ranger's way of showing his appreciation for a brave man. Boy that I was at the time, I understood that Mosby wanted Puryear to fight for him, but not to think for him.

What I have said of John Puryear will apply to fifty other boys of the Command. He was a fair sample of the younger element. When they were not fighting, they were generally playing. While on a raid they were as light-hearted as school boys at recess, and I have seen them chasing each other up and down the line of march oblivious of any discipline or of any approximate danger. It was fine sport for them to see how well a new recruit could ride, and this was ascertained by playing tricks on his horse to make the animal kick or buck.

One of our men had been shot in the mouth and his tongue healed with a big ridge on top, which made it quite an interesting organ. Every boy in the Command knew about this tongue of "B's," and often, when they were having fun on a raid, they would ride to him and offer to pay him if he would poke his tongue out for five minutes.

Mosby's correct estimate of men, his absolute freedom from jealousy and selfishness, his unerring judgment at critical moments, his devotion to his men, his eternal vigilance, his unobtrusive bravery and his exalted sense of personal honour, all combined to create in the mind and hearts of those who served him a sort of hero worship. Long before I ever set eyes on him I looked forward to the day when I would be able to take my hat off in his presence, and offer to follow him.

CHAPTER 2

Joining the Rangers

When the Civil War broke out I had just passed fifteen years of age, and I spent most of my time wondering what it all meant. One Sunday in the early Spring of 1861, a report came to Richmond that the U. S. gunboat *Pawnee* was coming up the James River to attack the city. The whole population was worked up to a high pitch of excitement. The governor at once ordered out all the local troops. Dignified old citizens appeared on the streets armed and equipped with weapons that had upheld the cause of the colonies against the invasion of the British in the Revolutionary war. A schooner laden with pig-iron was ordered sunk in the channel of the river below the city. The local cavalry company of Richmond was known as the Governor's Guard, and it was ordered to proceed down the river and capture the *Pawnee* and bring it up to town. The old governor probably had an idea that it could be hauled out on the river bank like a skiff and brought to town on a farm wagon.

Military companies in those days each had one or two markers, boys who carried little flags and whose duty it was to run out in front of the company to a given point, and stand there like statues, while the company marched up to and around them. I went down the river road that Sunday afternoon with the Governor's Guard, as marker, and we slept out of doors for three nights, for the first time in our lives. The Pawnee did not pass Norfolk, and at last we marched back to Richmond, covered with the dust of the campaign. A boot-black offered to "shine" some of us, and he came near being mobbed for the indignity. Every grain of that dust was precious to its possessor; we had been to the front and were real soldiers at last, and not militia.

This was my first soldiering of the war, and I believe it was the first that was done in Virginia.

Once in a while at night after that, when I was lying abed in Richmond all a-tremble for fear the war would not last long enough for me to get into it, the snarl of a snare drum would echo up and down the street, followed by the steady tramp of the regulars coming and going. It was tremendously alluring to me, as it was to every other boy living in that period. After a time, however, we became accustomed to seeing the men in grey and, as the country began to experience the agonies that grew out of the conflict, the romance faded out of the situation.

Then it was that we began to hear about Mosby and his men. To my mind Mosby was the ideal fighting man, from the tip of his plume to the rowel of his spur. Stories of his wonderful achievements came into Richmond from every direction. Joan of Arc never felt the call to go to battle any stronger than I felt it to join Mosby. I had not any doubt of my desirability, and figured out that all the Partisan Ranger required of his men was willingness to get shot, as occasion might require, and sleep out of doors in any kind of weather. Accordingly I curbed my appetite and discarded all the comforts within easy reach, assuming that suffering, starvation and self-inflicted misery would in time season me to undertake the rigors of a campaign with the Rangers. Whenever any other information came in concerning Mosby's movements I added new discomforts to my daily existence, looking forward to the time when I could stand before my hero, whom I had never seen, and let him discover, with his own eyes, that I was a seasoned man, no stranger to hardships, and altogether a valuable addition to his band of guerrillas.

One day I got wind of his whereabouts. As a rule he was a hard individual to locate, although a great many men in the Union army were engaged in looking for him; on the other hand a great many of the same army found him when they were not seeking him, and were surprised to see him so unexpectedly. News that came to me from several sources made it pretty certain that I could locate him in upper Fauquier County, Va., near the Blue Ridge Mountains, about one hundred and fifty miles from Richmond. I had nothing else in my mind but to make my way to him and that as soon as possible. Horses were scarce and hard to get and, besides, my departure on horseback in any direction out of Richmond would have caused remark among my young friends, and aroused curiosity, and I was nursing my patriotic zeal in secret.

There was nothing left for me to do but to set out ingloriously on foot. In fitting myself out for the guerrilla life, I figured on rapid physical development, and selected a dingy-grey suit cut for a man about six feet tall. I also had my hair cut close and this added nothing to my favour. The blouse of my suit was a sickly yellow shade of grey, and it came down halfway to my knees. I was perhaps the most unpromising looking candidate for military glory ever turned out of Richmond. For some reason that has never been satisfactorily explained, I had not so much as a pocket-knife for a weapon. A large crop of freckles spangled my sunburned face, and a *retroussé* nose that never entirely lost its tip shone red with fire gathered in the open air. I left Richmond under cover of night, fearful lest some inquisitive neighbour should see me making my initial dash for the front, a calamity that would have been tragic in case I should have the ill luck to be rejected by Mosby.

Ten days afterward, having passed through a country that was not too well supplied with luxury, I tramped into the foot-hills of the Blue Ridge Mountains, near Markham Station, where Mosby and his men were supposed to be. Arriving late in the afternoon, it took about two hours of my valuable time to scout out their whereabouts. As a matter of fact anybody in that neighbourhood could have directed me to him in five minutes after I arrived; but that did not seem the proper way for a prospective Mosby man to set to work. The guerrilla leader was fresh from one of his successful raids, and the admiring country people were vying with one another to do him honour and to throw their homes open for the convenience and entertainment of his partisans. I finally located him at the residence of Mr. Jamieson Ashby, a Southern sympathiser, with a large heart and a house always open to his friends; an old time Virginia gentleman, living in an old time Virginia mansion, and entertaining in the traditional manner.

Tired and footsore I came toward the building and, through the trees surrounding it, dimly saw some of Mosby's men moving around on the lawn and the wide veranda. Nervously I swept my eyes over the band in search of a big man with a showy uniform, a flowing plume and a flashing sabre. Gradually there had come into my mind on my tramp from Richmond an ideal figure that seemed to represent Mosby. I associated him in my imagination with Generals Lee and Jackson and Stuart, and I am not sure that I did not liken him to Robin Hood or Richard Coeur de Lion. By the time I set foot on the steps leading to the wide porch I was beginning to be disappointed at my failure to see and recognise the tall commanding warrior whose leadership I burned to follow. Where was Mosby? Suddenly I felt a tug at my elbow and, in the hushed silence that seemed to almost smother me, I heard a voice saying,

"There he is. Look!"

The moment I had longed for had arrived. I followed the direction of a finger that was thrust past my freckled nose, and the shock was something considerable. I beheld a small, plainly attired man, fair of complexion, slight but wiry, standing with his arms behind his back, talking quietly to one of his men. A military belt girded his waist, from which hung two Colt's army pistols.

The visions of splendour and magnificence that had filled my mind were swept away. The total absence of visible might, the lack of swagger, the quiet demeanour of the man, all contributed to my astonishment and chagrin. He did not even strut.

I stood rooted to the spot, speculating as to whether it was best to engage him at close range, or to take the road back to Richmond. The raiment that flapped about my person began to expand, or possibly I was shrinking.

The stalwarts grouped near Mosby, or sitting idly along the veranda, were not calculated to lighten the humiliation that was crushing me. They were fully up to the standard of the real live guerrillas that I had come so far to see.

My eyes sought out Mosby again. What a pity! He had not grown an inch, nor emitted a single war whoop; and his voice was so low that not a syllable of his conversation reached me.

At this juncture Mr. Ashby appeared on the veranda, smiling, and announced that supper was ready, inviting Mosby and his men inside. They heard him and, one by one, disappeared indoors with alacrity. I learned later that the guerrillas always carried their appetites with them on a raid, as well as elsewhere. Mosby was borne in with the rush, and I was left standing outside, with a confused idea that perhaps it would be necessary for me to start back to Richmond without even my supper.

"Come in, Sir, and sup with us, and you will have a chance to meet Mosby."

I looked up and saw Mr. Ashby standing in the doorway, extending his right hand in greeting, while his left pointed the way to the feast.

I lost no time in thanking him and accepting the invitation.

Whether it was by chance or intention I never learned; but Mr. Ashby placed me in a chair by Mosby's side. He was busily engaged upon the appetizing meal when I took my seat by him, and he did not notice me. From my position on his immediate right I saw only the profile of his face. It was as clean cut as a cameo, and the lips were straight and firm. His nose, with a slight suggestion of the eagle's beak, was finely chiselled. He was the smallest man at the table, weighing at that time about one hundred and twenty-five pounds, and was but a little more than five feet eight or nine inches in height.

Sittings by his side I measured our differences in build with my eye I was nearly three inches taller, and weighed twenty pounds more than he.

After what seemed to me an eternity, during which I did pot eat a mouthful, Mosby appeared to realise that there was a human being, a stranger, beside him. He turned upon me suddenly, meeting my full glance. At that instant the secret of his power over his men was disclosed. It was in his eyes, which were deep blue, luminous, clear, piercing; when he spoke they flashed the punctuations of his sentence. He looked at me intently for at least half a minute, the expression in his eyes merging from searching inquisition into astonishment, and from that to amusement. He took in every inch of me, from my cropped head to the baggy trousers that disappeared under the table. I had reckoned that the yellow blouse I wore would make a hit with him, but he displayed no perceptible interest in it.

When he spoke to me every man at the table stopped eating and looked in my direction.

"Who are you?" was his first question.

"John W. Munson," I replied, with a clumsy attempt at a salute.

"Where are you from?"

"Richmond, sir."

"What do you want?"

I keyed myself up to the grand declaration.

"I want to join the Partisan Rangers under Mosby."

The sentence escaped from my lips with accumulating force, exploding with renewed energy at the conclusion. I expected to hear some laughter from the men around the table. Instead, however, they all took on a serious look, and gave me their close attention. Mosby threw his arm over the back of his chair and continued.

"Are you equipped?"

"I have only my clothes," I answered.

In this particular I was somewhat over equipped, but I was woefully shy of arms and ammunition. The full magnitude of my audacity now burst upon the guests at the Ashby table. One man whose chair

JOHN W. MUNSON,
At the time of his enlistment in Mosby's
Partisan Rangers.

was turned away from the table, and who had lighted a cigar (captured) began to laugh. Mosby turned upon him, and with one look silenced the disturber. Of all the favours for which I am indebted to Colonel Mosby, none was ever more appreciated than this.

"Can you get a horse anywhere?" he resumed when quiet was restored.

"Certainly, sir," I answered with grave doubts as to my ability in that direction.

"All right; meet me at Blackwell's tomorrow morning at sunrise, and I will talk to you again."

He then returned to his meal and finished it in silence and, from any outward indication on his part for the rest of the evening, he completely forgot my existence. After this I proceeded leisurely with my supper, for I was not disturbed by a word addressed to me by anyone at the table. When we were finished and, one by one, the men went out of the house, I followed some of them to the stable, and found two of them saddling their horses. I asked them the way to Mr. Blackwell's, and learned that it was about ten miles distant. I did not want them to know that I was particularly anxious to get there, so I crawled into the hay-mow and went to sleep.

Long before daylight next morning I was awake and thinking of the horse that I had promised to secure. Striking out alone across the country, in the direction I had been told Blackwell's lay, I stopped at a farmhouse about sunrise, and spoke to a farmer who was going towards his barn. I told him who I was and where I was going, and asked him if he could tell me where I could capture a horse. Looking at me in some surprise, and suspecting that I was joking, which I was not, for I would really have been a horse thief if I could have secured a good animal, he told me he had a horse to spare and would sell her to me on credit. This proposition struck me at the time as manna falling in the desert, and I gladly agreed to his terms for the purchase of his mare, and borrowed his saddle and bridle.

Not very long after sunrise I rode, well mounted, but perspiring, into Mr. Blackwell's yard, and greatly to my astonishment found that Mosby and a few of his men had arrived there several hours previously.

I threw the bridle of my mare over the hitching post and, in addition, tied a good strong rope around her neck and fastened it to a tree nearby for fear she might get homesick, and strode into the house to announce my arrival. At that early day, only twelve hours after being ushered into the august presence, I began to feel my oats. Mosby turned and looked at me as I entered, and I think he recognised my yellow blouse or my freckled nose or possibly my reserve. In those days I had reserve. At any rate when I told him I had got a horse he smiled and put his hand on my shoulder as he asked me if it were a good one. Somehow I got the idea that he thought I had been on a lone scout and captured it from some picket. Youth can be buoyant in imagination. At any rate I shall not forget his merry humour nor the twinkle in his eye.

From that moment my clothes began to fit me better. I followed Mosby around the room and out on the porch and, after talking to him for ten minutes, somewhere or somehow a pistol came into my possession, with a belt and holster for it, and I was received into the ranks of the Mosby Guerrillas, all ready for action.

CHAPTER 3

How We Lived

The life led by Mosby's men was entirely different from that of any other body of soldiers during the war. His men had no camps nor fixed quarters, and never slept in tents. They did not even know anything about pitching a tent. The idea of making coffee, frying bacon, or soaking hard-tack was never entertained. When we wanted to eat we stopped at a friendly farm house, or went into some little town and bought what we wanted. Every man in the Command had some special farm he could call his home.

The people in that part of the state which was designated "Mosby's Confederacy," embracing in a general way the counties of Fauquier and Loudoun, were loyal to the South, though frequently outside the lines of the Southern army, and they were glad to have Mosby's men among them, not only to show their sympathy with the South, but also to have the protection which the presence of the Partisans afforded them.

During the war all local government in that country was suspended. There were no courts nor court officers. The people looked to Mosby to make the necessary laws and to enforce them, and no country before, during or since the war was ever better governed. Mosby would not permit any man to commit a crime, or even a misdemeanour, in his domain. One of our men, in a spirit of deviltry, once turned over an old Quaker farmer's milk cans, and when Mosby heard of it he ordered me to take the man over to the army, which was then near Winchester, and turn him over to General Early, with the message that such a man was not fitted to be a guerrilla.

As a Command we had no knowledge of the first principles of cavalry drill, and could not have formed in a straight line had there ever been any need for our doing so. We did not know the bugle-calls, and very rarely had roll-call. Our dress was not uniform in make or colour; we did not address our officers, except Mosby, by their titles; in fact, we did not practice anything usually required of a soldier; and yet withal there was not another body of men in the army under better or more willing control of their leader. Two things were impressed upon us well, however; to obey orders, and to fight.

We carried no sabres, being in no manner familiar with the weapon's use. My keenest recollection of the value of a sabre takes me back to the time when a large curved blade, sheathed in clanking steel, was brought in with some captured Union man. None of us dared swing it at arm's length, for fear of killing a neighbour, but we subsequently found it was a splendid weapon with which to bat a refractory mule over the back. When a captured mule received the sabre treatment with the flat side, he forged ahead and stayed in front of the procession from that time on. The jingle of the steel against his sides or back seemed to frighten him more than all the black-snake whips in the Union army. Once only did I see this deadly engine of war in bloody action, and that was when young Emory Pitts of my Company playfully drove its point into the body of a Thirteenth New Yorker who had fired at him and then dodged under an army wagon to escape.

Contrary to a popular impression we did not carry carbines at any time during the war. Each of Mosby's men was armed with two muzzle-loading Colt's army revolvers of forty-four calibre. They were worn in belt holsters. Some few who could afford it, or who had succeeded in capturing extra pistols or who wanted to gratify a sort of vanity, wore an extra pair in their saddle-holsters or stuck into their boot legs. These weapons were extremely deadly and effective in the hand-to-hand engagements in which our men indulged. Long and frequent practice had made every man in the Command a good shot, and each was as sure with his revolver as every cowboy is with his six-shooter. As a general thing our real fights were fast and furious and quickly over, one or the other side withdrawing at a dead run when the pistols were empty.

At the present time, (1906), the question of discarding the sabre in the United States Army is being discussed very generally by officers, and I believe before long they will be relegated to the museums and the junk piles. I received a letter from an officer of one of the crack cavalry regiments asking me for a more extended opinion of the sabre than I had expressed in my published reminiscences, and with hesitation, I told him how poor an opinion Mosby and his men had of the blade. I said that an Irishman with a *shillelah* in a close-quarter fight, would make the average cavalryman ashamed of himself. I never actually saw blood drawn with a sabre but twice in our war, though I saw them flash by the thousand at Brandy Station.

The Federal cavalry generally fought with sabres; at any rate they all carried them, and Mosby used to say they were as useless against a skilfully handled revolver as the wooden swords of harlequins. As the Mosby tactics became better known, scouting parties from the Northern Army began to develop an affection for the pistol, with increasing success, I might add, in the later engagements. In stubborn fights I have seen the men on both sides sit on their restless horses and reload their pistols under a galling fire. This was not a custom, however; someone generally, ran to cover after the revolvers were emptied. We both did this a good many times, but I believe, without bragging at the expense of truth, that we saw the back seams of the enemy's jackets oftener than they saw ours. I attribute this largely to the fact that we attacked them unexpectedly oftener than they attacked us.

Revolvers in the hands of Mosby's men were as effective in surprise engagements as a whole line of light ordnance in the hands of the enemy. This was largely due to the fact that Mosby admonished his men never to fire a shot until the eyes of the other fellow were visible. It was no uncommon thing for one of our men to gallop by a tree at full tilt, and put three bullets into its trunk in succession.

This sort of shooting left the enemy with a good many empty saddles after an engagement.

The standard uniform simply meant "something gray." It has been said that we wore blue to deceive the enemy, but this is ridiculous, for we were always in the enemy's country where a Southern soldier caught dressed in a blue uniform would have been treated to a swift court-martial and shot as a spy. I never knew, nor did I ever hear, of any man in our Command wearing a blue uniform under any circumstances, and moreover I never heard of one of our men making any use whatever of a blue uniform or ever taking a blue uniform from a prisoner. We had no reason to use a blue uniform as a disguise and, in fact, never used anything for a disguise, for there was no occasion to do so. Many of our attacks were made at night, when all colours looked alike, and in daytime we did not have to deceive the Yankees in order to get at them. On the other hand the men who were known as "Jesse's Scouts" in the Northern Army were always dressed in gray, and my experience with them justifies me in saying that they seemed to fully appreciate the risk of their disguise if they fell into our hands.

"Something gray" was the one requisite of our dress and the cost of it mattered little. Much of it was paid for by Uncle Sam out of the money we got from him directly and indirectly. Like gamblers we took chances with fate. We had ups and downs; but after our successful raids we were the best dressed, best equipped, and best mounted Command in the Confederate Army. There were meek and lowly privates among us, of whom it might truly be said that Solomon in all his glory was not arrayed as one of these. Union army sutlers supplied us with a varied assortment of luxuries, and I cannot recall an instance when we rejected what they had on hand on overhauling their stock, or when we threatened to take our trade to some competitor.

If we wanted anything that we could not take by force of arms we sent North for it and paid for it with money that was not Confederate.

Some of the Command were extremely fastidious in the matter of dress and affected gold braid, buff trimmings, and ostrich plumes in their hats. After the "greenback raid" when we captured General Sheridan's paymasters with a hundred and seventy thousand dollars in crisp new government notes, each man received as his share more than twenty-one hundred dollars. The result was that all had clothes and accoutrements such as had never gladdened their hearts before. At all times, whether things went well or ill, the guerrillas were as vain a lot of dandies as one would wish to see; blithe in the face of danger, full of song and story, indifferent to the events of tomorrow, and keyed up to a high pitch of anticipation; mingled with this was the pride that goes hand in hand with repeated victories and the possession of spoils.

I was soon possessed with the desire for finery, and forthwith sent North by a sutler for gray corduroy with which to make a full suit, as well as the necessary gold braid, buff trimmings, gilt buttons, high top boots, gauntlets, a soft hat, and three ostrich feathers to match. I made up my mind to dress for the part if it took my last dollar, and such was the case, for when the goods and baubles arrived, I found that the honest merchant wanted about two hundred in cash from me. I made a few trades, juggled my possessions around a little, and got the money together, adjusting the account in a measure, by charging the sutler five dollars a pound for some tobacco that I happened to have, which he wanted badly. I was quite a swell for a time until the fellow who had laughed at me at Mr. Ashby's house, on my first appearance, tackled me one afternoon, and we both showed the effect of the argument.

Mosby encouraged the men in their vanities, although personally he favoured the neatest and plainest of attire. Only when he came in touch with the generals, which he did once in awhile, did he make any attempt at display in his dress. On these occasions he always wore a new suit of the best the tailor could procure, a red-lined cape, gold braid, and ostrich plume in his hat, as gayly as did his men. I have always believed that he did it for the purpose of impressing the regulars with the importance of his Partisan Rangers, in whom he took the greatest pride. He wanted the army to think, when they saw him in his finery, that he was a fair sample of the entire band.

In a fight a conspicuous uniform, a waving plume, a flashing sabre, or a white horse, always attracted the fire of the enemy, and Mosby never went into a fight that his actions were not so conspicuous and his red-lined cape so prominently displayed that he drew on himself a concentrated fire. I believe he enjoyed such special attentions; not that he was reckless, for recklessness is not always bravery, but he was unconsciously brave, and loved war for itself; it was never "Hell "to him, as it was to Sherman, but on the whole he rather looked on it as a sort of martial picnic. If he had lived in France at the time of the Empire he would have been a field-marshal. If he had been at Balaklava he would have led the Six Hundred. In his own little circumscribed fighting grounds.

> *Where'er wild war's sirocco breath*
> *Its deadliest impress made,*
> *And revelled midst its feast of death.*
> *There flashed his battle blade.*

. . . . or, more correctly, there flashed his smoking Colt, for he had positively no use for a blade of any kind.

Whenever we made a successful raid, we made it a point to repay the farmers and country people whose bounty we enjoyed, in live stock and supplies. The return from a sutler's raid was a holiday occasion, for everybody got something. On one occasion we captured about two hundred and fifty fat cattle from General Sheridan's supply train, and we gave our country friends half of them, dividing them among all the people living within range.

On one occasion, we got into some sutler's stores at Duffield depot on the Baltimore & Ohio Railroad and the goods were so tempting that I concluded to carry an assortment back to our lady hostess and her household. I loaded up a sack with all sorts of useful and ornamental goods, and fastened it to my saddle securely. Then, going back into the store and looking around, I spied some hoop-skirts which the sutler had no doubt bought for some special order from an army officer's wife. I took these and strapped them to my saddle. Then I made another and final round of the store, and began stuffing my many pockets with notions, such as buttons, hair pins, thread, hooks and eyes, and the like; finally I found a lot of papers of needles, and I thrust a handful of these into my trousers' pocket.

Just then some one poked his head into the door and cried:
"The Yankees are coming."

We made a break for our horses and galloped away with our plunder, and our prisoners; keeping up a pretty fast gait for some miles for fear our burdens would slacken the usual speed we practiced when we were retreating. I had not gone a mile before my papers of needles began to come undone in my pocket, and at every jump of my horse a newly released needle would remind me that I had captured it, until at the end of our run I had dozens of needle marks on my anatomy, and two or three points were left inside, to work upward or downward, or out, as they severally saw fit I recollect that I delivered all my presents safely to my kind friends, except needles, and I made no reference to these in my account of the raid. In all my later raids on sutler's stores I contented myself with things that were not likely to prove troublesome, or stick into me, such as boots, and gloves, and furnishing goods; but I ignored needles.

While there was more or less risk in sleeping in houses inside the enemy's lines, our losses were comparatively small from this cause, as our men were always on the lookout for reprisals from the night raiding parties, who had learned that part of our tactics and were continually on our trail. We knew the country a great deal better than the Union soldiers did and, in time of danger, it was a simple matter to shift our quarters. Whenever there was an over-supply of raiders in the neighbourhood we took our blankets or robes and slept in the woods or orchards or fields till the danger was past. Mosby not infrequently slept alone in such places, but as he and I each had a fine buffalo robe it was my happy privilege frequently to snuggle up to him between these two robes, and "*dream of battlefields no more.*"

Mosby sometimes did his scouting alone, but generally he was accompanied by one or more men, selected because of their intimate knowledge of a certain part of the country to which he was going. Under cover of the night he would move with the stealth that would have put an Indian to shame. No sabre was ever worn on such a trip and if a spur or a curb chain jingled it was taken off. A neighing horse would have been murdered on the spot. Our animals seemed to know instinctively that they must keep still; at any rate they always did so.

Mosby was the fastest "scouter" I ever knew, and in the saddle could cover a dozen objective points, over a course of fifty miles from sunset to sunrise, gathering information of vital importance at each halt. He would send out messengers whenever necessary from any point wherever it seemed advisable to do so, regardless of the hour of day or night, or the proximity of friend or foe. I never knew one of his messengers to go wrong. No one ever heard of one of Mosby's dispatches being captured.

Horses, of course, were indispensable to Mosby's men. On whatever else we were obliged, or chose, to stint ourselves, it was necessary to have good horses. Nearly all the men kept at least two, and many of us who rode constantly had more. The work was too hard for one horse. I have known the colonel to have six at one time, all of them fine animals, but generally half his stud would be temporarily disabled from hard riding or wounds. When we started on a scout or a raid, his old coloured groom, Aaron, would take up from pasture one or two of his horses and begin to get them into shape for him by the time he returned. Thus he always had a fresh horse to depend on. Each man kept his horses at the farmhouse where he made his home, and there was not a barn or corral owned by our friendly allies that did not contain one or more of Mosby's cavalry horses, waiting to be saddled for a long, hard ride.

When a raiding party came through our neighbourhood and the men were at their respective homes, each would mount a good horse and take the rest off to hide in the woods till the raiders passed by. If we happened to be away the farmers would hide our horses for us, and instances were not rare when the ladies and children of a household would do the kindly office.

Mosby's old negro, Aaron, was fanatical on the subject of his own importance, and had an unconquerable fear of the Yankees. He used to tell us when we chaffed him that it was not "Mars Jack" that the Yankees came up there looking for, but it was "Aaron," and that, if they could catch him and take him to Washington, President Lincoln would have him handed around on a big silver waiter for all the people in the world to gaze at. The moment the report, or even the rumour, came to headquarters that the Yankees were coming, old Aaron would start off with his horses for the mountains and we would not see or hear from him till after dark, when he would sneak in at the back door and ask the first one he met, "Is dey gone yet?"

Once, as a joke, Johnny Edmonds and I galloped into the barnyard where Aaron was currying one of the colonel's horses and closed the big gate behind us. We fired our pistols and yelled to him to look out for the Yankees. Without waiting an instant he mounted his horse bareback, jumped the gate and flew for the hills. At each jump we fired a pistol and yelled to him to stop, but he kept on and we did not see him again till next morning. He never quite forgave us when he found out the facts.

Aaron accompanied Mosby in the regular service before the Command was organised. There was a fight near Barbee's cross-roads in Fauquier County in which Mosby was engaged, and old Aaron accompanied him at an entirely safe distance, leading one of his extra horses. He sat down on the porch of an old house to listen to the noise of the firing, "sniffing the battle from afar," and waiting for his master to come back and give him orders. Suddenly, and without warning, a misdirected shell swept high over the old building and burst in the air, a part of it striking the roof and scattering splinters all over Aaron.

He jumped upon his horse, leading the extra and much needed animal, galloped away and did not stop, or make any perceptible slackening of his speed, until he reached the old Mosby plantation, about one hundred and fifty miles away. It was three months before he could be persuaded to return to the army.

When my captain, "Billy" Smith, was killed in January, 1864, I was anxious to possess his favourite horse and I purchased him from Mrs. Smith, but it was necessary for me to sell three pretty good ones of my own to raise sufficient money to pay for him. I never complained of the price, and was never sorry I bought him, for there was not a better known horse in Stuart's cavalry, nor a better war horse in the whole army. My captain had been orderly-sergeant of the "Black Horse" troop, and used to ride old "Champ" in the regular service; and from Stuart down to the humblest private he was well and favourably known.

Norman Smith was killed while riding him in one of our fights, in August, 1863, and his brother, captain "Billy," was also killed on him in January, 1864. When the war ended I turned him over to a third brother, Captain Towson Smith, in whose possession he died. Some time after the war, the captain wanted to drive to church, and hooked up old Champ to the family carryall and got into it. The old horse looked around at it and, with a far-away look in his eyes, apparently more in sorrow than in anger, kicked the old carriage into splinters.

On one occasion Colonel Mosby took me with him on a trip to Richmond and we stopped at General Stuart's headquarters, then in Orange County, and left our horses with him. His own horses were pretty badly used up and we asked him to ride ours in a fight which he was to have early the next day. When we returned a few days afterwards, the general asked me if I would put a price on Champ. I told him he would honour me by letting me give the old fellow to him, but he would not consent to such an arrangement; therefore, as he would not allow me to give him the horse and I would not let him buy, he reluctantly saw me ride back to Northern Virginia. He told me he had never enjoyed riding a horse in a fight as much as he did old Champ.

The horse was absolutely controllable in the hottest sort of action, and never lost his head; but, as he had been badly shot twice, once in his head and the next time in his hip, he knew the sound of flying bullets and would shake his old head and apparently dodge when he heard them going by; but he did not know that dodging was unnecessary.

Mosby would send his men out in different directions on individual scouting trips with orders, perhaps, to meet him at a designated point fifty or more miles away. In this way he kept an eye on the enemy all around the circle and when, acting on one of his men's reports, he decided to strike a blow, he would take the necessary number of men with him or have them meet him at some point near the scene of the expected attack and, after verifying the man's report by his own actual observation, the trouble would begin. It was his constant care not to take his men into any place that he could not bring them out of, and they felt perfectly safe in following him.

His instructions to the various detachments of his battalion frequently covered three days ahead, and the instances were very rare when he did not keep his appointments to the hour. He knew the theatre of war so well, and was so complete a master of his own work, that it was impossible to confuse him. He never lost his self-possession; never got rattled. If he could make a raid at midnight it pleased him greatly, as he held that sleeping men are easy to surround, and that it required at least five minutes for an awakened soldier to get into shape to fight.

That is the explanation why so many of Mosby's performances were planned and came off at an hour of the night when most good people were in the land of dreams; it also explains how it frequently happened that our men attacked many times their own numbers. Seldom did Mosby return empty handed from a raid. On the march he was usually very quiet and uncommunicative; riding by himself a little ahead of the Command, apparently plunged in the consideration of some future problem, the germ of which had already begun to formulate in his brain. On a raid, however, when his mind was fully made up, he was the gayest of us all, joking and laughing with the men and looking forward eagerly to the clash of arms, these occasions he would direct one of the boys near him to ride back down the line and bring Jim Sinclair to the front to tell us all about the confusion of the mule-drivers; or to another one he would say, "Go back and ask Captain Bill Kennon to come up here and tell us a good lie." Captain Bill could charm the birds off their nests with his wonderful romancing.

Mosby never took anyone into his confidence. When he got an idea that he thought worth while, he immediately worked toward its development. I do not remember ever hearing anybody ask Mosby where he was going or what his plans were. One instance of his taciturnity will suffice. We met one afternoon in Upperville, Virginia, where the colonel told Major Richards to take the Command to a designated place in Fairfax County and await his coming late that night. Turning to me he said:

"Munson, get on your horse and come with me."

He was off at a trot. I followed him down the Little River turnpike and caught up with him, where we trotted and galloped, boot-leg to boot-leg, for twenty miles. Not once did he look at me, nor one word did he utter in all that ride. He was planning one of those sensational raids of his, which, before the next sunset, startled Washington, and kept the Federal commanders in a flutter for many days afterward. I thought my tongue would become paralyzed from long disuse.

Finally we drew up at a farmhouse, where the colonel reined his horse with the remark: "Let's stop here for a cup of coffee." His ideas had crystallized and he was normal again. In that silent gallop he had planned a victory. Not long ago, he told a friend of ours in New York, Mr. Frank Pemberton, that he liked to ride with me during the war because I did not talk.

Mosby maintained a discipline that was remarkable, considering the kind of men who made up his Command and the character of the service. Young men, especially, chafe under too much restraint; yet he made rules that were never broken and established rewards which, when won, were as highly prized by his followers as the medal of honour by the heroes of Austerlitz. He divided all captured horses by lot, among those who figured in the particular raid in which the animals were secured. Sutler's supplies, army equipment and personal property belonged to the man brave enough to take the risk of capturing it Men who went alone, or in small groups, on scouting parties divided their spoils as they saw fit. "*To the victor belonged the spoils*" was a satisfactory doctrine for Mosby, but during the whole war he never appropriated to himself as much as a halter-strap. The very horses he rode and the old coloured body-servant who accompanied him throughout the campaign, came with him from the Mosby homestead.

Once only did I know of any departure from this strict rule of his independence, and that was an occasion when all his horses were in a bad way, and the men purchased and presented to him a splendid charger which had belonged to one of his officers. He protested a great deal, but the men insisted.

The men always assembled at a designated place to go on a raid, but it did not make any difference to Mosby where they disbanded when the purpose of the raid was accomplished. For instance, he would give notice to a few men whom he might meet, to notify a given number of the Command to meet him at a certain cross-roads, or blacksmith's shop, or a village. If more of the men assembled than he wanted, he would dismiss such as he did not need, sometimes sending them on a scout under one of the officers, or letting them return to their homes; and, taking his force, would go on his raid. When the purpose was accomplished, he did not care how many of the boys left him, or what became of them, so long as enough remained to take care of the prisoners and horses and bring them out safely. I have returned with him from a raid that covered two or three days of almost constant riding, only to be told to get ready to start on another expedition at once.

In such cases we would take a hurried bath, put on clean clothes, get a fresh horse from the stable, pocket a few extra cartridges, eat something if it was ready, and gallop away. I used to think it was glorious sport in those days.

Every affair in which Mosby and his men figured had in it something novel, something romantic, something which is worth the telling; and many of those in which I took part, or with which I am at all familiar through the stories of others or the tradition of the Command, will be mentioned in the following pages. I would like to tell of some individual act of each man in the Command, and record the hundreds of brave deeds I witnessed or knew of, but I can only repeat what I once heard Mosby say when he was writing one of his reports to General Stuart. I said to him, when he told me he had put my name with three or four others, in his report of a fight, "Why don't you say something about —— and —— and —— and ——?" He replied:

"I can't call the roll in every fight, Munson."

CHAPTER 6

The Capture of General Stoughton

The only way I have of fixing the date of Mosby's first operations as an independent Ranger is his report to General Stuart, which is dated February 4, 1863, in which he says he arrived in Fauquier County about one week previously and had been quite actively engaged with the enemy, capturing twenty-eight prisoners with their horses and equipments. He signed the report "John S. Mosby." General Stuart endorsed the report on February 8, as follows:

> Respectively forwarded as additional proof of the prowess, daring and efficiency of Mosby (without commission) and his band of a dozen followers."

General Stuart made a little raid about Christmas time 1862, to Dumfries, and took Mosby with him. When he left there to go on to Fairfax he sent Mosby ahead and, when they reached Loudoun county and rested for a day before returning, Mosby got permission to remain there with nine men of the First Virginia Cavalry. Among them was Fount Beattie who, from that day till the war ended, was one of the best known men and one of the best men in the Command. He was Mosby's most intimate companion and friend, for they had enlisted together when the war broke out and were never separated.

With these nine men Mosby once went down into Fairfax County and in two days captured twenty Yankees with their horses. He took his men and prisoners back to Stuart's headquarters at Fredericksburg and the general was so pleased with the result of Mosby's experiment that he promised to let him go back again with fifteen men. This really was the beginning of his Partisan career, for later when he started North with his fifteen men he never again went back to regular army life. These fifteen men were not members of Mosby's Command for, shortly after he took them, some were ordered back to their regiment. The fact is that, strictly speaking, Mosby had no Command of his own until June 10, 1863, when he organised his first company, "A". Up to that time the men he had in all his brilliant engagements were volunteers. He utilised every man who, came to him.

A hospital at Middleburg served him as a recruiting station. The convalescent men, some of them on crutches, others bandaged and patched up in other ways, would go with him on a raid, make havoc among the Yankees, and return to the hospital and get into their beds. When the raiding parties who followed Mosby up to that part of the country would see these poor wounded rebels in their beds in the hospital, they never suspected them of being "guerrillas *pro tem*." On February 27, Mosby had twenty-seven of these new recruits with him in one of those Fairfax County raids, and although the post he attacked was defended by a force of fifty cavalrymen he captured five men and thirty-nine horses. He killed the lieutenant commanding, and three of his men.

Out of these early volunteers a number remained permanently with Mosby and became actual "Mosby men," but until his first company was formed he never could count, with any degree of certainty, upon any given number of men responding to his call for a meeting. Many of his volunteers were dismounted cavalrymen from Stuart's division who came over to Mosby to get horses and who returned to their regiments after the horses were secured and he never saw them again. At every meeting held for the first few months of his Partisan career entirely new faces would appear ready for the fray, and most of those with which, in a measure, he had become familiar on previous raids would be missing.

One of the first men of any importance to join him was John Underwood, a native of Fairfax County. Two of John's brothers, Sam and Bush, joined him later and served with him to the end of the war, but John was killed a few months after becoming a "guerrilla."

These Underwoods knew that country better than the wild animals that roamed over it by night or by day, and they were Mosby's guides on many of his scouts and raids and never led him astray. By night or by day any of these boys could thread his way through any swamp or tangled forest in Fairfax County, and personal fear was a thing unknown to them.

Another early recruit was Billy Hibbs, a blacksmith of Loudoun County, who had two grown sons in the regular army. By general consent he was known throughout the entire Command as "Major" Hibbs, a title bestowed on him in a joke by Mosby who, however, had great respect for the "Major's" loyalty and courage and ability. Another early acquisition was Dick Moran. Mosby used to say that these few men actually started his Command into being and that the real recruits came to his standard only after it bore their names.

Not because the capture of General Stoughton was the first affair of importance which Mosby accomplished in his career as a Partisan Ranger, is it recorded here, but because the, name of Mosby inevitably couples itself with the event. It was typical. While many other of his exploits far exceeded it in importance to our side and in loss to the enemy, there was nothing in boldness or originality which surpassed it during the entire war; nor did anything reflect more credit on the little Command or create any more notoriety than his capture. It seems to me that this exploit gave Mosby more deserved fame than any single achievement of any officer or commander in either the Northern or Southern Army during the war, and I desire to tell it more in detail than do the official records.

The following official report, which is given *verbatim*, of the United States provost marshal at the post, makes a good preface for my story. His report is much more accurate than was usual under such circumstances, and the exaggeration of our number from thirty to three hundred, was not at all an exceptional case.

Provost Marshal's Office.
Fairfax, C. H., Va., March 10, 1863.

Colonel Wyndham, Commanding Cavalry Brigade and Post.

Sir: On the night of the 8th instant, say about two, or half past two, a.m., Captain Mosby, with his Command, entered this village by an easterly direction, then advanced upon my outer vedette, when he challenged (no countersign out). The rebel picket or scout advanced presenting at the same time two revolvers to his head and threatening to blow his brains out if he said a word, demanding his arms, etc., when the force came up and captured every man on patrol, with horses, equipments, etc., until reaching the provost marshal's stables, when they halted and entered the stables, taking every horse available with them. They then proceeded to Colonel Stoughton's stables, captured his guard, took his horses and those of his aides; they then proceeded to Colonel Wyndham's headquarters and took all the

The House where Gen. Stoughton was Captured, Showing a Group of Mosby Men. Taken at the Reunion in 1904.

Hugh McIlhaney. Col. W. H. Chapman. Lt. Ben. Palmer. J. H. Alexander. F. Beattie. Lt. Jas. G. Wiltshire. Tom Lake. L. Hutchinson. Frank Angelo. Stacy Bispham.

horses and movable property with them. In the meantime others of Captain Mosby's Command were despatched to all quarters where officers were lodged, taking them out of their beds, together with the telegraph operator, assistant, etc., etc.

They searched the provost marshal's office, and finding him absent went to the post hospital and there made diligent search for him, offering a reward for him. The provost marshal had just left the street, say ten minutes before they entered, and went across some vacant lots to ascertain from one of his vedettes if he had caught any horses or horse thieves. Another party ten in number, proceeded to Colonel Stoughton's headquarters, taking him and one of his *aides* named Prentiss, who afterwards escaped prisoners. They then proceeded to Colonel Wyndham's headquarters and took Captain Barker of the Fifth New York Cavalry, and also Baron Vardner, who was stopping at the colonel's.

In the meantime another party of them entered the residence of Colonel Johnston and searched the house for him. He had, previous to their entering the town, heard of their movements, and, believing them to be the patrol, went out to halt them, but soon found out his mistake. He then entered the house again, he being in a nude state, and got out backwards, they in hot pursuit of him. He, however, evaded them by getting under a barn and had scarcely concealed himself when a guard of three men were placed upon it. It is supposed that they entered our lines between Frying Pan and Herndon Station, taking a diagonal course to come in at the lower end of the village. On leaving they went out by way of Colonel Wyndham's stables (southwest) and proceeded towards Centreville, cutting telegraph wires as they went along. I am told by parties who had seen them that they were some three hundred strong. I have the honour to remain.

    Respectfully, your obedient servant,

                          Lieut. D. L. O'Connor,
                                   Provost Marshal.

The following are some of the details, and I am indebted for them to Mosby's report of the affair to General Stuart, in the Confederate War Records, to his account of it, written many years ago for publication, and to the traditions of our Command, which are the priceless heritage of all its members.

Mosby started on his Partisan Ranger career early in February, 1863, with fifteen men not members of his Command, for he had no Command. They were members of his old regiment, the First Virginia Cavalry, and were loaned to him by General Stuart. On the twenty-fifth of the month, a deserter from the Fifth New York Cavalry, then stationed at or near Fairfax Court House, named Ames, came up to join Mosby. Little attention was paid to him by any of the men except by Walter Frankland, who had no horse, and who had joined Mosby a few days previously. Ames told Frankland he could lead him back to his camp at Germantown and get horses for both of them and, on the twenty-eighth they started on foot for the camp, reaching it at midnight on the night of March first. They entered the camp, talked to the sentinels and, in their presence, saddled two of the finest horses and came back safely to their starting point.

One week afterwards, Mosby took his little Command of only twenty-nine men and, with Ames as guide, started from Aldie in Loudoun County, to enter the camp at Fairfax Court House. What will be difficult for the general reader to believe is that Mosby, from the first meeting with the deserter Ames, had confidence in him and used him to pilot himself and his little band into the very jaws of the enemy, not communicating his intention of going to the commanding general's headquarters to any of the men except to Ames. I have already spoken of Mosby's correct estimate of men and of his unerring judgment in critical moments. This case of Ames was an illustration of it, for he proved worthy of Mosby's confidence, became one of the safest and best soldiers in our Command, was later made a lieutenant for gallantry and efficiency, and was finally killed in a fight at close quarters.

At the time Ames came to him, Mosby had already determined to make a raid on Fairfax Court House for he had gathered information to warrant it, and this Ames verified. This was only a month after Mosby had started upon his career as a Partisan Ranger and at the time he had made only a few experimental dashes at the enemy. Here was a very serious proposition to tackle. Fairfax Court House was invested and surrounded by thousands of soldiers—infantry, cavalry and artillery. At Centreville a few miles away there was a brigade of mixed troops with heavy artillery in the works. Another brigade of cavalry was located near Fairfax Court House on the pike. The adjacent railroad was heavily guarded and cavalry outposts completely encircled the town for miles, extending to the Potomac River. The headquarters were girdled with soldiers. There was only one weak spot in the entire line of outposts, and that was weak only in comparison with the rest. No man could have passed through any part of the lines by daylight, without being seen by hundreds of Union soldiers.

Mosby knew where that weak spot was and, after midnight, in a darkness so intense that he could hardly see a man ahead of him, took his twenty-nine men through it. Not until he was within the lines and almost at the headquarters of the officers, did he tell his men what he was doing and where he was going. At that early day there was already grounded in them the blind faith in their leader which continued until the end of the war, and which with me continues to this day. Just before reaching the headquarters he explained the situation to one of his men, Hunter, and touched upon its danger. The little band rode into the town and stopped at the Court-House Square, challenged now and then by a picket who was immediately quieted, and still they did not know what the program was nor where they were.

The men were divided into squads, each with its separate duty to perform. Some went to the stables to get the best horses; others to the officers' quarters to capture them; all of them with orders to return to the square when their allotted tasks were completed. General Stoughton and Colonel Wyndham, the latter commanding the cavalry, were the principal game sought by Mosby. He had been annoying the troops about Fairfax in the few weeks he had been operating in that country, and Wyndham had sent him some impudent messages. Mosby was anxious to take him out of his bed, but the colonel had gone by rail to Washington the afternoon before, and so Mosby missed him. When Ames with a few men went to Wyndham's quarters and found that the bird had flown they stripped his apartments of all his valuable effects and took all the fine horses in the stables. It fell to the lot of Ames to capture his former captain, Barker, of the Fifth New York. What the feelings of a deserter under the circumstances were must be left to the imagination, but he treated his old superior with great respect and deference, and took special pleasure in presenting him to Mosby.

While the men were scattered about the town performing their respective tasks, Mosby, with a few men, had looked up Stoughton's headquarters and knocking at the door they were admitted by an officer, Lieutenant Prentiss, *en deshabille*. Mosby took him gently by the collar and, in a whisper, ordered him to show him where Stoughton was. On reaching the general's room that officer was found asleep in bed and, as time was precious, Mosby unceremoniously woke him up by spanking him on his bare skin. The general was properly horrified at such a liberty and, when asked if he ever heard of Mosby, quickly answered, "Yes; have you got him?"

Mosby replied,

"No, but he has got you."

The general was made to dress in a hurry and, with his *aide*. Lieutenant Prentiss, taken down stairs and outside where two of our men were waiting, having in the meantime taken a lot of seven couriers and their horses. Hunter was given special instructions to guard the general at all hazards, and the little squad started toward the Court-House Square which was the rendezvous for the whole band.

All the squads had done their allotted work well and Mosby started off with one hundred prisoners and horses. In the darkness a few of the prisoners escaped. Passing a dwelling in the town the men were halted by a voice at a window inquiring, in an authoritative tone, who they were. Two of Mosby's men, Joe Nelson and Welt Hatcher, were sent into the house to bring the man out, but he took the alarm and escaped by the back door in his nightshirt. It was Lieutenant. Colonel Johnston, of the Fifth New York, and it was said that he hid under the floor of a house in the garden. In the morning he got his men together and started in pursuit of Mosby but took the wrong direction.

To get his men out of the trouble into which it had been so easy to get, was now Mosby's care, for he always looked after that part of his exploits. The troops in the town were apprised of his presence, but each man of them seemed to be looking out for himself, and there was no concert of action. Mosby started towards Fairfax Station to throw his pursuers off guard, and then suddenly turned off towards Centreville. To pass that point meant a great deal to him. The heavy guns looked down frowningly on him only a few hundred feet away, and the sentinels on the works, with "Who goes there?" halted him as he passed under them; but he made no reply. Silently the little troop passed along by the big guns of the forts with their prisoners, and vanished into the darkness. Captain Barker made a dash towards the fort but was shot at by one of the men and recaptured, just as his horse fell into a ditch.

One more serious danger confronted Mosby. Cub Run, just beyond Centreville, was overflowing. Back of the little band was the fort with its brigade of soldiers, soon to be, if not already, alarmed; in front of them a raging torrent. There was not an instant of hesitation but, plunging into the mad stream, the whole party swam safely across, though many were carried down stream with the current. Once on the other side pursuit seemed impossible and, as the sun rose above the eastern horizon, Mosby breathed his first sigh of relief. Even at that hour he knew he had graven his name in history never to be effaced. He had performed another feat entirely new in the annals of war and one that has never been repeated. In time he reached Culpeper Court-House and turned his prisoners over to General Fitzhugh Lee, who was a classmate of Stoughton's at West Point.

On the Federal side the result of this brilliant affair of Mosby's was the early resignation of Stoughton from the army. His reputation was gone. A general must not be captured in his nightshirt. Colonel Percy Wyndham was relieved and his successor, failing to wipe out Mosby, was soon transferred. Colonel Johnston soon retired from army life. On the other hand General Stuart issued the following General Order, and Mosby, about a month later, was promoted to a Majority.

General Order.

Captain John S. Mosby has for a long time attracted the attention of his generals by his boldness, skill and success, so signally displayed in his numerous forays upon the invaders of his native state.

None know his daring enterprise and dashing heroism better than those foul invaders, though strangers themselves to such noble traits.

His late brilliant exploit, the capture of General Stoughton, U. S. A., two captains, thirty other prisoners, together with their arms, equipments and fifty-eight horses, justifies this recognition in General Orders. The feat, almost unparalleled in the war, was performed in the midst of the enemy's troops, at Fairfax C. H., without loss or injury.

The gallant band of Captain Mosby share the glory as they did the danger of this enterprise, and are worthy of such a leader.

J. E. B. Stuart,
Brigadier-General, Commanding.

The Chantilly fight, which occurred on the twenty-third, scarcely two weeks later, while Mosby still had only these migratory volunteers with him, was as well conducted as though it were the work of veterans. He had gathered about fifty of them together and taken them down into Fairfax County to "do something." His previous attacks had so aroused the camps in that part of the country that everyone was on the lookout; for him. He tried to get through their lines into their rear, in order to surprise them, but they were too wide-awake. The men he had with him wanted to fight, but they were more eager to capture some horses. The magnet of spoils attracted every man to Mosby's standard in that early day.

> *Sweet is revenge, especially to women;*
> *Pillage to soldiers, and prize-money to seamen.*

Rather than disappoint his men by returning home he concluded to try to draw the enemy out on the pike and trust to getting a running fight. He sent a few men out in sight, and the ruse was successful. They drove in the pickets and were immediately chased back up the pike, in which several of them were killed and captured. The noise of the firing brought out the reserves, and Mosby hurried over to head them off and prevent being cut off himself, for he knew re-enforcements would soon arrive. He retreated up the pike in a trot, and was followed by the Fifth New York. When he came to a little piece of woods he halted his men and faced his pursuers. Just as they came in sight he ordered a charge and his men dashed into them. Utterly astonished and confused, they turned and, rushing back down the pike, ran into their re-enforcements, who in turn also retreated. It was a senseless, inexcusable rout, for they were four to Mosby's one.

His men never questioned the safety or the danger of the charge: Mosby ordered them to charge an attacking force, and that order was sufficient, for they had seen him win in every affair in which they had been engaged and they believed he could do no wrong. He never stood still and accepted an attack. His men chased the flying enemy several miles, leaving a number of killed and wounded in the road, and bringing out thirty-six prisoners and fifty horses. His men were happy, for there was a horse for each man; and Mosby was the happiest of all, for his little band, to a man, had behaved gloriously, and he had not lost one. "Major" Hibbs was uncontrollable in his joy and, to emphasise it, Mosby publicly proclaimed him the "hero of the fight," in the presence of all the men, and gave him a fine horse as a reward. By turns he laughed and cried and finally he said: "Well, Captain, I knew the work had to be done, and that was the only way to do it."

When the affair was reported to Stuart, he sent back this reply:

Headquarters Cavalry Division,
Army of Northern Virginia, March 27th, 1863.

Captain: Your telegram announcing your brilliant achievement near Chantilly was duly received and forwarded to General Lee. He exclaimed upon reading it: "Hurrah for Mosby! I wish I had a hundred like him." Heartily wishing you continued success, I remain your obedient servant,

                                        J. E. B. Stuart,
                            Major-General, Commanding.

Captain John S. Mosby, Commanding, etc.

No man was prouder of Mosby's achievements than General Stuart. Not two months before that time Mosby the scout had left headquarters with a little handful of borrowed men on a dangerous experiment. Now he was a captain and a proved success as a leader. Stuart took part of the credit for making it possible to develop such a raider.

CHAPTER 5

The Fight at Miskell's Barn

The capture of General Stoughton so early in Mosby's career as a Partisan Ranger whetted the appetite of the people for more of his brilliant achievements and when, three weeks later, they heard of his fight at Miskell's barn, there was no limit to their amazement and enthusiasm. Like the Stoughton affair it was never repeated for he never permitted the possibility of it to occur again. It took place on April 1, 1863, appropriately enough, for it proved to be a sad April fool joke upon the enemies who had planned Mosby's capture.

On the previous day Mosby, at that time a captain, had been scouting through Fairfax and Loudoun Counties with his men, arriving at Miskell's farm near Dranesville at ten o'clock at night, tired, hungry and utterly exhausted. Supper was eaten by some of the men fortunate enough to get it, and the horses were unsaddled and unbridled and tied, some in the barn, and others to the fences that surrounded it. The men tumbled in upon the hay and under the eaves outside the barn, falling asleep instantly. Not one of the horses was saddled or bridled, and the thought of fighting was far from all.

Early the next morning some of the men noticed the Federal troops across the Potomac River signalling and called Mosby's attention to it. It is strange that a Command usually so alert should have been taken so completely by surprise, but it is true that before Mosby could express an opinion about the signals, Dick Moran, one of our men who had been in the neighbourhood with friends and who was doing a little looking out on his own hook, galloped into the barn-yard, yelling at the top of his voice, "Mount your horses; the Yankees are coming."

Moran's voice served to awaken some of the men who were still sleeping when the alarm came. Before they could arouse themselves or throw a saddle on a horse, in fact before most of them had lifted their weary heads from the ground, two hundred of the First Vermont Cavalry, under Captain Flint, charged through the farm gate which opened into the road and surrounded the barnyard, pouring their fire in volleys into Mosby's men. It looked as though the light and life of the guerrillas must be swept from the face of the earth. Never before or after had the Federal troops such another chance to secure Mosby and wipe out his men. They were three or more to his one, and they had him corralled in a perfect trap, as perfect as they could possibly have made it. The first shots brought every member of the Command out of the barn half awake, wondering what had happened.

In an open space in the barnyard stood Mosby on foot: in each hand holding a smoking Colt. As soon as a handful of his men gathered around him he ordered them to mount and "Charge 'em: charge 'em, and go through 'em." A movement of his hand indicated that he did not care just where the charge was made, only that he wanted his men to get into the open where he could handle them. He made no reckoning of the numbers of the enemy; he gave it no thought; he only knew that he and his men were in a trap and he did not intend they should be murdered like a lot of sheep in the shambles, if grit and ammunition held out. No thought of the disparity in numbers nor of their apparently desperate situation checked the impetuosity of the little band for an instant. They knew only one word: "Fight." The next instant Mosby was in the saddle. Harry Hatcher, seeing him on foot, insisted on giving up his horse, which Mosby at once mounted; and the Mosby yell to which no person has yet been able to do full justice, rose on the wings of that memorable morning.

Under the furious fire of the Vermonters most of the men saddled and bridled their horses, and mounting them, made a dash for Captain Flint's men. Like an avalanche the Guerrillas, with Mosby at their head, rushed through the barnyard gate and into the thick of the enemy, plying their revolvers with deadly effect. Every shot seemed to drop a Yankee from his saddle, so fast did they fall. In the panic that followed Mosby's unexpected and audacious counter-charge, Flint's men retreated to the gate leading into the turnpike and became jammed in a mass at the exit. Most of Mosby's men, being mounted by this time, poured a withering fire into the struggling, cursing, howling mob packed at the gate. When an opening was made Flint tried gallantly to rally his troopers but fell mortally shot in the effort, his body pierced by six bullets; fitting tribute to his courage, and evidence of the Mosby tactics, which always was to try to kill the man in command.

Nothing could now gather the remnant of the panic-stricken troop together, and the rout began. Mosby following some of the flying Vermonters for miles down the pike, while others scattered in different directions. By all the rules of war, Flint's men, numbering more than three to Mosby's one and completely surprising him, should have annihilated his entire force. The Rangers were completely entrapped in a corral with only one exit; not a single man with the exception of Dick Moran was mounted, and most of them were asleep. Notwithstanding these facts one sentence sums up Mosby's report, the report of a miracle. "Our loss was four men wounded; one of whom died later." The enemy's loss required more space in the report in summing it up as follows:

> Ten killed and fifteen mortally or dangerously wounded and left on the field and counted by us. Eighty-four prisoners and one hundred horses captured; among the prisoners a number were found to be wounded.

William H. Chapman, who afterwards became lieutenant-colonel of our battalion and second in command to Mosby, was a volunteer that day. He held a commission as captain of artillery and was in our part of the country on recruiting service. He was one of the first to get into action although he had to rush from the farmhouse to the barn to saddle his horse. Through the cracks in the barn he could see the Yankees surrounding the side of it and, though the temptation to pick off a few of them was great, he thought Mosby's men should put on a bold front, and accordingly he mounted and galloped out of the barn, and with a few others who were mounted, dashed through the gate which was held open by John Farrar, who was on foot.

He was in the midst of the fray immediately and encountered his first man at close range. The pistols were not a foot apart. The Yankee's pistol snapped but Chapman's did its deadly work. He fired six shots and emptied five saddles.

On one occasion I begged him to tell me about that fight. He had nothing to say about his own behaviour, and I was forced to hear it from others. Explaining Flint's awful mistake and the poor showing his men made under fire, he said, however, that our men were fresh from a good night's sleep on comfortable, sweet smelling hay, while Flint had been marching all night from Dranesville to Miskell's in the face of a cold wind, which was so benumbing that some of the men could hardly use their pistols. Chapman should have been named Charity. Our men were probably just as numb when they woke up that morning as were Flint's, and if the cold night had not made them so the sight of that crowd of blue-coats around the barnyard fence was enough. Furthermore, Mosby had given his men a march of forty miles the day before through mud and snow and slush, and a night's rest had done very little to restore them to their normal condition.

Sam Chapman, a brother of William H., was another conspicuous figure in the fight at Miskell's barn. I can not refrain from inserting here an extract concerning him, from Colonel Mosby's pen:

> There was with me that day a young artillery officer, Samuel F. Chapman who, at the first call of his state to arms, had quit the study of divinity and became, like Stonewall Jackson, a sort of military Calvin, singing the psalms of David as he went into battle. I must confess that his character as a soldier was more on the model of the Hebrew prophets than the Apostles, or the Baptist in whom he was so devout a believer. Before he got to the gate Sam had already exhausted every barrel of his two pistols and drawn his sabre. As the fiery Covenanter rode on his predestined course, the enemy's ranks withered wherever he went. He was just in front of me. He was generally in front of everybody in a fight. At the gate, it was no fault of the Union cavalry that they did not get through any faster than they did, but Sam seemed to think it was. Even at that supreme moment in my life, when I had just stood on the brink of ruin and had barely escaped, I could not restrain a propensity to laugh. Sam, to give more vigour to his blows, was standing straight up in his stirrups, dealing them right and left with all the theological fervour of Burly of Balfour. I made him a captain for it.[1]

On the following day United States troops were sent up to Miskell's to bury the dead and gather up the wounded. A hospital was established there to care for, those who were so seriously injured that their removal was impossible. The surgeon reported to Washington that a large number among those who escaped were found to have wounds.

Major General Julius Stahel, U. S. A., commanding a cavalry divi-

---

1. *The Gray Raiders*—Volume 1 published by Leonaur contains *Mosby's War Reminiscences* by John S. Mosby along with *Reminiscences by the Surgeon of Mosby's Command* by Aristedes Monteiro.

sion, in reporting this fight to Major-General Heintzelman, wrote as follows:

> Captain Flint took his men through the gate and fired a volley at Mosby and his men, doing slight damage, and then ordered a sabre charge which was also ineffectual. Mosby waited until his men were checked by the fence, and then opened his fire on them. The men here became panic-stricken and fled precipitately towards the gate through which to make their escape. The opening was small and they got wedged together.
>
> A fearful state of confusion followed, while Mosby's men followed them up and poured into the crowd a serious fire. I regret to be obliged to inform the commanding general that the forces sent out by Major Taggart missed so good an opportunity of capturing this rebel Guerrilla. It is only to be ascribed to the bad management on the part of the officers and the cowardice of the men. I have ordered Colonel Price to make a thorough investigation of the matter, and shall recommend those officers who are guilty to be stricken from the rolls.

Mosby reported the affair promptly to both General Lee and Stuart, and General Lee issued the following order:

> Headquarters, April 4, 1863.
>
> Mr. President: Major John S. Mosby reported that he was attacked early on the morning of the 1st inst., near Dranesville, by about two hundred Vermont Cavalry. He promptly repulsed them, leaving on the field twenty-five killed and wounded, including three officers, and brought off eighty-two prisoners with their horses, arms and equipment. His force consisted of sixty-four men, and his loss was four wounded. I had the pleasure to send by return courier to Major Mosby his commission of Major of Partisan Rangers, for which I am obliged to your Excellency.
>
> I am with great respect
>
> Your obedient servant,
>
> R. E. Lee, General.
>
> To His Excellency, President Davis,
> President Confederate States of America.

At the time that this fight occurred Mosby had not been quite two months engaged in Partisan Ranger warfare, but he had amply demonstrated to his generals that he was the man for this peculiar work.

Two such achievements as the capture of Stoughton and the victory at Miskell's, with a mere handful of newly acquired men and within three weeks of each other, stamped him as a phenomenal leader; a man with magnetism to attract to himself the right sort of followers for his unique work and to impart that force to them when once they had come under his spell. I cannot conceive of any of the noted generals or colonels of either army carrying through successfully, with a detachment of men, two such affairs as these.

They were both to become classics in Partisan Ranger warfare though entirely different in kind, and Mosby's men, flushed with their victories redoubled their energies, and for two years following made history that will last when the stories of big battles and retreats and victories are forgotten. There were hundreds of regiments and brigades and divisions, but there was only one Mosby's Command.

In the official report of the fight at Miskell's the Federal officer said:

Lieutenant Grout mortally wounded; will die tomorrow.

But Lieutenant Grout did not die. In 1896, on account of this wound, he was nominated as Republican candidate for Governor of Vermont. At the time of President McKinley's first inauguration Colonel Mosby saw by the papers that Governor Grout, his family and his staff were at the Arlington hotel. Sam Chapman, who took such an enviable part in the Miskell fight, was with Colonel Mosby in Washington at this time, and together they called upon Governor Grout at the Arlington, sent up their cards, and soon the governor, his wife, son and staff received them most cordially.

Not long after that Colonel Mosby was badly injured in Charlottesville, Va., by a horse and, while lying in bed, received a very kind letter from Governor Grout. He reminded the colonel of something which he had forgotten. After the fight at Miskell's was I over Mosby went into a house into which all the wounded had been brought, and Lieutenant Grout, severely wounded, asked him to let two of his Vermont soldiers remain there as nurses. Mosby let him select two from among the prisoners who remained.

CHAPTER 6

Warrenton Junction and Catlett's Station

On a bright spring morning, May 3rd, 1863, Mosby took his one hundred men down to Warrenton Junction, on the old Orange and Alexandria railroad, now the main line of the Southern, and ran into a hundred or more of the First Virginia Cavalry, Federal. I say we ran into them, but the fact is we slipped in and found the Yankees lolling around the station, some asleep, some idling, all unprepared for the suddenness with which we rushed them. There was a wild scattering in different directions, but the main body took refuge in a large building nearby and refused to surrender, defending their position with a shower of bullets fired from cracks and windows. Finally Mosby decided to smoke them out, and ordered that the building be set on fire, but some of our men under cover of the trees got near the entrance, made a bold dash for it, and broke the door down. The whole crowd capitulated at once and Mosby gathered them in as prisoners.

In the meantime the Fifth New York, and the First Vermont Cavalry, encamped at Cedar Run a short distance away, had heard the firing and came up on the run. This overwhelming force turned the tables on us with a vengeance. They chased us in a running fight towards Warrenton, recaptured most of their prisoners and horses, and made it generally disagreeable for the Partisan Rangers. They killed a scout named Templeton, a member of the regular army who had volunteered with our Command that day. We also lost about twenty of our men wounded and taken prisoners. The killed on the other side were Major Steele, of the First Virginia and one private. Ten of their men were wounded. Of the Fifth New York, Captain Krom was severely wounded, and Lieutenants Frank A. Monson, and McBride were wounded, but not dangerously.

Our men succeeded in getting away with ten prisoners and their horses. Among our wounded and captured was Captain Sam Ducheane, a soldier of fortune, who had served under Walker in his Nicaragua expedition before the war. Another was Dick Moran, who gave the alarm to Mosby at Miskell's barn on April 1st, just one month before; and still another was Tom Richards who captured Major Forbes in the fight at Mount Zion Church on July 6th, 1864, and who became one of the most conspicuous members of our Command and was made captain for bravery.

This engagement was a most disastrous one for Mosby. The loss of twenty men wounded and captured, where only one hundred were engaged, was something serious and unprecedented.

While writing the account of this fight at Warrenton Junction I had a letter from Captain Elmer Barker, of the Fifth New York, suggesting that I get Captain Frank A. Monson, of the same regiment, to tell me something about the fight from the other side. I opened a correspondence with Captain Monson, who is a business man of New Haven, Conn., which has resulted in the following interesting story:

> Sunday morning, May 3rd, 1863, found the Fifth New York Cavalry encamped about one quarter of a mile north of Warrenton Junction. For four or five days previous to the above date we had scoured the country for many miles looking for Mosby's men, having been to Upperville, Salem, The Plains, Rectortown, Aldie, and Middleburg without finding them.
>
> The First Virginia Federal Cavalry was encamped at Warrenton Junction. Both regiments were taking it rather easy after the five days of scouting. Many of the horses were grazing in the field. It was about six o'clock and we could hear the booming of the guns at Chancellorsville. There was some cheering up at the junction. At first we thought there was good news from the battle but the shots that followed told us that the First Virginia had been attacked.
>
> We jumped for our horses, which were unsaddled, and in less time than it takes to tell it the First Virginia horses came on a stampede through our camp, stampeding many of our horses. Two of my horses got away. I put the saddle on a horse and had only time to buckle one girth. The other, as well as the breast strap, girth and throat strap, were hanging. We started out from

Mosby planning an attack on a Federal Convoy

the Junction with only forty men in line. More joined us after we got into the fight. Major Hammond led the men, Captain Penfield, Captain Krom and myself were at his heels.

As we approached the house at the junction we divided, one-half went one way and one-half went the other. Mosby had captured the whole First Virginia regiment, which he had drawn up in line and was about ready to march them off as prisoners. A running fight commenced. Mosby had to abandon the First Virginia boys. We followed them to Warrenton, about ten miles. A little way south of the junction, one of Mosby's men was a little behind the others and was shooting at me all the time. I thought I would have him, so I put spurs to my horse and was alongside of him in a minute and ordered him to surrender. He turned on me and we both fired; my revolver missed fire; his bullet whizzed past my head. I had to turn and run; he followed me. I lay over on the side of my horse out of his aim. He put a ball through my boot leg. Captain Penfield came to my assistance and captured the man.

About a mile south of the junction one of Mosby's men introduced a piece of cold lead into my left shoulder which made me go to the rear. I did not get quite back to the junction before I fell from my I horse from weakness from loss of blood. When I recovered consciousness two hours later I was in the junction house with other wounded, among them Captain Krom of the Fifth and Major Steele of the First Virginia. Major Steele did not recover.

In the latter part of the same month General Stuart sent to Mosby, at his request, a little howitzer, but nobody dreamed then what a hot and meteoric career it was destined to have. The old Orange and Alexandria Railroad was used for the transportation of all the supplies of the Union Army which was then on the Rappahannock and, as a consequence, it was heavily guarded at every weak point. It's trains were all protected by sufficient troops to prevent an attack from our men, and cavalry patrols were constantly on the move from post to post along the whole line. This condition made it a mark for Mosby, as it was his mission to annoy the enemy, and the fight at Catlett's was one of the blows he struck.

On the 29th of May he had the Command, about one hundred men, meet him at Patterson's, and the wonderful little howitzer was run out for inspection and criticism. Some of the men thought it a bit too large to carry in a holster, but not big enough to be called a cannon. Sam Chapman was one of the few men in the Command who knew the difference between a howitzer, and a saw-log, and Mosby told Sam to show some of the boys what to do with it. He was an officer in the Dixie Battery when he came to us. He spent a few minutes instructing the men in the artillery tactics, showing them the difference between the muzzle and the touch-hole, and finally reported to Mosby that his battery of one twelve-pound gun was thoroughly and efficiently manned.

Mosby then started for the railroad, stopping at Greenwich for supper, and camping not far from there for the night. Early on the morning of the 30th the Command was pushed on towards Catlett's Station, where the gun was to have its baptism of fire. When they reached the railroad a section of the track was torn up and the telegraph wires were cut. A train, heavily guarded, soon came up and stopped before it reached the torn-up rails. Sam Chapman turned his howitzer loose upon it, and the men charged it and scattered the guard. The train of eleven cars was plundered of its contents and then burned. The boys got all sorts of good things and a lot of miscellaneous supplies that were of no earthly use to them, but which they could not resist the temptation to carry off. Among these latter were big' bundles of sole leather and a lot of fresh shad.

Cavalry camps were near by on each side of the station and the firing of our guns and the pistol shooting that followed attracted their attention; relief parties were at once sent out.

Colonel Mann was in command of the cavalry at Bristoe Station, and he immediately started Captain Hasbrouck with a detachment of the Fifth New York cavalry to intercept Mosby, while he followed along the railroad with his own Seventh Michigan and the First Vermont. Mosby had only gone a few miles when the men of the Fifth New York faced him, having cut across from their camp. Chapman used his howitzer again and sent a shell into them which stopped them, and Mosby then proceeded. Colonel Mann came up very soon with his Seventh Michigan and First Vermont, and the odds were too great for us.

It was decided to make a last stand. Sam Chapman placed his little gun to the best advantage near the residence of Mr. Green not far from Greenwich, and when Captain Barker of the Fifth New York charged him, Sam cut loose with a charge of grape and canister, and killed three or four and wounded seven of them; but, though our men repulsed them and drove them back, we finally had to retreat and lost the gun. The pursuit was not kept up.

The enemy admitted a loss of five killed and fifteen wounded. Our loss was five killed and about twenty wounded and captured. Sam Chapman was desperately wounded and left at Mr. Charles Green's house, presumably to die. Captain B. E. Hoskins, an English Army officer serving with us, was also badly wounded and taken to Mr. Green's house where he died, and was buried in the little family churchyard at Greenwich, where over his grave, there is now a beautiful monument placed by the kindly hands of Mr. Green at the request of Captain Hoskins' father, who was an English rector. Captain Hoskins had served in the Crimean war and had won the Crimean medal as a captain in the English Army, and was a splendid specimen of the gentleman adventurer, which our Command attracted to its ranks. He sold his commission and joined Garibaldi in one of his campaigns, and later came to America for adventure. I am indebted for a very fine photograph of old Greenwich Church and Captain Hoskins' tombstone, to Mr. Douglas Green, a New York broker, son of Mr. Charles Green. He was a boy at the time of our fight, but remembers it distinctly, and says he gave up his room and his bed to our two wounded officers, Hoskins dying in his bed. Sam Chapman went down at his gun, and Fount Beattie and Montjoy were captured trying to save it.

It was of this fight that Major Boutelle, a retired army officer now living in the State of Washington, wrote me he thought the bringing out and handling of our gun that day was one of the most romantic affairs of the war. The major was a lieutenant of the Fifth Cavalry at the time of the fight and had his horse killed under him by a shot from Sam Chapman's little cannon at close range. He suggested that I write to Major Barker of Crown Point, N.Y., who led his men against us so successfully that day, and get him to give me his version of the fight, which I did, and got the following interesting story from him, which I here insert with his permission.

> The morning of May 30th, 1863, found detachments of the First Vermont, Seventh Michigan and Fifth New York Cavalry, in which latter regiment I was then Second Lieutenant, guarding the railroad near Bristoe Station. A train came out from Washington and, stopping at our camp, left papers and supplies and passed on. It had gone but a few moments when we

heard an artillery shot from its direction. We knew Mosby had never had any cannon, and so supposed it must be General Stuart who had attacked the train. Colonel Mann of the Seventh Michigan, in command, ordered Captain Hasbrouck, in command of the detachment of the Fifth New York, to strike across the country and get in the rear of the enemy, he himself taking Lieutenant-Colonel Preston with the First Vermont and the Seventh Michigan directly to where the train was attacked. Our detachment started out and met Mosby's Command face to face in the road. He immediately put his gun into position and sent us his compliments by way of a shell, which killed Lieutenant Boutelle's horse. Captain Hasbrouck, instead of charging as he should have done, marched his men up on a hill and allowed Mosby to march by us in good order. I rode up to Captain Hasbrouck and asked him what he intended to do, and he replied that he could do nothing with his small command. This made me very angry. I was nothing but a boy anxious for a fight and I turned around and gave the order, 'By fours from the right, trot, march,' and started after Mosby, most of the command following me. We had gone three or four miles on the run, tracking the enemy by the shad and other things which they dropped, which they had captured from the train, and were pretty well strung out when, going around a turn in the road in a small piece of timber, we suddenly ran into their rear guard.

It proved to be Mosby himself. Captain Hoskins of the British army, and three others. Corporal Wooster of Company H, Corporal Jenkins of Company F, and myself were too near to halt and ran right into them. At the first fire Wooster and Jenkins were both wounded and their horses shot. Colonel Hoskins was mortally wounded, and one of Mosby's men killed. This left me alone with the other three for probably one or two minutes (it seemed hours). I fired all the shots in my revolver, and then drew my sabre, they trying to shoot me, crying 'Surrender, Yank,' and I trying to kill them.

Hiram Underhill was the first of my men to get up to us. He undoubtedly saved my life. I have seen an article written by a Confederate officer stating that Mosby was slightly wounded on the arm that day by a sabre. It must have been my sabre, as I hit someone, but did not know then who it was. They got away but we soon caught up with them. They had their gun posted on a knoll in a lane, and as we came up they fired a shell into us. I said to the boys, 'I think we can get that gun before they can fire again,' and they all said, 'Let's go.'

We got very near to the gun, probably within twenty feet, when it was fired, killing the gallant Corporal Drake, poor brave fellow, a grape shot passing through his head. Two others were also killed and a number wounded. Two grape shot entered my left thigh, one carrying off my stirrup and the sole of my boot, and four or five entered my horse.

At this time Colonel Preston came in with the Vermont men and we took the gun, the brave Lieutenant Chapman fighting to the last, though mortally wounded. I then rode back about one mile and met Doctor Edson of the First Vermont. I got off my horse and laid down under a tree, having lost considerable blood, and feeling rather weak. The doctor took off my boot and found one ball in it and the other he cut out of my leg. At this time a Mr. Green, a quiet elderly gentleman, came out with an ox team, some ice water and a bottle of brandy, the contents of which revived me amazingly. He kindly invited me to remain at his house until I convalesced, but I declined, with thanks, as it was in the enemy's lines. I waited until they sent to camp for an ambulance, in which I rode back to camp, arriving about dark, and remained in the ambulance all night.

Official reports say that we lost four killed and one officer and seven men wounded out of one hundred and seventy-one engaged. Mosby's Command numbered about two hundred men, but I am unable to give his loss.

General Stahel in his report of June 3rd, said:

> The advance of the Fifth New York, led by Lieutenant Elmer Barker, came up with the enemy first. . . . with his small detachment dashed up the hill and when within about fifty yards of the gun received a charge of grape and canister, which killed three and wounded seven of our men and several horses; the enemy had then charged upon us, but were met with a stubborn resistance by the lieutenant and his men although the lieutenant had received two grape shot in his thigh. We were, however, overpowered and driven back a short distance. Just then Colonel Preston of the First Vermont, came up at a full

charge upon their flank and was again received with a discharge from the Howitzer of grape and canister. Our men pushed on, until they came to a hand-to-hand conflict, when the enemy gradually fell back.

On the day of the fight Colonel Mann reported very promptly to General Stahel, commanding, a very graphic account of the affair, and on the following day, after returning from a visit to the grounds, he reported to Major Baldwin as follows:

> Returned at dark, bringing in one cannon and all our dead and wounded. The wounded number fifteen on our side. It was an extremely hot affair for a small one. Many of the wounds very severe. Our captures of the day are ten prisoners, including Captain Hoskins, an English officer of seven years' service, now in the Confederate service, and Lieutenant Chapman, who had charge of the artillery. Both these officers so severely wounded could not be removed and were paroled. I sent in prisoners by train today. The enemy lost heavy in wounded, as they received a terrific fire from revolvers at close range, followed by a determined sabre charge. Many were severely cut by sabre, but clung to their horses and fell back into the thicket. (Not a man of Mosby's was so much as scratched with a sabre. The colonel had been misinformed. J. W. Munson.) Lieutenant Barker had two grape shot through his thigh, but is quite comfortable. He crossed sabres with them and fought desperately after this wound.

Chapter 7

Dranesville and Elsewhere

When the two armies under Lee and Meade were coming back from the disastrous Gettysburg campaign, Mosby's little Confederacy was overrun with troops, and his men, at the time only one company, were kept on the alert; but they were well paid for the annoyance Meade's army gave them. Singly and in groups, men were picked up and gathered into the Mosby fold and as it was impossible or, more properly speaking, inconvenient, to carry them out of the enemy's lines to turn them over to General Lee, a temporary camp for them was established in the Bull Run Mountain, where they were as securely kept, though in full sight of their own passing troops, as if they were in Libby prison.

By the 21st of July, Mosby had captured forty-seven men, two sutler's wagons and a headquarters wagon. To retain them, however, was an annoying task, for Mosby wanted every available man for active service. Tom Lake, with seven men, was detailed to carry the prisoners out, much to Tom's disgust, for the boy was eager to stay where he could participate in the fighting. The sutler's wagons proved a treat to the boys, for they contained all sorts of good things. From the appetising contents of one, Lake prepared a supper of canned turkey and hot corn bread with a bottle of wine. That was Tom's idea of a feast. He invited his chief to share the meal and during its progress he was ordered to carry out the forty-seven prisoners. Three wagons were burned and the captors and captured started along the mountain side to worm their way toward the Southern Army at Culpeper.

A few days later Mosby sent the following report to General Stuart:

I sent you in charge of Sergeant Beattie, one hundred and forty-one prisoners which we captured from the enemy during their march through this county. I also sent off forty-five several days ago. Included in the number, one major, one captain and two lieutenants. I also captured one hundred and twenty-five horses and mules, twelve wagons (only three of which I was able to destroy), fifty sets of fine harness, arms, etc., etc.

Beattie carried these prisoners out safely with a guard of only seventeen men, and when they were approaching our army it is said that the alarm was given that Meade was making a flank movement on Lee. Beattie was so completely lost to sight among his men in blue that our troops could not distinguish any of our men and supposed it must be a flank movement or a daring raid.

The first night that Tom Lake and his forty-seven prisoners were on their journey South, he ran into Hancock's column not far from Warrenton and, remembering that Mosby once carried two prisoners safely through an entire regiment of the enemy, he struck out boldly with his little crowd and piloted them through without a challenge or the loss of a prisoner. It was then not yet dusk, and immediately afterward he went into camp for the night at the home of one of the Blackwells. He resumed his march the next morning, escaping a raiding party who had heard of his being there half an hour previously. Not content with the number of prisoners he already had, he gathered in several of Hancock's men as he passed through that column. At three o'clock he turned his prisoners over to General Longstreet, at Culpeper Court House and started back to the Command. This daring journey was made entirely by day.

Charley Hall was one of the seven men detailed to accompany Tom Lake, and the mere mention of his name recalls enough incidents connected with him to fill a book. I reluctantly resist the impulse to chronicle them at length, but as he is one of our dead heroes I must make suitable mention of him. Though he was a mature man, thirty years old, as I recall him, he was companionable with the younger set, and especially popular with the daredevil element. At times he drifted away from the truly exemplary paths of the regular Mosby Guerrillas and went off on wild adventures with Nick Carter and Charley McDonough, two brevet-outlaws who accompanied us only by tolerance of the colonel. When these three started out on a business trip there were always results. Colonel Mosby would not permit Charley and Nick to indulge in reprehensible actions when they were with us, but I think he had a sneaking admiration for their bravery, for neither of them knew what fear was. There was a reward for Charley McDonough's apprehension, and once he was chased by a raiding party near Middleburg. His horse having fallen the boy realised that he was to be taken prisoner, and accordingly emptied all but one load of his pistols into his pursuers, and the last into his own brain.

Carter belonged to one of the oldest and most aristocratic families in Virginia, but he accumulated such a load of undesirable responsibility and notoriety during the war that he thought it best to leave the country mysteriously at its close.

Charley Hall was always picturesque. He was a particularly handsome man, and always went faultlessly mounted and equipped; in fact he was one of our pronounced dandies. I have seen him emerge from a fight, brushing the dust from his clothes and smoothing out his ruffled plume as though nothing unusual had occurred. There was a story current in the Command that, in the "Greenback Raid," he had relieved a cattle dealer of more than five thousand dollars, in addition to his share of the greenbacks captured from Sheridan's paymasters. The cattle dealer was a government contractor.

Charley and John Puryear were riding down the Snickersville turnpike one dark night and, as they crossed a little stream, they stopped their horses to let them drink. While they stood there two men rode up alongside of them and also stopped their horses. Not a word was spoken for a moment and then Puryear whispered softly: "Charley, they are Yankees." Knowing full well that the newcomers were the extreme advance of a raiding party and that any attempt to run would only hasten their own capture or their death they quietly drew their pistols and, each selecting the nearest man, fired. There were cries of pain; a splash in the little stream; two riderless horses dashing by them down the pike; and the clatter of hoofs back of them. That was all. War is not play.

On the 20th of February, 1864, two days before the Dranesville Fight, frequently referred to as "the other Dranesville fight," because Miskell's was not far from Dranesville, and they used to call that the first fight at Dranesville), Colonel Mosby. Johnny Edmonds, Jake Lavinder and I were seated at breakfast in Mr. Blackwell's home in the Blue Ridge foothills; the same house at which I joined the Partisan Rangers the year previous, and which I had made my home ever since. It was known by all our men and by the citizens generally, as Mosby's Headquarters, for he was there more than anywhere else when not in the saddle. Before we had completed our meal Jimmy Edmonds, Johnny's little brother, burst into the room panting from his long run and yelling:—

"The Yankees are on the pike: it's just blue with 'em."

We saddled our horses at once and galloped out to the pike to see how much of it they occupied, as such action seemed like trespassing on our preserve. To compliment a faithful follower, the colonel had appointed Lavinder Ordnance Sergeant of the battalion; in fact he had created the office to give it to Jake, and incidentally to please Jake's sweetheart, who was a sister of Mrs. Blackwell. The colonel was ever a gallant, and had a warm spot in his heart for lovers.

During Jake's term of office he had gathered, though from what source no ever knew, two carbines and a few rounds of cartridges which, at a pinch, might be used safely, if not effectually. We laughed at his arsenal, preferring our pistol to anything else, but Jake halted long enough to seize his collection before he galloped after us. I recollect how encumbered he appeared as he followed in our rear, carrying his guns in every possible position, and hanging on to them in the face of our ridicule.

When we reached the pike not far from Piedmont Depot, on the old Manassas Gap Railroad, we discovered a raiding party of about two hundred and fifty men. They proved to be Cole's Maryland Battalion and they were looking for trouble. We four were so absolutely out of proportion to their number that the colonel sent a messenger off to spread the news and gather the Mosby clans. While we were waiting for enough of our men to gather for an attack, we could do nothing except ride along in the wake of the enemy and keep a sharp watch on their movements. Meantime someone was riding frantically from house to house, crying out:—

> The colonel is down on the pike with only three men, trying to hold a whole Yankee column: hurry over to him and send to him all the men you can! Spread the news!

And so on to the next farm rode the Guerrilla Paul Revere.

It soon became evident that Mosby's men were what the Yankees were looking for. Shortly after we came in sight of them they turned back on the route upon which we first saw them. Presently they dropped down a little hill and stopped for a moment at a creek that ran at its base. This was the moment for which Jake had been waiting. He passed us the two carbines and insisted that now was the time to try their range and effectiveness. Colonel Mosby did not care to use a strange and suspicious looking weapon, and I was equally reluctant, for I had never fired a carbine in my life, and I did not want to be killed by a bursting gun. Jake insisted and finally talked us into it. We selected a couple of shells that seemed to fit into the guns without their sticking or dropping through all the way and, after warning Jake to stand back out of danger if anything unusual happened, we blazed away. A horse and a man, far apart, dropped dead in the road. Jake let out a whoop and pressed us to try it again, but we knew when we had enough, especially as a rain of bullets from Cole's men fell around us. It was never known which of us killed the man and which the horse, for neither of us aimed at either, but I claimed the animal as my prize because it had on a bridle and saddle which I wanted for a friend. The dead man was carried off by his men.

This carbine shooting woke things up. Some of our men, rounded up by the messengers, began to appear; more joined us along the pike as we started after Cole's men, whom we pursued for miles into Loudoun County in a running fight. Just as we passed through the town of Upperville, the boys' school was dismissed for recess. One very fat boy took in the situation at once and, jumping on his pony with his McGuffy's Third Reader for his only weapon, which he waved aloft, he dashed into the chase with us, whooping and yelling and never stopping until we all quit the chase. That day was the boy's last at school, for he insisted on joining the Command and, until the end of the war, was one of the gamest and best soldiers Mosby had. He was Cab Maddox. known to every man in the Command and to everybody in that country, as a fighter.

One man, McCobb, was killed, and a few captured, among them Bartlet and John Bolling, who were at their father's home when Colonel Cole pounced down upon them. The Command was called together the next day to attend the funeral of our dead comrade. We gave our dead Christian burial whenever possible and they sleep today in many an unmarked grave in northern Virginia.

While we were gathering for the funeral at the house of Mr. Jeffries, one of our scouts brought in the report that the Yankees were about. We jumped into our saddles, leaving McCobb's body to be buried by others, and rode away at a stiff gallop in the direction where our scout had last seen the enemy. We had about one hundred and fifty men and Mosby was in Command. Late that same afternoon we overtook the raiders and ascertained that they were a part of the Second Massachusetts Cavalry under Captain Reed. They had about two hundred men which included a number of Californians belonging to a California battalion that formed part of the Massachusetts regiment.

We followed them quietly all the afternoon and when they camped at nightfall, not very far from Dranesville, we camped on their trail. They were joined that night by another party of the Sixteenth New York Cavalry under Major Frazer, but the next morning Frazer and his men quitted them and went to his camp by a road in our rear which left us between the two forces. The outlook was exceedingly promising for a pitched battle on a small scale. Mosby was in a very cheerful mood, looking forward to a fitting celebration of Washington's birthday, which was to fall upon the morrow.

Most of us "retired" to our saddle blankets on the frozen ground later than usual as the imminence of a splendid fight made sleep impossible to many. The hot-headed youngsters among us wanted to begin at once. We were astir about sunrise the next morning, saddled up and mounted quickly, and moved over to the Dranesville pike, a mile or so below town. Colonel Mosby split his force, placing the two divisions two or three hundred yards apart, near the pike. From the two sections he selected fifteen men whom he stationed, dismounted, in the pines immediately beside the pike. Down the road he placed three men, Frank Rahm and two others, to attract the attention of the Yankees when they came along and to draw them out. Mosby gave strict orders that not a shot was to be fired by any man until he gave the signal, which was to be a sharp blast from a whistle, and, taking with him Companies A and B a little way below where he had stationed the fifteen men, he left Chapman in charge of Companies C, D and E above the fifteen men. All were near the road but hidden from view.

Presently some of Reed's men saw Frank Rahm and the two men down the pike and started for them, passing our first division under Chapman concealed in the woods. Not a shot was fired and the enemy following the pickets rode blindly into the trap. Our men, who had been ordered to remain quiet and await the signal, were tremblingly eager to begin firing, but a Command from Mosby was not to be disobeyed. We could see the Yankees moving cautiously along the pike, but inevitably into the jaws of death. After a time the advance column came opposite our fifteen dismounted men, and a shrill blast came from Mosby's whistle. Instantly fifteen pairs of six-shooters were emptied into the enemy's ranks. They halted and wavered, some of them throwing up their hands as if to ward off a sudden slap in the face. Almost simultaneously our mounted detachments, right and left, on the pike, descended like wolves on the fold, with the unearthly Mosby yell spreading terror and confusion everywhere. Our attack seemed to be a complete surprise, although they were out "looking for Mosby."

The whistle had been blown just a little too soon, for what we supposed was the main body of Reed's men and had fired into proved to be only an advance guard and, when Chapman charged upon the pike, he was abreast of the main body which had turned and begun retreating. When Mosby appeared on the pike with Companies A and B none of the enemy were in front of him and we had to gallop up the pike to catch up with them. When we reached them Chapman and his men were already there, and all of a sudden it became a hand-to-hand affair. It was soon evident to Reed that he was in for a whipping, and his men began breaking through the fences and into the fields, but fighting all the while. His Californians, especially notoriously good fighters, were standing up to the rack like men, dealing out to us the best they had. They rallied at every call on them and went down with banners flying. The road was rapidly filled up with dead and wounded men and horses, and riderless horses were galloping in terror everywhere. We chased the flying men in every direction, constantly emitting the Mosby yell to give speed to their heels. Many of them were driven into the Potomac River, and dead and drowned bodies were found around the neighbourhood for several days afterwards.

No man in the Command was nearer to the thick of that fight than Mosby himself. There was no room, after once we got started, to lead a charge, and the chief got right in the middle. I saw him weaving in and out of the fighting mass like a ferret, fighting hand-to-hand with every man who would stand before him. His fine mare was shot early in the action, and he sat her firmly throughout the entire fight, though she was on three legs only.

There was in our Command one Baron von Massow, a Prussian officer, whom came to us with letters, looking for adventure and desiring to study our tactics, like the Austrian officer of whom I shall speak in my account of the Greenback Raid. Since 1865 he has been identified with the German Army and has had part in every war since. Today he commands the crack cavalry corps, the Ninth, of the Imperial German Army, and as I write these lines his photograph is before me, showing his breast covered with medals of honour. He was one of the handsomest men I ever saw.

That morning, at Dranesville, the baron rode into the fight in the squad in front of me. A long redlined cape was thrown back from his shoulders exposing his glittering uniform. From his hat waved a big ostrich plume and he dashed into the fray with a bright German sabre flashing in the light. I have not the slightest doubt that he was mistaken for Mosby, for he was a very conspicuous figure and drew a perfect rain of bullets and sabre thrusts from the enemy. He saw Captain Reed and charged him. Reed threw up his pistol hand and surrendered to the baron, who passed him by to charge on the next man. When his back was turned Reed shot him through the body. Seeing Captain Wm. H. Chapman rushing towards him to avenge the deed, he started on a run but was immediately overtaken by Chapman who shot him through the body, falling dead near the baron who was lying in the road where he was shot. I was near enough to see him hit and remember he tried to raise his weapon for another shot, found his strength going, and plunged forward on his face dead.

I saw the baron lying in the road with his martial cloak around him, magnificent in his colours, and looking every inch a hero. I had no time at that moment to stand in contemplation of the real military man among us, so I jumped my horse over him and rode on. The brave German pulled through after a long and hard siege, and made up his mind to return to his native land; the following summer he bade many of us an affectionate farewell, and left us. Some of our old Command correspond with him to this day. I got the facts of Captain Reed's death from Colonel Wm. H. Chapman.

Before we went into the action that day I loaned one of my pistols to a new man who had none, which left me but one for my own use. I did fairly well until the end of the action, when I got the drop on a Californian with my last shot. He threw up his pistol and exclaimed, "I surrender."

I took it for granted he meant what he said, and rode past him, firing at a man beyond who was trying to work his way through a wedge of his men, on the roadside. Then the man who so readily surrendered turned and shot me in the back as I passed him. I don't blame him in the least, for I ought to have had the sense to take his pistol from him when he held it up. Lud Lake, who was an eyewitness to his attempt on my life, shot and killed him. When the bullet struck me only a half inch from my backbone, I felt a numbness coming over my legs first and then my body. One of our men reached out and held me on my horse. At that instant Harry Sweeting was shot at my side and the

BARON ROBERT VON MASSOW,
Private in Mosby's Command, and now General of Ninth Cavalry Corps, the Crack Corps of the German Army.

same man reached out and seized him, too: but Harry's wound hurt him so badly he pulled away and fell from his horse into the road. He managed to drag himself to a little stream trickling along the roadside, where he bathed his wound in the cold water and stopped the flow of blood. He recovered.

My friend who held me on my horse (I never learned his name), succeeded in getting me into a nearby house and placing me on a lounge, after which he rushed off to finish his engagement with the Yankees. The wounding of a man in our Command was of little moment and my friend never thought enough of the incident to look me up later and receive my thanks. Shortly afterward, when the fight was over and the men started home, some of them, seeing my horse tied to the fence, came in and found me trying to amuse myself by counting the clock ticks, and took me away.

At the beginning of the fight the family had run out of the house and gone to the woods for protection and I was alone when the boys found me. I must have been an attractive object, for I had put my hand back of me to ease my pain and got it smeared with warm blood, and then wiped my face with my bloody hand. My wound kept me out of service for a few weeks, but I had gentle nursing by Mrs. Edmonds and her daughters and the best of medical care from Dr. Dunn, who, having no nitrate of silver, used to dress my wound with burnt alum; he had me on a diet of bacon and cabbage till he could get my stomach strong.

The result of the fight on our side was the loss of one man, Chappalier, killed, and eight wounded, five of them seriously. The Federal loss was fifteen killed, twenty-five wounded, seventy-five prisoners and one hundred horses captured. The Yankees, had been piloted on their raid by Charley Binns, a deserter from our Command. When the first shot was fired Charley started to run and was never heard of by the Californians or our men. It was said that he stopped for one night in Winnipeg to get a bite and then went on towards the North Pole. His name became a by-word in Mosby's Command.

There is another incident of this second Dranesville fight, that is entitled to a space in these recollections. Johnny Edmonds was my "bunky" in Mosby's Command. Mr. Blackwell, at whose house we lived and where Mosby made his headquarters, was Johnny's brother-in-law. The whole family resided in the neighbourhood. The day before when we started from Mr. Blackwell's to go to McCobb's funeral, Johnny's mother insisted that he should take a little pocket Bible along with him. "You can't tell how soon you may need the good book, my son," was her parting advice. She was a very devout Episcopalian, and, while her heart was in the cause for which her sons were fighting, she had an abiding faith in the supreme strength and wisdom to be gained from the word of God.

Johnny took the book, thrust it into his trousers' pocket and forgot all about it. In the fight the next day he fired at a man at close range and missed him, something he did not do often, and the Union man fired back and hit Johnny with a forty-four calibre slug which ploughed through the little pocket Bible, lodged against Johnny's thigh-bone and put him out of the game. Had it not been for the Bible, however, the bullet would surely have shattered the bone. We were taken home in the same carriage from the fight, and both were nursed back to strength at Mr, Blackwell's home by his mother and sisters. Mrs. Edmonds bent over her boy when they brought him in all covered with dry blood and I heard something about a Bible as they embraced each other in tears.

Johnny went to Texas after the war ended and he had finished his education, became a leading attorney, and was elected mayor of Sherman; he went to the Spanish-American war as a colonel. His old wound began to bother him in Texas and, in 1896, he went to St. Louis, where the X-ray located the bullet in his thigh. He had it cut out and now wears it on his watch chain as a cheerful reminder of the good old days. My own sons sat at his bedside in the hospital after the operation and heard him tell of his experiences with Mosby when he was my "bunky." When he got well enough to go out, the boys went to see a game of base ball with him. John L. Sullivan sat near them and was creating some annoyance by his hilarity. Edmonds did not know who he was and did not care, but told him to "shut up," or he would "fire him out." I suppose he thought it was the old Mosby days when the size of a man made not the slightest difference.

CHAPTER 8

A Narrow Escape

On July 3rd, 1864, the Command was assembled to make a raid into Maryland and, marching north through Loudoun county, reached the Potomac river opposite the Federal post at Point of Rocks, on the morning of the Fourth of July. We had a small cannon with us and we opened fire on the troops on the opposite side, and then, the whole Command under Mosby's lead, forded the stream. Mosby had dismounted a few of the men who had carbines, which they had picked up somewhere, and started them in ahead of the rest to wade the river and act as a sort of long-range advance guard. The higher the water came up around them the more exasperated they became, especially as sharpshooters on the other side were trying to pick them off. There was one standing on the bridge that crossed the canal on the Maryland side, where we could see him loading and firing, and every shot striking annoyingly near our men. The colonel rode up to one of our dismounted men, Emory Pitts, and asked:

"Pitts, can you stop that Yankee over there from sucking eggs?"

"I'll try," answered Pitts; and standing there with the water up to his breast, he raised his carbine and fired; the sharpshooter fell.

Reaching the Maryland side we found that the bridge across the canal had been torn up, but repaired it so the men could cross. We attacked the garrison, drove it out, captured the camp and a lot of stores, destroyed all the government property, burned a freight-boat, cut the wires, helped ourselves to everything we could handle, and came back to the Virginia side in safety, bringing our prisoners with us.

All this Fourth of July celebrating was decidedly annoying to the enemy, and it kept us busy all forenoon. The afternoon was spent in getting things straightened out after the frolic and late the next day, after operating along the Potomac in sight of the enemy all day, hearing that Major Forbes, with the Second Massachusetts Cavalry was somewhere in the neighbourhood and looking for us, we started towards Leesburg and stopped for the night. A scouting party that had been sent by Mosby towards the town returned after nightfall and reported that Major Forbes's Command, together with some of the Thirteenth New York Cavalry were encamped near Leesburg, that the major knew of our raid at Point of Rocks, and that he had spread the report among the residents of Leesburg that he had Mosby's men in a tray which he would spring the next day, July 6th.

This was not the pleasantest thing that could have been said to us just then and, for better safety, the men were ordered to saddle up; in the darkness we moved in a wide circle around the town towards Waterford and camped for the remainder of the night. Whenever I use the expression *"camped for the night,"* I mean only that we unsaddled and laid down on the ground among the horses, with saddles for pillows and the starry firmament for bed clothing.

We had about one hundred and fifty men at this time, for a number had gone back home after the Point of Rocks raid. Undisturbed by the presence of Major Forbes in our vicinity, with no thought of his making an attack on us at night, and with the desire to have it out with him by daylight in a fair field, the colonel and the men slept soundly all night. Early the next morning we were up and in the saddle, singing cheerfully. We followed our leader into Leesburg where we learned that the Major's Command had moved towards Aldie, a few miles south.

We followed, trying to cut him off at Ball's Mill, but he had already crossed the ford when we arrived and was headed for Mount Zion church. We took a straight cut to reach the turnpike east of Mount Zion, so as to get in between Forbes and his headquarters, which were at or near Falls Church in Fairfax County. We knew that he had heard of our movements and began to suspect that he was not half as anxious to get us into his trap as he was to keep out of Mosby's. When we broke into the pike a mile and a half below Mount Zion, Forbes had not yet come in sight, so we took time to plant our cannon in the middle of the road and arrange to receive him.

Presently Forbes and his two hundred men came into view near Mount Zion. The major did not see us until he got started down the pike again. Our artillery squad which was more or less afraid of the little twelve-pounder, yanked the lanyard and a shell went howling up the road only to burst well out of range without doing the slightest damage. The two commands were then several hundred yards apart and Major Forbes instantly crossed with his men into a field on the south side of the road, passing through a gap in the fence. Here he drew his entire command up in line to await our attack which he knew was about due.

In order to get at him we had to move along the road in his front and take the concentrated fire of his men. Mosby ordered us to hold our fire until we could get into the field and we went along the pike rather leisurely, not giving our horses full rein until we got through the gap in the fence. Forbes had not the same idea about where the fight should begin. His men began raking us along the road and were ready with more ammunition when we wheeled and sent up the yell which was so much a part of our tactics. That we had better horses than our opponents there is not any possible doubt. At any rate we swept into their line like a hurricane, each man with a drawn six-shooter.

At first Forbes' men made a good fight, but they could not stand the rain of our pistol balls. We split their front rank asunder and broke their spirit Half of them, in a mad and helpless scramble, got into the next field, where they rallied around Major Forbes and fought as gallantly as any men could fight. We crashed into them again and the battle became a hand-to-hand conflict, revolvers against sabres and revolvers, Mosby's men discharging their weapons into the very faces of Forbes's troopers. It was a mass of struggling, cursing maniacs, each striving to slay his antagonist. Some of this same Second Massachusetts Cavalry were the men we had met at Dranesville on February 22 previously.

Major Forbes occupied the centre of the action, standing in his stirrups with sabre drawn, fighting desperately. He thrust his sabre through the shoulder of Captain Tom Richards who had marked him for single combat. Richards snapped his pistol in the major's face, but it failed to explode. In that instant a bullet ripped into Forbes's horse, and he went down under the dying animal, pinned helplessly, and had to surrender. One of his officers, Lieutenant Amory, now a prominent citizen of Boston, fell side by side with his commander, while his men were flying in every direction. To show how we were interwoven with the enemy it may be mentioned that one of our boys, Willie Martin, was so closely surrounded by Forbes's man that they were obliged to club him into insensibility because there was no room to fire a carbine with safety to their own men.

When Forbes and Amory fell, their men were getting into full rout with Mosby at their heels. The flight and the pursuit were strung out from the scene of the first engagement to old Sudley Church, a distance of ten miles. I followed Colonel Mosby and Johnny Edmonds over the entire stretch and when we returned we found dead and wounded men and horses all along the road and in the fields. We found a man kneeling near the fence by the roadside, with his head bent forward touching the ground in front of him and his left hand clutching a gaping wound in his side. I was ordered to go to his assistance, but when I dismounted and tried to raise him or ease his position, I found a corpse.

The fighting and the rout lasted until late in the afternoon, and there were so many wounded men to help, and so many prisoners to look after, that we did not start homeward till long after dark.

Our loss was seven wounded, one of whom died later. Forbes had twenty men killed on the field and forty wounded, about fifteen of them mortally; a very handsome tribute alike to their staying qualities and the accuracy of Mosby markmanship. Forbes also lost sixty prisoners and one hundred horses.

Colonel C. R. Lowell Jr., commanding the brigade of which the Second Massachusetts was a part, said in his official report of the fight that only forty-five men got back to camp alive.

Although Tom Richards did his best to kill the Federal commanding officer in this fight, I am pleased to record the fact that we captured him alive, which was a much more satisfactory achievement, because Major William H. Forbes returned to Massachusetts after the war, and up to the time of his death, a short time ago, he was one of the most influential, beloved and respected citizens in that commonwealth. I called on him several years ago in his Boston office and we fought the war over again with all the zest at our Command. In the course of our conversation he put his hand on my knee and said: "Tell me, Munson how is my old friend, Tom Richards?" Surely to recall Tom Richards as his friend was enough to convince any listener that the North and the South are again united.

Charley Dear sent me the following story of a little side issue which fits in very well with the story of the Mount Zion fight:

On the evening of the Fourth of July, 1864, after Colonel Mosby had captured the Point of Rocks and the Command had returned to the south side of the Potomac River the colonel ordered Wat Bow to take ten men and recross the river and to cut the telegraph wires and to stir up the Yankees. The men who composed the scouting party were Jim Wiltshire, Charley Dear, Steney Mason, Bush Underwood, Carlisle, Jim Lowndes, Ned Gibson, Clay Adams, Monroe Heiskell, and Kane. They crossed the Potomac River at Edwards's Ferry, swimming the river part of the way. After they crossed they cut the telegraph wires and went down the river on the towpath. When they came to the aqueduct at the mouth of the Monocacy River they found it guarded by some of the troops of the Eighth Illinois. They charged down the tow-path in single file, Bowie leading the way. They went over the flag-stones at a dead run, the enemy on the other side of the canal firing at them. If a man or a horse had been wounded there it would have been death to him, with the river on the right, twenty feet below, and the canal on their left; but fortunately the Yankees did not hurt any of them.

Bowie ordered Heiskell and Kane to stand on the aqueduct, and fire at the enemy, while our men charged down the tow-path and came on the road under the aqueduct, where they found some of the enemy disputing their way. Wiltshire, Dear and Mason each dropped a man and then charged down the road to the store where they found four canal boats tied up, which they burned, and also captured a few horses. After loading down their horses with goods they started to return, as they had stirred up a hornet's nest. Up the towpath they went at a dead run, with calico streaming, shoes scattering in every direction, and hoop-skirts, of which they had captured a goodly number, flying in the air, the Eighth Illinois, from their camp at Muddy Branch, a mile below, coming after them, as they could see by the dust.

Cole's battalion had returned to the Point of Rocks, and were coming down to cut them off from Edwards's Ferry. Wiltshire called to Bowie to look behind at what was coming, as the dust seemed to be nearing them. Bowie said: "Yes, they are in front, too; we are between the devil and the deep sea." Cut off from Edwards's Ferry, with the Potomac on one side and the canal on the other, death or capture seemed to be inevitable.

Among the prisoners was a negro about fifty years of age. Wiltshire said: "If you will show us the way out of here we will turn you loose and give you a horse and money and goods." To their surprise he said they were close to a riffle, where they could ford, and that he would take them across, which he did. The dust from both directions was coming nearer and nearer, but the old negro got them over safely; soon after they entered the brush the enemy met in the tow-path, but our men were in old Virginia again.

Jim Lowndes was so much delighted with getting home that he embraced the old negro and blessed him; he and Heiskell began to sing "I am going back to old Virginia shore," and all joined in. The boys gave the old negro what they promised him and, after he received his reward, he raised his hat and said: "Mars Bowie, when you and Mars Dear and Mars Wiltshire and the other gentlemen come again, let me know and I will help you out: I am rich." The boys had made him rich indeed, and as they rode off he was waving his hat to them.

CHAPTER 9

The Berryville Fight

On the 7th of August, 1864, Major-General Philip H. Sheridan assumed Command of the Middle Military Division of the Federal Army, with headquarters at Harper's Ferry, Virginia. Colonel Mosby set to work on a large scale to "annoy" Sheridan. On the 13th Mosby took three hundred of his Command, the largest number he had ever had in any single engagement up to that time, and marched from Upperville in Fauquier County over into the valley. We went into camp about midnight not far from Berryville in Clark County a manoeuvre which consisted of unsaddling our horses and lying down on the landscape to sleep. Scouts sent out to look the situation over presently returned with the information that a wagon train was moving up the pike a few miles distant While John Russell, our most prominent valley scout, was reporting to the colonel, I was engaged just at that moment in trying to spread my saddle blanket among the rocks and tree roots, so it would resemble a curled hair mattress as nearly as possible. I stopped for a moment to listen to John's report, hoping secretly that it did not mean any change in the camping program, but my hopes faded away when the colonel said:

"Saddle up, Munson, and come along with me."

Taking a few more of us, we started off for the Valley turnpike, leaving the rest of the Command to get some much needed sleep. We struck out in the direction whence, in the stillness of the night, came the rumbling echoes of the heavily laden wagons. In olden times, when the stages were run up and down the valley turnpike, it was said that the rumbling of the coach on the hard, rocky road could be heard for miles on a still night and, on this quiet August night of which I am writing, we heard the wagon train long before we came in sight of it, which we did in an hour after Russell reported to the colonel. We found a long line of wagons winding along the road and stretching away into the darkness as far as the eye could reach.

We rode among the drivers and the guards, looking the stock over and chatting with the men in a friendly way. I asked one of the cavalrymen for a match to light my pipe and he gave it to me, and when I struck it, revealing his face and mine by its light, he did not know I was pretty soon going to begin chasing him. It was too dark to distinguish us from their own men and we mingled with them so freely that our presence created no suspicion.

Colonel Mosby asked them whatever questions he chose to, and learned that there were one hundred and fifty wagons in the train, with more than a thousand head of horses, mules, and cattle guarded by about two thousand men, consisting of two Ohio regiments and one Maryland regiment, besides cavalry distributed along the line; all under orders of Brigadier-General Kenly, commanding. Having pumped the men dry of all the information he needed, the colonel withdrew us from their line into the field, one by one, and sent me back to our sleeping comrades to arouse them and bring the full force up in a hurry. Just as day was beginning to dawn Chapman and Richards, with the whole Command of about three hundred men and two pieces of light artillery, twelve-pounders, came out of the woods on a run and met the colonel, who was impatiently awaiting them in full view of the wagon train. I believe it was one of these little guns that made so much noise and did so little harm at Mount Zion Church on July 6, but I am not sure.

In the hurried rush through the woods to get to the colonel, or immediately after it was fired, I don't remember which, one of these guns commanded by Lieutenant Frank Rahm of Richmond, was disabled and drawn out of the way. The other was posted on a little eminence looking down on the turnpike along which the wagon train was moving. A streak of light broke in the east, and our force was hustled into position, Mosby giving his instructions to the Command. His trouble seemed to be to keep the men from charging before he was ready. Three hundred against over two thousand meant carefulness. The flush of the morning began to blow over that beautiful valley landscape,—there are few lovelier spots than the Valley of Virginia around Berryville,—and down on the pike we saw a cloud of dust rising as though a giant serpent was creeping along towards Berryville from Harper's Ferry.

The entire train was soon in sight, all unmindful of our presence.

From our position on the low hill, while we watched them in breathless suspense, Frank Rahm sent a twelve-pound shell over the train. It exploded like a clap of thunder out of a clear sky, and was followed by another which burst in the midst of the enemy. The whole train stopped and writhed in its centre as if a wound had been opened in its vitals. Apparently its guards did not see us and we got another charge into the little twelve-pounder and let it fly, and then; oh then! What on earth ever possessed them I am unable even at this date to say. Two thousand infantry and a force of cavalry all at sea, but, as with one mind, and without making the least concerted resistance, the train began to retreat. Then we rushed them, the whole Command charging from the slope, not in columns, but spread out all over creation, each man doing his best to outyell his comrade and emptying revolvers, when we got among them, right and left.

The whole wagon train was thrown into panic. Teamsters wheeled their horses and mules into the road and, plying their black-snake whips, sent the animals galloping madly down the pike, crashing into other teams which, in turn, ran away. Infantry stampeded in every direction. Cavalry, uncertain from which point the attack came, bolted backward and forward without any definite plan. Wounded animals all along the train were neighing and braying, adding to the confusion. Pistols and rifles were cracking singly and in volleys.

Colonel Mosby was dashing up and down the line of battle on his horse, urging the men by voice and gesture. I never saw him quite so busy or so interested in the total demolition of things.

Before the attack he expressed the hope and the belief that his men would give Kenly the worst whipping any of Sheridan's men ever got, and it delighted him to see the work progressing so satisfactorily. At several points along the line Kenly's men made stands behind the stone fences, and poured volleys into us but, when charged, they invariably retreated from their positions. The conflict was strung out over a mile and a half, which was the length of the wagon train when the fight was at its best. Our men were yelling, galloping, charging, firing, stampeding mules and horses and creating pandemonium everywhere. It was not long before we had the enemy thoroughly demoralised and were able to turn our attention to the prisoners and the spoils.

Mosby gave orders to unhitch all the teams that had not run away and to set fire to the wagons, and very soon smoke and flames filled the air and made a grand picture. Among the wagons burned was one containing a safe in which an army paymaster had his greenbacks, said

Mosby attacking the Federal Convoy at Berryville in August, 1863

to be over one hundred thousand dollars. We overlooked it, unfortunately, and it was recovered the next day by the enemy, as we always supposed; but there is a story afloat in the town of Berryville that a shoemaker who lived there at the time of the fight got hold of something very valuable among the wreckage of our raid and suddenly blossomed out into a man of means, marrying later into one of the best families of the Valley. He never would tell what his new-found treasure was. Maybe he got the safe and greenbacks.

By eight o'clock in the morning the fight was over, the enemy ours, and the wagons burning. Then a serious problem arose: how were we to get three hundred prisoners, nearly nine hundred head of captured stock, and the other spoils of war out of Sheridan's country into our own? News of the raid had gone in every direction and we were threatened with an overwhelming assault at any moment. I should have said the problem was serious to the men only. Mosby solved it very promptly by saying: "We will go directly to Rectortown and take all the prisoners and animals and booty with us." There was not anything more to be said on the subject. Rectortown lay twenty-five miles to the south, back in Fauquier County. Stonewall Jackson's forced marches and Stuart's rides were not in it with this one of ours. Our disabled cannon had to be taken care of. When Mosby asked Frank Rahm what he proposed to do with his broken-down gun, Frank promptly replied; "I'm going to take it back home on the other gun, if I have to hold it there," and he did.

We fastened the loose harness as best we could and, herding the animals into one drove, started at a trot down the pike towards the Shenandoah River several miles away. It was the most extraordinary procession that ever headed for that historic stream; our captives were on foot while we were mounted, the victors and vanquished chatting freely together and speculating on the trip before them. A number of the Rangers, in a spirit of gayety, had decked themselves out in the fine uniforms found in the baggage of the Northern officers. Some of the coats were turned inside out so as to display the fine linings. From one of the wagons we had resurrected a lot bf musical instruments and the leaders of the mounted vanguard made the morning hideous with attempts to play plantation melodies on tuneless fiddles.

No more motley throng ever came back from a successful raid. There was a song on every man's lips and those who had yelled or sung themselves hoarse waved captured flags. In the midst of the nondescript legion the nine hundred head of stock, bellowing, neighing, and braying, wallowed along in the hot dust of that August morning, the steam rising from their bodies and the saliva dripping from the mouths of the fat steers, of which we had nearly two hundred and fifty head. Down the turnpike into the rushing Shenandoah, regardless of ford or pass, dashed the whole cavalcade; some swimming, some wading, others finding ferriage at the tail of a horse or steer. The orchestra in the lead scraped away bravely at their fiddles. Only the unhorsing of some of the worst of the performers saved them from bodily violence at the hands of their justly indignant comrades. In a short time, dripping but refreshed, we emerged from the stream, struggled on up the road and began the ascent of the Blue Ridge Mountains.

Strange to say, not a man nor an animal was lost in the passage. We crossed the mountain at a breakneck pace, made a rapid descent into the Piedmont Valley, and at four o'clock that afternoon, with all hands present, the captured property was divided at Rectortown, twenty-five miles from the scene of the action fought on the morning of the same day!

Our loss in the affair was two killed and two wounded; the number of the enemy's casualties we could not ascertain, but Major Wm. E. Beardsley of the Sixth New York Cavalry, reported from Winchester on the day after the fight, to Colonel Devine, commanding the Second Brigade of the First Cavalry Division, as follows:

> We were attacked by Mosby at daylight yesterday morning at Berryville, and a disgraceful panic ensued, resulting in the entire destruction of the reserve brigade's train and a portion of ours, with battery forges, etc., the running off of nearly all the mules, the capture of a large number of prisoners, the killing of five of our men, with many wounded.

We brought out more than six hundred horses and mules, more than two hundred and fifty head of fat cattle, and about three hundred prisoners, destroying more than one hundred wagons with their valuable contents.

After dividing the horses and plunder among the men we sent the mules and a large number of cattle to General Lee for the use of the army. They were driven through Fauquier, Rappahannock, Culpeper and Orange counties, as far as Gordonsville. On my return to the Command from carrying reports and despatches of this affair to General Lee, I could follow the trail of the captured animals by bits of broken harness, here and there, for nearly the entire route. By six o'clock that afternoon everything was in order where a short time before all seemed to be tumult and confusion. The horses were divided, the mules and cattle corralled ready for their long drive, the guards to take the prisoners over to Gordonsville had been detailed and given their instructions and the Command was disbanded, and each member was starting home with his share of the spoils, when the colonel came to me and said:

"Munson, don't you want to see your sweetheart?" I was willing. We rode together to our headquarters at Mr. Blackwell's, a few miles distant, where I got a bath and a clean outfit and a good supper and a fresh horse and, with the colonel's written despatches, got in the saddle and galloped to Warrenton, twenty miles away. As I was about to leave, the colonel put his arm around my shoulder and said: "Don't let the Command suffer while you are gone." That meant, that if occasion should arise, and I found the opportunity to brag any about our Command, or to tell any Munchausen stories, I was to lie like a gentleman. My instructions, however, did not include these details, but were to ride as far as Warrenton that night, go to church the next morning and drive with the young lady referred to, who is now and has long been the happy wife of a much handsomer member of our Command, and then gallop on to Culpeper Court House, twenty-five miles, and take the cars there for General Lee's headquarters, then near Petersburg. I was so utterly worn out by my long ride of two or three days and the loss of sleep that, by the time I had galloped and trotted fifteen miles, I could stand it no longer; I unsaddled and tied my horse to a sapling on the roadside and laid down on my saddle blanket at my horse's feet where I slept till sunrise, when I got up and galloped into Warrenton as fresh as a lark.

At General Lee's headquarters I broke in on that ragged crowd like a vision. I think I was the only well-dressed man in his army at that time. I had on my best, and it was the best that money could buy in the North. My boots came half way up my thighs, and my spurs were hand-made with silver rowels. My entire suit was gray corduroy trimmed with buff and gold lace, my hat had a double gold cord and an ostrich plume on it, and I carried a pair of high gauntlets carelessly in one hand, while with the other I toyed with a handsome enamelled belt and a pair of Colt's revolvers.

And I was only an humble private of Mosby's Guerrillas, and not nineteen years old!

If any officers or men around the headquarters of the Army of

Northern Virginia failed to be impressed with my appearance or with the stories I related of our Command and its doings, it was certainly not my fault. I tried to obey the colonel's injunction not to let the Command suffer, and when I left there I believe every man who saw and heard me thought I was only a fair sample of our entire battalion.

The result of this raid was shown by the rapidity with which Sheridan at once fell back to his old position down the Valley, where three days later he received the following telegram from General Grant:

When any of Mosby's men are caught, hang them without trial.

No one who is at all familiar with Grant's admiration for a fighter will be surprised to learn that a strong friendship sprung up between the two men after the war; that Mosby stumped the state of Virginia for Grant in 1872, against Greeley; that, when he became President, Grant offered appointments to Mosby which were declined and that the last autograph letter ever written by General Grant was a request to Mr. Huntington to appoint Colonel Mosby to a good position in the law department of the Southern Pacific Railroad when he returned to California from his consulship at Hong Kong. Grant meant it when he said "Let us have peace."

Sheridan's reply to Grant's telegram was as follows:

Mosby has annoyed me and captured a few wagons. We hung one and shot six of his men yesterday.

There was no truth in this statement that he had hung one and shot six of our men that day.

In the busiest part of the Berryville affair, when teams were running wild in every direction and the confusion was at its worst, Colonel Mosby saw a splendid four-in-hand team of big bays attached to a heavy portable army forge which had become upset on the pike and from which the horses were struggling in vain to free themselves. Turning to me he ordered me to take a man and extricate the team from the tangle they were in, and bring them out safely. That sounded just as easy as if he had said, "Take a cigar," but I did not find it so. I took with me a young fellow who had joined the Command only a few days. When we galloped up to the struggling team and began to untangle them we were fired upon by a lot of infantrymen hidden behind a stone fence. When the rain of bullets flattened against the metal forge it sounded as if there were a thousand of them and my young companion, this being his first engagement, toppled over in the road in a dead faint.

It was no time just then to look after a sick man, for our horses were frantic with fear and excitement, and I had to hold both of them when the boy fell. I let him lie where he was and in time got my team untangled and tied securely; I was just ready to lead them out, when, very opportunely, my youngster revived. Getting up in a surprised way he jumped on his horse and galloped off, leaving me to mount my half mad charger and get my team out as best I could. That boy developed into one of the best soldiers in the Command and, until the end of the war, was up near the front in every engagement. It was his baptism of blood, and his confirmation followed immediately after it. This was one of the ways a beginner had to be initiated into our service.

While I am in the neighbourhood of Berryville I recall a fight Captain A. E. Richards had only a few days after the foregoing affair, and almost on the same ground, while he was scouting with a small squad of men in the Valley. He ran into a body of Yankee cavalry and killed the commanding officer. Lieutenant J. S. Walker of the First United States Cavalry; wounded and captured Lieutenant Philip Dwyer of the Fifth United States Cavalry, and captured all the rest of the squad but one. When Richards reported to Colonel Mosby on this affair the Colonel replied that he was glad one man got away so he could tell Sheridan what had happened to the rest of them.

CHAPTER 10

Turning the Tables

The neighbourhood of Harper's Ferry was very warm in that month of August, 1864. Sheridan was much irritated by the persistent annoyance of Mosby's men. In fact the relations between us and the other side were daily growing more bitter, and General Grant's telegram would have been obeyed if the Federals had captured any of us.

Among others who wanted to have a tilt with us was Captain Blazer, of Crook's Division. The result of his uncontrollable desire is set forth in two war despatches subsequently published by the government. The first, dated August 20th, 1864, is from General Sheridan to General Augur, and reads:

> I have one hundred picked men who will take the contract to clean out Mosby's gang. I want one hundred Spencer rifles for them. Send them to me if they can be found in Washington.

Captain Blazer was to command these one hundred men who stood ready to "clean out Mosby's gang." The second despatch is dated at Harper's Ferry, November 19, and is from General Stevenson to General Forsythe. It follows:

> Two of Captain Blazer's men came in this morning, Privates Harris and Johnson. They report that Mosby attacked Blazer near Kabletown yesterday I about eleven o'clock. They say the entire command with the exception of themselves were either captured or killed.

It may be interesting to know just what developed between the dates of the two telegrams. Captain Blazer thought, and General Sheridan agreed with him, that the Northern Army could find some work for a husky little guerrilla band of its own to fight the devil with fire, as it were. The captain was put at the head of one hundred picked men, selected by himself from Crook's entire division, and there is no doubt he succeeded in getting some fine material. He was provided with his Spencer rifles and, shortly after the 20th of August, started to work. He began under very favourable conditions, as Colonel Mosby was busy with bigger game than Blazer all during the summer and autumn of 1864, and paid little heed to the buzzing of the new Captain's wings around our doors. Blazer went to work at once, coming after us in our own territory, surprising a few of the Rangers here and there and generally whipping them. His first official report was that he had captured one Mosby man after chasing the guerrillas three miles.

Early in September while on a scouting expedition in the Valley of Virginia, he surprised one of our scouting parties under Lieutenant Joe Nelson and gave it a good whipping, killing two men, wounding five and taking five prisoners. Blazer reported one killed and six wounded in the engagement. If he only had one man killed we knew where to locate the fatality, for in the running fight a Blazer man rode up alongside of Emory Pitts, of our company "B" and snapped a pistol at his head but it missed fire. Pitts greatly surprised to find his brains were still intact used them with rapidity. He leaned from his saddle, seized his antagonist by the scruff of the neck with his left hand, lifted the man from his saddle almost over on to his own lap and with his right hand held a revolver under his captive's breast and fired a bullet through him, dropping the corpse to the ground as he galloped away. The soldier happened to fall on one of our men who had been unhorsed and who was lying, half hidden among the rocks, playing possum. He reported that the body that dropped from Pitt's grip after the shot was fired never so much as quivered. Death came on swift wings to that poor fellow. But that is war.

I don't remember ever hearing Mosby mention Blazer's name or make any reference to his movements, until he finally ordered Major Richards to go over to the Valley and wipe him from the map. Mosby treated his forays into our territory merely as incidents of our regular life as Partisan Rangers. To him Blazer and his men were "a raiding party of Yankees." We made no special attempts to capture him, nor any special pains to keep out of his way. During those three eventful months in our history we were after bigger game, and the stakes were always higher than "a captain and one hundred picked men." In fact they were General Phil. Sheridan and his army; and nobody knew better than Sheridan how often we won part of the stakes. Nevertheless, he was a foe to be reckoned with, and the boys who had felt his hard knocks remembered it against a day of reckoning.

On the tenth of November, Captain Montjoy took his company to the Shenandoah Valley and, early the next day, attacked a company of Federal cavalry on the pike between Winchester and Newtown. He defeated them, capturing about twenty of them with their horses, and recrossed the river near Berry's Ferry. All but thirty had started for their homes when suddenly Blazer's hundred men made a fierce attack. In less time, almost, than it takes to tell it, they recaptured the prisoners and horses, killed two of our men, wounded five others and galloped away, while Montjoy and his badly whipped men sought much needed cover in the direction of the river.

It happened that, at the time the news of this affair reached Colonel Mosby, Companies A and B of our Command had nothing special to do. The colonel summoned Major A. E. Richards and told him to take some of the men of each company over into the Valley and, "Wipe Blazer out! go through him." He did not think it necessary to go in person to command the men of A and B for, whenever he told Richards to do anything, no matter how difficult, and especially if A and B went along, Richards was sure to do it. Mosby has claimed full credit for the victories achieved by his officers when they worked by his direction. He argued that he had the judgment not only to dictate the work, and the manner of doing it, but also the discrimination to pick the officers best suited to the work. And every officer of the Command was glad to have our colonel get the honour.

Major Richards started on the seventeenth of November with one hundred Rangers to look for Blazer. Most of his men were specially anxious to set eyes on the Northener who had turned the trick so neatly on Montjoy and Nelson. They were not picked men, however, but just plain, ordinary, every-day A and B Guerrillas. When he reached Castleman's Ferry he heard that Blazer was then on one of his raids, having fully made up his mind to finish the contract about which Sheridan had wired Augur nearly three months before. Our men located him in camp near Kabletown, a favourite stopping place of his, in Jefferson county. West Virginia. Major Richards preferring a daylight fight with him, where there would be no odds in our favour, camped near him. In the morning the men were so anxious for a final settlement of old scores with Blazer and his command, that they did not wait for breakfast, but at sunrise charged into Kabletown only to find that Blazer had left but shortly before and was looking for them.

When both sides were out for scalps and each looking for the other, the end could not be far off, and it took only a few hours to find the blue column. Richards turned his men from the road to draw Blazer into the field but Blazer was busy taking down the fence and dismounting his men so as to use his carbines at long range. This was a good sign. If he had been spoiling for a fight he would have charged Richards in the road but he was apparently just as careful as our major. It also meant a carefully planned conflict if he could have his way. But Richards upset his calculations by dividing his men and starting off with half of them as if retreating. Blazer swallowed the bait and ordered his men to mount and charge. It puts a lot of courage into a cavalry company to see the enemy galloping away. When his men got entirely clear of the woods and into the open where there was nothing in the way of either party, Richards turned suddenly, and our two divisions charged simultaneously.

Blazer's men used their Spencer rifles until our men got close up to them when they dropped them and drew revolvers. Richards's attack was very much like a dynamite explosion at close range, inasmuch as it was entirely unexpected; for, while there is no doubt Blazer counted on a fight, and really wanted one, he had made no preparations whatever for a massacre, and that is what, all of a sudden, seemed to be imminent, for Richards and his men looked and acted like a band of Apaches. Blazer's men broke before our onslaught, defying all their Commander's efforts to rally them as they saw their ranks thinning, and, in a few minutes the flight became a panic and a rout. Richards was in their midst, each of his men apparently picking out a special victim. They were fading away before our deadly fire, and Blazer, catching the infection of retreat from his men, did the fastest riding of his life.

One of our men, Syd Ferguson, who rode one of the handsomest and best animals in our Command, marked Blazer for his own and, touching his mare, Fashion, lightly with the spur, was soon at the captain's side, ordering him to surrender. His pistols had been emptied in the fight and as the captain did not, or could not stop, Syd knocked him from his horse as he dashed by. As soon as he could check and turn his mare he rode back and found his man lying apparently dead in the road but, thinking the blow of a pistol could hardly have killed a man, he got down to examine, when Blazer got up smiling and admitted who he was and that he was only stunned. He took his medicine cheerfully. His loss was more than twenty men killed, many more wounded, most of them mortally, and over thirty taken prisoners. General Stevenson's despatch of November 30, heretofore quoted, summed up the situation briefly and truthfully:

> Two of Captain Blazer's men came in.

In this connection I cannot pass over an incident that, at the time of its occurrence, was widely discussed among our men. It involves the Richmond boy, John Puryear, that gallant daredevil youth of whom I have written in the first instalment of these recollections.

On the morning of the day we had balanced our books with Blazer, Puryear and Charley McDonough were ostensibly scouting for Richards but really looking up trouble for trouble's sake. They were approached by a few men dressed in gray who McDonough instinctively feared, believing them to be some of Blazer's men. He would not stay to decide the matter but turned and galloped away. John Puryear, with his trust in everybody, stood his ground and heard them address him as they came near, "Hello Johnny," which completely disarmed any suspicion which he may have had. When they reached him they pounced on him in true guerrilla style and disarmed him. Then they took him back to Blazer and he was turned over to the tender mercy of Lieutenant Cole, of Blazer's Command, who gave orders that steps be taken to extract information from the prisoner.

He was brow-beaten, cuffed and threatened in a fruitless effort to loosen his tongue. Finally a halter was put around his neck and he was drawn up in the air, clear of his toes, several times; but Cole finally wearied of his attempt to make the boy tell anything and ordered him to mount the worst horse they had and follow Blazer and his men. The beast was so weary that Puryear had no difficulty in making it appear that movement was next to impossible, a state of affairs that justified him in requesting permission to dismount and cut a stick big enough to induce the animal to step lively. No objection was offered, and Puryear proceeded to get a club that was about right for the plans that were forming in his mind.

It was not long before Mosby's men came into view, and Blazer ordered the boy to the rear. This did not suit him at all, and he insisted on staying where he was, up near the front. There was no time to argue, for the long looked for moment had come. Puryear stayed. Richards told his men to watch him and try not to shoot him when they came together; and one of our men, Graf Carlisle, yelled encouragingly to Puryear to "keep his spirits up, for everything would be lovely by-and-bye."

At the moment Richards's men came swinging down on Blazer in two divisions, Puryear rose in his stirrups, let out his rebel yell and, with a swinging, back-hand movement, dealt his guard a killing blow in the face with his club. Then he slipped from his horse in the thick of the *mêlée*, stripped his fallen enemy of his pistols, remounted on the fellow's horse and lit into the ranks of Blazer's crowd which surrounded him with an expression of ferocity that it is impossible to describe. His black eyes literally blazed and, with the perspiration standing on his forehead, his jaws set, and his whole face livid, he started on his errand of vengeance.

Nearly every man in our Command saw him swirl into the fight. His rage was something terrible to look upon. Presently his eye found Lieutenant Cole and without delay he was after him. He chased that Federal officer around the old blacksmith's shop and overtook him just at the moment he was surrendering to John Alexander, now a prominent attorney of Leesburg, Va., who tried to restrain Puryear from wreaking his vengeance upon a man who had quit. But Puryear declared that Cole had ordered him hanged, and had abused him, a charge admitted by Cole. The next instant Puryear fired his pistol into Cole's chest and stood back to contemplate his work. Cole fell limp and gasping against Alexander's horse, sinking gradually to the ground. He was dead in less than a minute. Puryear burst out crying like a child, and collapsed, sob after sob shaking his body. He was useless for the rest of the fight. Nature had given way to the strain.

When Alexander took Cole's pistols from his body he found them both empty. It is only fair to say, however, that Puryear did not know this till Alexander told him; in other words until he had wreaked his ghastly vengeance. Puryear at the time was not out of his teens.

In 1865, when most of our men went over in a body to General Hancock's headquarters in the Valley of Virginia, to surrender, Blazer and Syd Ferguson met and hugged each other like long lost brothers.

Blazer furnished a striking illustration of the difficulty of conducting Partisan Ranger warfare successfully. He possessed advantages greater than Mosby in some respects. He picked his men carefully from an entire Division, and had seen much hard service in West Virginia before coming to Sheridan, service of a kind to fit him for coping successfully with us. His entire Command was splendidly mounted, armed and equipped. He and his men were brave and hardened soldiers. He had a perfect country to operate in for guerrilla warfare.

He had, singular to relate, rather the good will of the people, especially of the Valley, for he permitted no vandalism among his men and, whenever occasion arose, he was courteous and kind to them. He had the protection of Sheridan's whole army when he was "at home," while we never closed our eyes in sleep free from liability to be stirred out of bed by him. If his ranks were thinned he had thousands of the same sort to draw on. He need ride only thirty miles from his base to be among us. The day he went down he had just as good a chance to whip us as we had to whip him. He had even more, for he was better armed to resist an attack than we. Seven shooting Spencer rifles are not to be despised in the hands of men who can stand still and receive an attack from charging horsemen. And yet, when he was put to the test of a fair, open, stand-up, hand-to-hand fight, with one of Mosby's boy officers, and only a part of Mosby's Command, he was simply annihilated.

Lieutenant W. Ben. Palmer in 1864.

CHAPTER 11

A Chapter of Personalities

Samuel Waggaman, who is now a prominent physician in Washington City, enjoys the distinction of being the only man who joined Mosby's Command in Richmond; he was duly enrolled there, and transportation given him by the War Department to Gordonsville. His uncle was a prominent officer in the Quartermaster's Department, and when Sam enlisted regularly in the Command this uncle fitted him out with gorgeous jacket and trousers and presented him to the Secretary of War. In the first fight he got into, which was the rather disastrous affair at Warrenton Junction, all his finery disappeared in some way and, when he reached Upperville, through the help of Ned Hurst, "the old reliable," he was picked clean. Ned Hurst seemed to be always on hand ready to help some youngster out of a hole. At the Warrenton Junction fight Sam's horse was shot while our men were retreating, and Ned helped him through.

When the colonel sent the cattle and mules we captured from Sheridan on August 13, 1864, over to the regular army, Sam was one of the detail to take them. At Culpeper Court House he turned them into an enclosure belonging to John Minor Botts, a prominent politician who had remained a Union man. Mr. Botts objected to the use of his farm as a corral for rebel livestock and, but for the timely arrival of General Stuart, they would not have gone into the enclosure. But Stuart ordered them in and told Mr. Botts he was the only man in Virginia who had a fence around his barn. So in they went. Stuart told Sam if it were not for Mosby all his wagons would have remained stuck in the mud.

Sam was captured in August, 1864, after he came back from Culpeper Court House in a house near Upperville, where he and Frank Darden had hidden in a garret. Frank Darden fell through the ceiling of the family living-room and lit in the bed with the lady of the house. Sam was in the dark, and when the enemy began firing he offered to surrender, but none of them would take him. There being nothing else to do, he began firing at them, and when both his pistols were empty he walked out and they seized him. He went to Fort Warren in handcuffs, and remained there till June, 1865.

John H. Alexander had a theory, or rather he had several, about our peculiar warfare. First, he believed the precarious life that we led made us vigilant, alert and self-reliant, so that in action each man was an independent, intelligent unit, and not a mere automaton to be manoeuvred by his officers. Second, he believed the enemy dreaded ambuscades, and that many of our escapes were due to their exceeding carefulness. And, third, he had an abiding faith in the advantage we had over the enemy in our experience with the pistol. He used to say, "There is a terrible difference between shooting to scare and shooting to kill," and he thought it did not require so much nerve to charge a platoon which was to fire by volley according to Hardee's tactics; but men had a prejudice against riding towards the muzzle of a pistol which they knew was going to hit something when it went off. They just would not go up against it.

Now, allow these theories, and it takes all the miraculous out of his story of how he held up a whole regiment of cavalry on an open highway, in broad daylight. Our Command had gone down to Fairfax on a raid the day before, and this young fellow who was convalescing from a wound which he had recently received, had been left behind. He had recovered so far as to be able to ride around and take notice of things; and this morning he had donned his best "blockade goods" and started from the Middleburg neighbourhood to call on some ladies at Dover. Between these two points, at Macksville, the turnpike passes over a level plateau about two hundred yards wide. It is approached from the Middleburg side by a rise about the height of a rider on a horse; on the other side the road dips into a considerable hollow, deep enough and wide enough to hide a regiment.

As he rode up the hill from one side, he saw the heads of four men abreast climbing the hill to the plateau at the farther side. His first impression was that they were some of our men returning from Fairfax. But as we never took the chances of letting men ride up on us whom we did not know, he halted on the brow of the hill and drew out and cocked his revolver. As he did so the approaching party dashed towards him, yelling and shooting. This dispelled his doubts as to who they were, and he knew that he had to get away from there. As he wheeled his horse he concluded he would give them an intimation not to crowd him too closely on his morning gallop. They offered a beautiful shot as they came four abreast over the plateau, and he held his horse a moment until they got within good range and then let go at the nearest one. He saw his victim throw his hand to his head and reel from his horse. His companions yielded to that prejudice which I mentioned above, and the promptness with which they jerked up their horses provoked a laughing ring in the tones in which our Ranger called to them to come on. But other heads were bobbing up the eastern rim of the level, and away he went.

A hundred yards up the road a lane opened into the pike at an acute angle from the south. Ere he reached the mouth of it, he recollected that his horse had a shoe off, and the thought occurred to him that in a long chase up the macadamized road his steed would go lame and be overtaken. The lane would bring him back in some degree toward the enemy and subject him to a broadside; but he was familiar with the ground and knew that it would be but a short run to the protection of a hollow in a piece of woods.

So he took the chances of the dash. Sure enough some Yankees had dismounted on the plateau as they saw him turn into the lane, and the whistling of the bullets from their carbines, and their pit-pat on the rail fence alongside him, made that one of the most exhilarating rides of his life. The occasion was enlivened, too, by an old negro, who happened to be mending the fence. As our rider passed him, the slapping of the bullets against the rails scared him nearly to death, and he fell on his back, striking arms and legs in the air and hallooing at the top of his voice that he was killed. The dash was over in a minute, and neither horse, rider nor negro got a scratch.

When he was out of range, in a hollow in the lane, Alexander held up his horse. He was about three hundred yards from the enemy and could not hear any signs of pursuit. He was unwilling to leave the vicinity without getting further information and, jumping over a fence into an adjoining field, he rode up on a hill. He saw the turnpike at Macksville full of cavalry.

As soon as he reappeared the long-range guns opened on him again, and a bullet which clipped his hat admonished him that there was a good marksman behind one of them. Yielding to an indisposition to furnish a living target for Uncle Sam's sharpshooters to practice on, he waved an *adieu* with his hat and cantered off to a piece of timber at the far end of the field.

The Yankees evidently thought the Ranger was waiting for them on the turnpike, for when their vanguard first caught sight of him he was sitting still on his horse on the brow of the hill. His subsequent movements, which must have appeared as eccentric, to say the least, were interpreted as attempts to draw them on. Assuming that he was a decoy, they naturally concluded that the woods into which he had ridden hid an ambuscade. And while he tarried under their shades he saw the regiment brought up and formed into a battle line, skirmishers deployed, and the whole array move in all pomp across the field toward him. He could linger but a short while, however, to view the striking pageant. He has assured me that one of the regrets of his life has been that he could not wait to witness their chagrin when they reached the woods and found that no more serious business awaited them than to scare the birds from the bushes.

The following contribution from Johnny Alexander I am sure will be read with interest after the foregoing article about him:

A Lively Ride Before Breakfast.

Hugh Waters and I lived at his mother's home, which was situated about one mile south of Middleburg. Her house was on the far edge of a large body of timber, which extended more than half way to the village. On the east side of her farm, and within a quarter of a mile of the house, ran the road from the Plains to Middleburg; and about the same distance to the west was the road from Salem (now Marshall) to Middleburg.

During the winter of 1864-5, there was a heavy snow which laid on the ground for some weeks and became covered with a thick crust. One cold night Hugh and I camped out in a rock-break on his mother's farm, within a few yards of the Plains road; but the rocky cliff, at the foot of which we made our bed and tied our horses, and the clump of trees about it, hid us from sight of the road. Indeed, we relied on the cold weather to keep our enemies at home, and the warning which we would get from the sounds of their travelling over the snow, if they should have the enterprise to turn out.

We slept the sleep of unconscious innocence. The next morning about sunrise we were awakened by Mrs. Waters's negro man, Edmond, with the information that a large body of Yankees had marched along the Plains road a short while before, had called at the house to pay their respects to us, and had gone on towards Middleburg. It is needless to say we made a very hasty toilet and did not stand much on the order of our going away from there. We left Edmond to take charge of our bedding, and hurried off towards Middleburg to take observations.

When we reached the Salem road we met Lieutenant Fount Beattie who had also been induced to rise early by a party scouting uncomfortably near his quarters. He assumed responsibility for our movements, and led us on toward Middleburg in pursuit of information and, incidentally, adventure. Well, we succeeding in finding both.

We followed the road to the top of a hill on the edge of the town and saw the streets filled with blue-coated cavalry. At the same time the wearers of the blue coats saw us, and hastened to exchange greetings with us. We felt, however, that salutes at a distance were all that the occasion required of us, and retired with some precipitancy in the direction whence we came. The Yankees insisted on closer relations, and pressed their attentions with ardour.

We were making good our courteous purpose to leave them in possession of that neighbourhood, and were getting out on the Salem road in fine shape, when we rose a little hill about a half a mile out. And there, coming towards us, and not more than two hundred yards away, was a road full of Yankee cavalry. On each side of us was an abominable stone fence, which, you know, very few horses would jump. As we pulled up, the enemy in front commenced paying us attentions. It did look like a hopeless situation.

But Beattie was not the man to give up as long as there was daylight between him and the toils. A short distance behind us we had passed a gap in the stone fence which would let us into a field and to the big woods beyond it; and our leader turned us back to it, as some of the Salem party sprung up the road toward us. The pursuers from Middleburg were scarcely within good range as the last one of us jumped through the gap, but a good shot gave pause to the foremost of them. Somehow, both parties of the Yankees found ways through the fence too; and in a moment the situation was this: we three, running by a straight line for the woods, the Yankees to the left oblique and Yankees to the right oblique, making after us with absolute assurance of running us down.

If we should make the woods, they were barren of foliage and almost as open as the field. But just within them was a hill, and just over it—well, the Yankees did not know what. And neither did we, for that matter; but the religion of a Mosby man was never to throw up his hands as long as he could stick to his horse, for he trusted much to that chapter of accidents which is in every book of Fate. It contained deliverance for us that morning.

The snow was at least a half foot deep and, as I stated, was covered with a thick crust, and it greatly affected the speed of all parties. I was riding a horse quite recently "acquired." I was soon dismayed to find he was falling behind and, what was worse, he did not seem to care if he was. The shooting and yelling and my rigorous application of the spur made no impression on him. Whether it was actual leg weariness, sheer brute stubbornness or the aroused affinity for his old companions, I do not know. But the cold fact is that, when Beattie and Waters rode into the woods, my horse slowed down into a walk and was a considerable distance behind them.

The pursuers were then scarcely a hundred yards from me, and were calling to me in jeering tones, between shots, "Come out of that overcoat, Johnny," and other pleasant salutations. The truth was, I had on a splendid new overcoat, one of the fruits of the greenback raid and their remarks about it made me feel sick. I verily believe it was my salvation at that moment, though. The heartless fellows were close enough to see that it was an unusually fine one, glistening with brass buttons and some other garish trimming, and they evidently took me for an officer. Now, do not lose sight of that, for I think it was the key to what followed.

As my companions were riding away over the hill, in the woods, and I realised that my horse had flunked on me, in my desperation I involuntarily called out to them to stop and take me up. They wheeled and commenced firing.

The enemy doubtless heard me call to them to stop, without distinguishing what I said about taking me up. They saw my horse drop into a quiet, dignified pace, and did not understand that it was not due to my own management of him. And, attributing to the officer a most magnificent nerve, they assumed that I was rallying my men from the ambush into which we had decoyed them. The manly response of Lieutenant Beattie and Waters clinched the matter. And I pledge you my word of honour that the whole party pulled up within almost touching distance of me, and let me march in a quiet walk over the hill. I soon came up with my friends and we rode away unpursued.

I submitted the above to Lieutenant Beattie who fully corroborates it, and expressed his gratification that I wrote it for you.

Joe Bryan, of Richmond, who belonged to Montjoy's company D, joined our Command about October, 1864, and his first raid was when we captured General Duffie in the Valley. Charley Dear says when a detachment of Company D, which was sent out to participate in the capture, returned, he found Joe with a lot of others chafing like a caged lion. In a sort of desperation he asked Charley how a man could make a reputation in Mosby's Command, and Charley was astonished at such a question, for just at that time the boy was standing among a lot of the best material in the Command. He told Joe, however, that it was easy enough and, as they were going to charge the Yankees in a few minutes, all he had to do, when the charge was ordered, was to break away from the ranks and ride at them full tilt.

To Charley's surprise a moment later he saw Joe break away in the charge and go it alone, trying to lead all the rest. Harry Hatcher was standing near and heard the conversation. Turning to Puryear he said, "John, did you hear what Charley Dear told that boy? He must be trying to get him killed in the first round, before the water gets hot." The boys came back from the charge for there were too many for us.

After company D re-formed, Montjoy rode up to Charley and asked, "What is the name of that boy you brought up to company D?" Charley told him he was Joe Bryan, and Montjoy said, "He'll do! he is one of the old blue hen's chickens and he has won his spurs in the first round. Let him ride in the first set of fours between you and Ned Gibson and fill out Louis Adie's place." Adie was killed in the Berryville fight only a short time before and was one of the gamest and best boys in Montjoy's company of all good ones.

Joe always sustained his reputation. A youngster who could keep up his end with Charley Dear and Ned Gibson, and stay up at the front, had to be made of the right stuff, and Joe had proven what sort of stuff it was, for his career since the war has been constantly upward, until today he is perhaps as prominent as any man in Virginia.

Frank Angelo, a member of company C, was captured near Milwood in the Valley late in November, 1864, by five men of the Twenty-first New York. He was taken to headquarters and the officers had a lot of amusement out of him, for he was a very bright and witty fellow. Major Otis and General Tibbits became quite interested in him, and finally the major bet his general that Frank would never be taken to Washington. The wager was a basket of champagne and the general lost. Frank was taken with a lot of others to Martinsburg and put in an old jail. The door leading into an adjoining yard was fastened by a railroad spike, driven into the floor, and he managed to get hold of an axe with which he loosened the spike so the door would open, and when the opportunity offered he marched out, taking several other prisoners with him, and all got safely out of the town. While in prison he made friends with a number of his guards. One of them, finding Frank was going to escape, and wishing to help one of his own friends who was confined for some offense, made Frank promise to take the imprisoned Yankee with him, which he did, and got him safely across the Potomac.

Frank found that escaping from jail was a small matter compared with escaping from the Valley, for the whole country was alive with camps and soldiers were on the move day and night in every direction. After almost countless narrow escapes he reached Mosby's Confederacy at last, to be welcomed by the colonel who told him he would take him on his next scout and give him the best horse captured as a reward for his troubles and losses. Before the colonel could keep his promise he was badly wounded at Lake's house on the 21st of December, and Chapman let Angelo go home to Richmond on a furlough.

Frank was quite a mimic, and the gift served him well in his efforts to escape from the enemy. In trying to get out of the Valley on foot, he ran unexpectedly on a picket, stationed on the railroad and, seeing that he was discovered, he rolled down the embankment into a swamp; as he waded off in the dark he imitated a sow and pigs. The Yankee was heard to say; "Damn that hog: if it was daylight I would have one of them pigs, sure." His next obstacle was a wagon camp nearby, which he found himself in before he realised it. He unhitched and saddled a good mule, and rode out safely, and finally landed his mule and himself at home. Angelo is living in Washington at present, and is a welcome attendant at most of the reunions of the Command.

John McCue was one of our youngsters who had a trying experience, entirely unique. He joined the Command the day before the

Berryville fight and saw one of his college mates, young Louis Adie, killed in that fight. His company was sent down with others to winter in Westmoreland county and, late in March, 1865, he went across the Potomac River with five others on a private scout, lured by the prospect of capturing a quarter of a million dollars supposed to be deposited in Leonardtown, Maryland.

They crossed the river near Stratford, the birthplace of General Robert E. Lee, and finding it impossible to do anything at Leonardtown they went to Croom, in Prince George County, where the party separated, three going to their homes, while McCue and two others concluded to capture the post office. I suppose "capture" is a good, harmless word to use, though the authorities said the post office was robbed.

While John and his two companions were going through Uncle Sam's mail the door was suddenly opened and six detectives rushed in on them, firing their pistols at close range. John stood his ground but his companions bolted through a side door and, mounting their horses, escaped, finally getting back to Virginia. John killed one of the men, Detective Ryan, and wounded another, Jerry Coffron. Ryan had rushed the boy and was shot in the bowels by him, but the shot did not kill him and he grabbed John around the arms and while holding him received two more shots. The captors tied the boy and threatened to lynch him, but an officer coming up prevented it. They took him to Annapolis and from there to Baltimore, where he was tried by military Commission, and found guilty of murder, assault with intent to kill and violation of the laws of war. He was sentenced to the penitentiary for life, sent to the prison at Clinton, N.Y. and put at hard labour. In the following November a petition, signed by thousands of influential Virginians, was presented to President Andrew Johnson asking for his pardon but not until General Grant had personally asked the president to release the boy was the pardon signed.

Raiding and scouting parties going into Maryland frequently had exciting experiences before they came back across the Potomac. This historic stream proved a deadline very often, which it was dangerous to cross. John McCue undertook his scouting expedition as a sort of an outlet for his enthusiasm, which had been pent up all the winter.

Colonel Chapman took part of the Command down to the Peninsula to winter and save the limited supply of forage in Loudoun and Fauquier counties for that part of the Command which remained there under Colonel Mosby. While Colonel Mosby found plenty of work to do all winter, Chapman and his men were idle nearly all the time they were there. Boys like McCue fretted and chafed in their enforced idleness, and finally the six I have spoken of started out to accomplish something, with the result that five of them did nothing, and McCue did more than he expected. The boy only thought he got what was coming to him until they clipped his hair short, put him in chains and dressed him in stripes. "Capturing" a post office is sometimes a serious affair.

Captain Montjoy was a Mississippian, and Mosby made him Captain for gallantry—but he created all the officers for the same reason, for that matter. Montjoy, however, was conspicuously gallant: a sort of meteor that we could all see as he moved across the horizon of war. He was a very handsome young man with black eyes and hair, and his manners were very fascinating and attractive to both men and women. In addition, he was fastidious in his dress and in his general equipment. I never saw him awry in any particular. He was one of our dandies and we were proud of him. He rode the finest horses that money could buy, and his accoutrements would have suited a general.

Somehow or other, when Company D was organised, it seemed to contain nothing but dandies. Possibly the boys composing it took the example from Montjoy; but at any rate they were, so far as dress and equipment and general appearance went, the flower of the battalion; and, in order to sustain their prestige among their comrades, they became known to us all, and deservedly so, as game fighters. Nearly every Marylander in our Command was in Company D and everyone of them was a fire eater. Montjoy was as proud of his company of fighting dandies as the colonel was of his entire Command of fighting Guerrillas.

The manner in which Montjoy met his death—a most serious loss to the Partisan Rangers—is worth recording. It occurred on the 27th of November, 1864. He was commanding his Company, on a raid into Loudoun county, where he was trying to round up a company of local Yankees known as the Loudoun Rangers. On the morning they came together Montjoy killed, wounded and captured about twenty-five of them, including among the latter two lieutenants in command of their two squads, He scattered them like chaff before the wind and they flew for their lives in every direction. Montjoy picked out one of them to follow, and was close on his heels when the man threw his six-shooter over his shoulder, pointed it backwards without aim and pulled the trigger. The bullet went straight into Montjoy's head. Every man of his company who witnessed the tragedy reined in his horse involuntarily and groaned. We never filled Montjoy's place. We never tried to. There was only one Captain Montjoy.

A few days later Colonel Mosby issued the following notice:

Partisan Rangers:
The Lieutenant-Colonel Commanding announces to the battalion, with emotions of deep sorrow, the death of Captain R. P. Montjoy, who fell in action near Leesburg on the twenty-seventh *ultimo*, a costly sacrifice to victory. He died too early for liberty and his country's cause, but not too early for his own fame. To his comrades in arms he has bequeathed an immortal example of daring and valour, and to his country a name that will brighten the pages of her history.

John S. Mosby,
Lieutenant-Colonel, Commanding.

One of the men killed in the Blazer fight was Edward Bredell of St. Louis. He had been an officer in the regular army before he came to us, and his parents were very wealthy. Moreover, he was an only child. On the day of the fight the boys laid him to rest where he fell, but afterwards we brought his body over to our side of the mountain and buried it near Oak Hill, the former home of Chief Justice Marshall. Before the war ended young Bredell's father came down to Virginia and took his dead son's body home. When he reached St. Louis, owing to the bitter feeling there towards the Southerners, he was informed that the body could not be buried in any of the cemeteries. He thereupon had a grave dug in his own handsome grounds, and his son's body found its final rest in the shadow of his old home.

At the close of the war, or rather two years after, I went to St. Louis to live, taking with me a letter of introduction to the father of Edward Bredell, whom I found to be an old Eastern shoreman of Maryland, and distantly related to family connections of mine. Upon my first visit to the old gentleman he took my hand and escorted me to the beautiful grounds in the rear of his house, where we two sat by the grave of the Partisan Ranger and talked of him as we had known him in the flesh. I called frequently at the Bredell home and I have not the slightest doubt that it gave the old man no little pleasure to hear me recount the exploits of his brave son, and to repeat, time and time again, the story of the fight in which the boy fell and died. Many a time I have sat near him in the shade of the trees that spread their limbs over the simple grave, and caught him gazing wistfully at the green mound that covered his son's body. He tried to take his sorrows philosophically, but I cannot forget his first remark as we stood together:

> Maybe it is all right to give your only boy to your country, but I wish I had mine back again.

Chapter 12

An Unpleasant Episode

As I have written before, the month of August, 1864, was one of the busiest in the history of our Command. Hardly a day passed without bloodshed. The Northern feeling against Mosby's men was intense and the opportunities to crush our Command were thrown away because of the enemy's anxiety to bring about instant annihilation. When concerted attacks were arranged, some hot-headed one, guilty only in judgment, would blaze away at us from ambush and sound the signal that enabled us to slip away in time. Mosby's men, it must be remembered, knew more about the country than did any of the visitors from the North, and we knew the game of guerrilla warfare thoroughly.

One afternoon in that busy month of August Colonel Mosby with about thirty or forty men of his Command, was riding through the woods in Fairfax County. He was not expecting immediate trouble. Suddenly bullets came singing through the trees from a party of Thirteenth New Yorkers who retreated in a gallop towards Fairfax station as soon as they had fired their volley. One of our men, George Slater, was wounded.

At the station the enemy was joined by some of the Sixteenth New York, about one hundred men in all. They came swinging back through the woods and prepared to attack us. Our scouts, scattered through the underbrush, heard their commander tell them to use their carbines in the preliminary rush and then charge with their sabres. Mosby heard the order and, realising that sabres were utterly worthless against our six-shooters, smiled when he told us simply to "Go through 'em." There was no excitement, no alarm at their greater number, three or four to our one, no surprise at the colonel's quiet order; everything seemed to be moving along in its usual way. The order was a common one to us. "There are the Yankees! Go through 'em."

What is there to write about? It was all over in a few minutes, and it was the same old monotonous story. We killed the commanding officer, Captain J. H. Fleming, of the Sixteenth New York and six of his men; we wounded Captain McMenamin, of the Thirteenth New York, a lieutenant and eight men, and we captured thirty prisoners and forty horses.

Why the Federal troopers so often went into battle with those clumsy, antiquated sabres was a mystery that none of Mosby's men ever found out They might just as well have walked up to a battery of howitzers with billiard cues. A good healthy Irishman with his *shillelagh* would make any cavalryman with his sabre ashamed of himself. In his report of this affair Colonel Lazelle said that:

> A board of investigation had been called to ascertain who was responsible.

The one man who could have best enlightened the board was dead, but it would not have been a bad idea to court-martial the officer who ordered the men to wear sabres.

There are some things in the lives of all of us that we can't refer to with pleasure, and the hanging and shooting of some of our men, by order of General Custer, and in his presence, is one of those which Mosby's men rarely refer to. Neither it, nor what followed as a result of it, are happy memories to any of us. We want to remember General Custer, and I believe we all do remember him, as the gallant martyr who went down at Little Big Horn, surrounded, almost covered up, with the dead bodies of his foes; his pistols smoking hot; his blue eyes flashing defiance; his voice ringing out in command of his brave companions. This was the real hero, the real Custer.

The Custer episode is part of our history, however, and its recital reflects nothing but credit on our Command. It was one of the important events of our career. Its effect was far reaching on both sides and I have no doubt that it was never generally approved throughout the North. The official records of the war will bear out my story of it.

At that time, August, 1864, Alger was operating in the lower Valley of Virginia, and we frequently exchanged shots with his men, picked off their sentries, chased them and were chased by them. One afternoon Lieutenant-Colonel Chapman of our Command, with a detachment of raiders, came upon some burning dwellings in the neighbourhood of Charlestown, in Jefferson County. We learned from the recent residents, huddled about their ruins, that General Alger's men had applied the torch. The entreaties of the women and children had been of no avail. The order had been given and the order was obeyed. The sight of those helpless non-combatants crouching in the rain, weeping over their burning homes, wrought up the resentment of the men and we started out to even things up in real guerrilla fashion. We passed the ruined and deserted homes of Mr. McCormick and Mr. Sowers and, learning that the burners were just ahead of us, went after them on a run, overtaking them at the residence of Colonel Morgan, to which they had just set fire. Our men were demons that day. Thirty of the burners were killed and wounded, mostly killed. We took no prisoners and gave no quarter. Forty horses fell into our hands and we retired without further concern. No more buildings were burned by the Federals in that valley.

In order to contrast this house burning with Mosby's idea and understanding of ethics I have only to recall the case of one of our men, recently recruited, who went down with us into Loudoun county, among the Quakers. He overturned an old Quaker's milk can. The fellow knew that all the Quakers were sympathizers with the North, at least not with us. Colonel Mosby had him arrested when he heard of it, and I was sent back with him to the regular army and instructed to turn him over to General Early, with the information that he was not sufficient of a gentleman to travel with Mosby's men and that he had a mistaken idea of the mission of the guerrillas. I had other prisoners to take on the same trip and, as I was starting, Colonel Mosby took me aside and told me to take the milk spiller along with me to help me guard the captured men and, when I got him to General Early's, to turn him over also.

When I reached the army and had unloaded my charges I reported to General Early's tent. The general and my father were great friends and he welcomed me. I told him all about the doings of Alger's men, how we met them at Colonel Morgan's and what we did to them, of course colouring the picture somewhat, as was my duty. He was so well pleased and so greatly interested in my recital and the result, that I did not attempt to restrain my talents, but added that we had killed every man that we could get at, and threw them all in the fire.

"I wish to heaven," he replied, "that you had thrown all of Sheridan's men in after them."

General Phil was worrying the old man greatly at the time, and I have not the slightest doubt that General Early meant just what he said.

The fight, or rather the onslaught, at Colonel Morgan's house, was not to be forgotten, however, for on the 23rd of September, General Custer, still breathing fire and vengeance, captured some of Mosby's men and had some of them hanged and others shot with their hands tied behind their backs. This was in Front Royal, Va. Mosby's men have erected a handsome monument to them in that pretty little town, and the ladies look after it for the Command. These seven men had been taken prisoners in a fair fight and by overwhelming numbers. They were captured doing the best they could and should have been sent to some northern prison like other prisoners of war. The men who did the work were, some of them, Alger's. I received only a short while ago a letter from a prominent business man living in the West who was a member of the Fifth Michigan. He said that affair was a disgrace to the army.

Reports of the unfortunate affair came very promptly to Colonel Mosby from many sources. One of our men, Frank Angelo, had cut down and removed the bodies of some of our boys who were hanged, and he gave all the particulars of it to us. There was at once a rumour set afloat that we were to fight thereafter under the black flag, and as a proof of it Custer's act was pointed to. Men examined their pistols more carefully. The price of good runners went up rapidly and, as the greenback raid followed the next month, and the men had money to burn, there were a number of fine horses bought. Where formerly the boys had slept with one eye open they now slept with both open, as it were. Mosby waited his time.

On the 6th of November following we got twenty-seven of these Michigan fellows in a raid. Mosby had them draw lots to determine which seven of them should be killed in retaliation for our men killed at Front Royal. It was an awful shock to the unlucky ones and a fearful suspense to all. Lieutenant Ed. Thomson was instructed to take the condemned men to a point across the Shenandoah River in the Valley and have them hanged or shot. It is safe to say he never had a more disagreeable duty to perform in all his life.

On the march one of his prisoners escaped in the darkness! A little farther on, while crossing the mountain at Ashby's gap, Thomson met Captain Montjoy returning from a raid in the Valley with some prisoners. Montjoy had recently become a Mason, and was a very enthusiastic craftsman. He ascertained in the usual way that two of the condemned men were brother Masons, and that they would be glad to enjoy any fraternal assistance that might be available at the moment;

so Montjoy took them from Thomson in exchange for two of his own prisoners, and passed on.

When Mosby heard of this transfer he called Montjoy to him and said, after delivering a lecture on discipline, "I want you to understand that my Command is not a Masonic lodge."

Of the seven men to be killed only three were hanged. Two of them were shot, but not killed, and recovered later; two got away. One of these latter, when the spot for the execution was reached, asked Thomson for time to pray, which was readily accorded; the lieutenant joining silently in the petition of the condemned. The whole job was ill-suited to Thomson's inclination, but he was too good a soldier to disobey orders.

While the Michigan man was making his peace with his Creator he was incidentally "sawing wood" vigorously. With his hands clasped apparently in prayer, he slowly worked away at the cords that bound his wrists, until they were free. His appeal to the Almighty was fervent in the extreme, and at the *Amen* which was uttered in a voice heavy with penitence, he turned to Thomson as if he were ready to have his head shot off. Instead, however, he planted a terrific blow with his right hand on Thomson's nose, knocked him flat on his back, jumped over his prostrate form and, without waiting to thank our men or tell them goodbye, disappeared in the darkness. I take off my hat to men who can do things like that.

Thomson, rather pleased at the celerity with which the Michigan man's appeal to heaven had been answered, picked himself up and finished his work.

To the clothing of one of the men he pinned the following note:

> These men have been hanged in retaliation for an equal number of Colonel Mosby's men hanged by order of General Custer at Front Royal. Measure for measure.

On November 11 Colonel Mosby wrote a letter to General Sheridan and sent it by John Russell. It read as follows:

> Major-General P. H. Sheridan,
> Commanding U. S. Forces in the Valley.
> General: Some time in the month of September, during my absence from my Command, six of my men, who had been captured by your forces, were hung and shot in the streets of Front Royal, by the order and in the presence of Brigadier-General Custer. Since then another (captured by a Colonel Powell on

a plundering expedition into Rappahannock) shared a similar fate. A label affixed to the coat of one of the murdered men declared that, "This will be the fate of Mosby and all his men." Since the murder of my men, not less than seven hundred prisoners, including many officers of high rank, captured from your army by this Command, have been forwarded to Richmond, but the execution of my purpose of retaliation was deferred in order, as far as possible, to confine its operation to the men of Custer and Powell.

Accordingly, on the 6th instant, seven of your men were, by my order, executed on the Valley pike, your highway of travel.

Hereafter any prisoners falling into my hands will be treated with the kindness due to their condition, unless some new act of barbarity shall compel me, reluctantly, to adopt a line of policy repugnant to humanity.

    Very respectfully.
     Your obedient servant,
      John S. Mosby, Lieut.-Colonel.

On the 29th of October, Colonel Mosby had written a letter to General Lee, telling him of the practice of compelling helpless old men to ride exposed on the trains running over the railroads from Alexandria into Fauquier County, and of his intention to continue attacking such trains. He also told him of the murder of our men by Custer and Powell, and his intention to retaliate.

The first endorsement of Mosby's letter was as follows:

> Respectfully referred to the Honourable Secretary of War for his information. I do not know how we can prevent the cruel conduct of the enemy toward our citizens. I have directed Colonel Mosby, through his adjutant, to hang an equal number of Custer's men in retaliation for those executed by him.
>
>   R. E. Lee, General.

The third endorsement was:

> General Lee's instructions are cordially approved. In addition, if our citizens are found exposed on any captured train, signal vengeance should be taken on all conductors and officers found on it, and every male passenger of the enemy's country should be treated as a prisoner. So instruct.
>
>   J. A. Seddon, Secretary.

Chapter 13

Incidents

In a raid we once made at midnight into the very heart of a cavalry camp near Fairfax Court House, where we were entirely surrounded by thousands of the enemy, it was necessary to go inside the stables to unfasten the horses. It was also necessary to keep absolutely quiet, for we were outnumbered a hundred to one. The pickets had been captured and ordered in whispers to follow us, and we made them unhitch the horses and help us to get them out

Captain Wm. Chapman had by his side Baron Von Massow, of whom I have spoken previously. In whispers he explained to the baron what we were doing, and how to do it artistically; incidentally, he told the baron of the boldness and the danger of it. The baron proved a very apt scholar but after awhile he whispered to Captain Chapman very quietly: "This is not fighting; this is horse-stealing." And who shall say he was wrong? But, before that job of horse-stealing was finished, and when each man had from one to five, or even more, haltered or bridled horses, and was starting to lead them out to safety, the alarm was given, the troops were aroused, firing and yelling began, and the wounded were groaning and dying. In the midst of the confusion the guerrillas mounted the captured horses and, leading others, dashed away to where their own horses were waiting, without the loss of a man.

This was one of the many affairs that read like romance when told in the newspapers. People asked how on earth Mosby could get his raiding party inside of a big cavalry camp and, once the camp aroused, how on earth he could get it out.

I do not know just how to explain it or to tell how easy it all appeared when it was over. But if you will bear in mind that everybody in the camp was fast asleep except the pickets; that we either crept stealthily upon these pickets, one by one, put pistols to their faces and told them to keep quiet, or that we rode up to them boldly and gobbled them up before they realised that we were not their own relief guard; and that, once inside, it was no more dangerous to move around quietly among five thousand sleeping men than among five; and that, when sleeping men awake suddenly, they never are instantly ready to fight; and that, when we began yelling and firing into them, they never knew whether we were five thousand or five; and that, by the time they were sufficiently aroused to fight intelligently, we had dashed out of the camp and disappeared in the darkness, it will not seem so strange.

It fell to my lot one dark night in winter to capture an infantry picket before our men could get into the camp, where we knew there were a lot of fine horses and mules. Not knowing how many pickets we might have to take the colonel had ordered another man to go with me. His orders were merely to "take the pickets." We left our horses and started towards the camp on foot. Within a few hundred yards of where our men were waiting for us I could see a figure moving along in the darkness, and we both dropped to the ground. I saw him march to the right and we crawled up a little and stopped. He turned and marched back, and as he passed us we crawled a little nearer. When he had gone up and down a few more times we were in his path, and just as he came up to me I jumped up and thrust my pistol in his face.

I do not recall that he said that he was pleased to make my acquaintance, but I do remember that, before we got him back to our base, he was taken suddenly sick. It was a simple case of extreme fright. He needed a good stiff drink. I captured a Yankee soldier on the 21st of November, 1863, who never ceased to be grateful to me for doing it. Mosby had about seventy-five men on a raid below Warrenton while General Gregg's Division of Federal cavalry was encamped there. We had stopped in a piece of pines near Bealton Station to watch "for something doing" in our line of business; it was raining, cold and disagreeable, and the boys were all feeling ugly and impatient. Mosby saw a cavalryman and a man on foot coming along the road, and told Walter Whaley and me to bring them in to him. We had on rubber *ponchos* which hid our bodies entirely and, drawing our pistols under them, we marched up to the two men; we spoke only when we were a step away, and then merely said, "Surrender." The mounted man's first impulse was to draw his pistol and fight us, but he thought better of it and gave himself up. Whaley disarmed him and I had laid violent hands on the one on foot, when his face broadened into a smile.

"Oh, thank God for this," he cried, "may God bless you my boy."

I did not know exactly what to make of this demonstration, for we were not accustomed to being thanked for gobbling up the boys of the other side but, when we went through the cavalryman, who proved to be a courier bearing important despatches and papers, we unravelled the mystery. My man on foot was his prisoner, and was being taken to a nearby camp to be shot, according to a sentence of a court-martial held the day before.

When we first took the men I asked the one on horseback if he carried any papers; he said he did not and, to prove that he was a good soldier and likely to be lying, I searched him thoroughly; I did not come across the prize envelope until I got inside of his inside shirt, next to his skin, where it was sticking to him like a porous plaster.

When we took our prisoners to Mosby he opened the envelope and found the order to have the man shot. We took him back with us to our part of the country, got him a suit of old clothes and, facing him Northward, turned him loose. He started for his home in Pennsylvania and no doubt he never stopped until he got there.

Among the courier's papers was an official order which informed us that some wagons would be along soon; in due time they arrived and we captured them, with their guard. Mosby said that it was clever of the enemy to inform us when to be on the lookout for their good things. With the wagons we captured fifteen prisoners together with thirty horses and mules, and helped ourselves to all the medical supplies we needed for our surgeon's use. Their wagons contained a supply greater in quantity, perhaps, at that time, than the Medical Department at Richmond could boast. I know of one old local doctor, to whom I gave a few bottles of morphine shortly afterwards, who thanked me actually with tears in his eyes, assuring me that the stuff was worth more to him than its weight in gold.

The courier also carried a bundle of letters to be mailed, and these we amused ourselves with while we waited for the wagons to come along. We did not think it was wrong to open other people's mail in those days. Among them were some love letters, which we sent to Warrenton later, one of which created a mighty stir and nearly split a church in twain. For there were many in that congregation who were horrified at the discovery that one of their number was corresponding with a "horrid Yankee officer."

Very few of the fights of Mosby's men were pitched battles. Most of them were little affairs hardly worth writing about. Yet they were part of the almost daily experience of some of the men. I recall one of them in which I took part, where my companions killed four-fifths of the enemy, and I captured the rest. We wiped the whole crowd out completely.

Colonel Mosby took five of us on a scout into Fairfax County, on one occasion, and about midnight we got information from a man living on the roadside which changed his plans and made him decide to go back home and try again a little later. We learned, however, that a picket post of five cavalrymen were stationed on the turnpike a few hundred yards below where we were, and that a vedette stood between them and us. Colonel Mosby told us to go down and bring them in while he took a little nap in the pines, as he did not think it at all necessary to lead in person such a formidable body as we were. We tied our horses and started on foot in a roundabout way, to get between the picket post and the supporting company, a hundred or two yards away and nearer their army corps. Captain Montjoy, being the only officer in our little party of five, assumed command without objection from any of us and suggested we string out, in line-of-battle style, a few yards apart, and stealthily approach the post, till we could jump on the pickets and whisper to them not to create unpleasantness by firing their weapons.

We crept along noiselessly, step by step, in the dark, circling around the vedette, and keeping the pickets in full view all the time, as they were grouped around a little smouldering fire. Each of us had his pistol drawn ready for an emergency, but we hardly expected to use them. When we were within twenty feet of them one of us stepped on a dry stick which broke with a snapping sound, and the five sentinels turning to us called out, "Halt, who goes there" Montjoy answered, "Surrender."

In an instant five carbines were emptied at us, and four of our pistols rang out, point-blank, at them. Four of them fell dead around their little fire.

In our advance on them Montjoy was on one end of our little "line-of-battle," and I was at the other, not dreaming we should have to fire on them, but thinking that we could take them noiselessly. I did not realise what Montjoy said, but mistook "Surrender" for "Friends;" and in my excitement I did not fire my pistol with the others.

We rushed on them immediately, and it fell to my lot to reach the only live one first. He understood the situation only too well, and in his anxiety to surrender to me and save his life, he pushed the muzzle of his carbine up against my stomach but, not knowing how to speak English he did not speak a word of anything. I mistook his action just as I had mistaken Montjoy's call and, as the carbine was pressed against me, I imagined I could feel my heart, liver, lungs and vermiform appendix flying through space out of the stove pipe hole in my back. I do not believe I ever suffered such suspense for about a half minute in all my life but, as the carbine failed to do its expected deadly work of exploration, I took the fellow a prisoner and threw the gun away.

We pulled the four dead bodies out of the fire, took their pistols and belts, mounted the five horses, put the captured German up behind me, and galloped back to where the colonel was peacefully sleeping in the pines.

As we rode away from our ghastly work we could hear the lone vedette crashing through the woods on his way around us, back to his company, but we did not try to head him off and, when daylight dawned we were twenty or thirty miles away, headed for the mountains, with five horses and no German. In the darkness he had slipped off the horse he was riding, and the man who was supposed to be guarding him did not seem to be very sorry to lose him. As we rode along through the darkness we each decided to keep the horse he was leading, instead of drawing lots for them and, as my captured animal was the friskiest of the lot, I believed I had the best. But oh! what a difference in the morning! I had a regular old plug.

One morning in the late summer, previous to my capture, I had been scouting with Colonel Mosby in the Valley, and a few of us were resting on the roadside, hidden under the trees from the view of any of the enemy who might be passing along the pike. While Sheridan was in the Valley all the roads in the vicinity of his army were pretty well covered by his cavalry in motion. Looking out under the trees from our hiding place the colonel saw the four legs of a gray horse coming toward us, and assumed that a horse's body and a man, mounted on it, accompanied the legs; so he told me to go out and bring the man in to him. I mounted my horse and rode out to see who the newcomer was and, as he was not looking for anybody from Mosby's Confederacy, I had no trouble in poking my pistol under his nose before he could draw his own from the holster. He surrendered very quietly and I took him back to the colonel, in the meantime searching him carefully to be sure that he had no dynamite about his person.

I was much relieved to find that he only had a harmless pocketbook and a pretty good watch which, in all kindness, I offered to keep for him and which, in equal kindness, he permitted me to do. He proved to be Lieutenant Wright, provost-marshal for General Merritt. During the morning we captured some other prisoners and, inasmuch as I had profited more than the other boys by the horse and the personal effects of the lieutenant, as well as some other trinkets obtained casually from other prisoners, the colonel made me take all the prisoners out. I had to get them from the rear of Sheridan's troops, and along the western base of the mountain till I came within the lines of our own army, which was facing Sheridan. In other words I had to describe a circle of about twenty miles to go what would have been only about five in a straight line. When I got to General Early's headquarters I tried to have Lieutenant Wright exchanged for one of our own lieutenants, Frank Fox, who had been wounded and captured only a few days before, but my good intentions were frustrated by the death of Frank Fox, and my captured provost-marshal was sent to Richmond.

The colonel enjoyed my ownership of the captured watch very much, and after that day he would frequently say, "What time is it, Munson, by Lieutenant Wright?" Years and years afterwards, in fact when he had returned from his long residence in Hong Kong, where he had represented the United States Consul, he was walking with me one day in St. Louis, and turning to me with his happy smile, asked me the same old question, "What time is it, Munson, by Lieutenant Wright?"

When I was captured my "Lieutenant Wright" watch became part of the spoils of my conquerors, but in all the excitement and terror of my downfall I noted the appearance of the fellow who took my watch and, when I arrived at the headquarters of my captors that night I asked the colonel of the regiment (I think it was Farnsworth of Illinois, who later was a Congressman) to try and get my family heirloom returned to me. I pointed out the man who had it and it was given up, but not to me. It was sent along to the Old Capitol prison accompanying the prisoners.

When I escaped from that prison early in 1865, I was in such a hurry that I forgot to ask for my watch.

In June, 1865, when the men who were in prison with me came home from Fort Warren, one of them told me that when my escape was discovered and our men were sent away to Boston, the superintendent of the prison restored to each man his personal effects, and when he held up that watch and asked who it belonged to, the boys told him it was Munson's. "Well," he remarked, "if Munson will call here for it he can have it." When I heard this I wrote him a request to send me the watch and, two days later, received it; as it is still among my possessions it has really now become an old family affair.

I met General Merritt at an entertainment in St. Louis, ten years after the war, and told him of my capture of Lieutenant Wright, and he said he was glad to learn the facts, because the lieutenant had disappeared from the face of the earth that morning and, as no word was ever heard of or from him, he always supposed he had deserted. I heard that he died in prison in Richmond, but if I am mistaken, and if he is still alive, and if he reads this and wants his watch I will send it to him; but not his pocket-book.

I captured another watch that same summer from another man of Sheridan's Command and, at the close of the war I gave it to Mr. John Carr, a citizen who lived on the mountainside near Paris. When most of our men went over to the Valley on April 22, 1865, to surrender to General Hancock, Mr. Carr went along to get his parole also, thinking perhaps that sympathizing citizens were included in the general terms of the surrender. The old gentleman was pretty well frightened at his surroundings when he reached the Valley, and told a friend of his he expected every minute to be his last. He wanted to know what time it was but he was afraid to pull out that watch on the street, for fear its former owner might recognise it and put him in jail. The possession of it worried him so that he slipped it down inside his trousers and let it drop into his sock, and getting on his horse he hurried out of town to his home.

Sam Alexander was one of our heavy-weights, though he was only a youngster. I would not like to say how much he weighed, but it was close around the two hundred and forty pound mark. It did not interfere in the least, however, with his riding. He came from Campbell Court House, Virginia, and was a son of Captain Jack Alexander, one of the best known men in the state and once the owner of the celebrated race horse "Red Eye," by Boston, the sire of Lexington. Sam came by his love for fine horses honestly, but I do not know where he got his fluent and variegated assortment of profanity. There was not a better rider in the Command, and there was not a gamer man. When he swept down on a sutler his process of absorption was unique. He could extract from the victim his last gasp of protest, as well as his last penny's worth of goods. I only mention this boy's name, among my stories of time-pieces, because I am reminded of him whenever I think of a captured watch. It was a fruitless raid for Sam when he did not come home with a newly absorbed watch.

There were other specialists in our Command. Some would have a peculiar fondness for new pistols, and in every fight would try to capture weapons newer than their own. Others made a point of getting handsome saddles, and still others wanted fancy saddle blankets. It is perhaps not strange that a number of the men made pocket-books a specialty. I believe I was of this number.

While the effect of robbing a captured soldier was felt largely by the victim, it formed its part of the general purpose of "harassing and annoying the enemy." It made a man in the service less anxious to fall into his captor's hands a second time, after one experience of being fleeced. I recall at even this late day that I never had any desire to become the guest of the Eighth Illinois Cavalry after that gallant band had gone through me. And that just reminds me: It was the major of the regiment who got my pipe and silk tobacco bag. Surely a poor private can be forgiven for indulging in his raids on the prisoners' pocket-books, when the commissioned officers set the example.

Chapter 14

I am Captured

After the war, when the Nation was healing its wounds and reminiscence was rife in the land, my dear old mother met a friend on the Richmond Capitol square and stopped to talk about the great conflict.

"Mrs. Munson," ventured the friend, who knew my connection with the Partisan Rangers, "what do you reckon was the worst whipping Colonel Mosby's men got during the war?"

"Well, I never heard anyone discuss it," replied my mother, smiling to herself, "but I reckon it must have been the day the Yankees captured my boy Johnny."

A good many mothers were under the impression that the entire conflict was fought right around their children, and those who sat waiting at home for the soldier who never came back had some reason for their beliefs. Fortunately for me and for the good woman who dated Mosby's greatest misfortune as simultaneous with my capture, I succeeded in escaping from the Yankees and in returning to the South before the trouble had ceased.

It was not strange that I should get into the Federal drag net sooner or later. I had been enjoying a lot of liberty during the two last years and, when it came time for me, as it did in the latter end of 1864, to throw up my hands and "come along with us," I did so with that same alacrity with which other hands had been thrown up to me.

It came about in this wise. A newly appointed captain, chosen by Mosby from what he used to call his blue hen's chickens, because of their unfailing excellence, had a chance to win his spurs in a fight that was about due to come off near Upperville. A detachment from the Eighth Illinois Cavalry was on a short raid from their camp near Rectortown, to Upperville, and Colonel Mosby ordered them attacked.

The officer to whom I refer had been with Mosby since the very inception of the Partisan Rangers and, as an individual fighting man, had no superior in the Command, his promotion from the ranks being a just reward for a continuous record of brilliant service. His waving plume was ever at the head of the column when there was fighting to be done, and everybody in the Command loved Walter Frankland.

Captain Frankland's plan was to divide his Command for the purpose of charging a stone-wall of Federal cavalry in front and flank simultaneously. It did not work if my memory serves me right, as the enemy had our first detachment whipped before Lieutenant Grogan with his flanking party reached the scene. Grogan had no idea that Frankland had been disposed of, until the Federals turned their attention to his little squad, and discomfited him at the same handy pace.

They poured a deadly carbine fire into us as we rushed on. We were charging in fours, and I was at the front, and did not know that our men had wavered and turned off from the hopeless attack until it was too late to follow them. When I discovered my predicament I believe it would have been a safe thing for me to have headed my horse straight at their line and trusted to my breaking my way through by the impetus of the charge. It takes a good strong horse to withstand the charge of another one, head on. What I should have done, and what I did, are two widely different things.

Luck, too, was against me. I only realised that I was up against it, and must try to get away. When I headed my mare for a high and forbidding stone fence the animal refused to take the leap. For an instant, as she approached the ugly barrier, I thought she would go over, but that short, firm step that a jumper makes just before rising failed, and a wave of anxiety passed through me as she hesitated. I tried to lift her with the movement that the rider involuntarily makes, and touched her with my spur. She trembled, gave a frightened little neigh, and fell back on her haunches.

It looked bad for me. I jumped from her back, scrambled over the wall on my own hook, and was breaking the world's record in a fine two hundred yard dash for some timber on the other side. At one time I thought I would actually get away, but the Yankees found a gap in the wall that I had overlooked and got on my trail at once. My mare jumped the wall after me like a deer, and with head and tail up defiantly, though really as badly scared as I, dashed away across the field and was found the next day riderless, miles away from the scene of my troubles. I fancied, as I saw her fading away from me, that she looked back pityingly, but I could fancy any old thing just then.

Before I got a hundred yards from the wall they pounced on me and made the most complete capture of a rebel ever witnessed. About twenty men made as many passes at me, and the baubles and splendours of guerrilla life disappeared. They got my hat and plumes, my gloves and pistols, my watch and belt, and all my personal belongings. Before I had time to make the slightest protest, one fellow sat me down abruptly, put his foot on me, and relieved me of my boots in a most startling and finished manner. Talk about Mosby's men going through a man! There was not a man in our Command who could swoop down and capture a pair of boots like the man who took mine! It was my initial touch at the game of retaliation, and the Yankees trimmed me well.

I have very recently received a letter from Mr. W. S. Freeman, who is now a prominent business man in Le Mars, Iowa, in which he said:

> I was one of the men who captured you, and my share of the swag was your spurs. I wish I had them now, so I could send them to you. Another one of our little party was Mr. James How, of Audubon, Iowa. You overrated the number of men who captured you; there were only a few of us.

I answered his friendly letter and told him my mental condition was such, when he claims to have first formed my acquaintance, that I could imagine his whole regiment had a hand in the affair.

I did not regret the loss of any of my belongings as much as that of my watch. Pocket-book, knife, pipe, tobacco-bag and everything else could be duplicated when I should come back home, but that watch was my pride.

Not many months before that day I had ridden out on the turnpike in the Valley and captured an officer who was riding towards me. He was Lieutenant Wright, provost-marshal for General Merritt. The first thing I took from him after disarming him was this watch. Everything else he had followed in the regular order, but I paid no special attention to them. I fondled that watch, for it was the first one I had ever captured.

I had learned to appreciate what we were pleased to call "a fat capture," for a great many of the men we took seemed to be waiting for the paymaster to arrive. I remember in a fight we had near Duffield Station on the Baltimore & Ohio Railroad, I captured, single handed, five poor, frightened infantrymen who had thrown down their guns and were absolutely harmless. From all the five men I only got sixty-five cents. I had no heart in the business for days after. One of the best men we had was big, fat Sam Alexander. He was a daredevil and much given to profanity. In an ugly fight one day Sam aimed his pistol at a man's head and said: "Give me your pocketbook, you blankety blank, blank."

"I have not got any pocket-book," he said.

"Well then, surrender," Sam said, as he proceeded to disarm the prisoner. But this is a digression.

I was taken with some other prisoners over to Rectortown, and locked up in the station of the old Manassas Gap Railroad. Had I known that the distance from the second story to the ground was less than fifteen feet, I might have jumped it and got away. As it was, I remained there that night and got some much-needed rest and sleep. The following day we were taken to Alexandria by rail. In my guard I recognised a man whom I had befriended the previous year, when he had been my prisoner in Fauquier County. He had not forgotten the circumstance and was willing that I should jump off the train when it came to the next stop. Here was a little light ahead; some of the bread I had cast upon the waters bid fair to return. The next thing I knew my friendly guard was relieved by another man, and the bread became dough.

I spent the next night in the old slave pen in Alexandria. "Served me right," remarked one of my fellow prisoners. On the following day I was marched into Washington to the Old Capitol prison. My raiment consisted of a suit of underclothes protected by a cast-off outfit that I had picked up somewhere after I had been put through the third degree by the Eighth Illinois boys, I carried a pair of rough horsehide boots that replaced the twenty-seven dollar Wellingtons which had been skinned off me. I could not wear the boots, but I did not care to give them up, for I had hopes that I might be able to exchange them for some others to suit my size and taste in foot-gear, so I carried them around with me.

From Alexandria we were marched up the road and across the long bridge to Washington and, when we swung into Pennsylvania Avenue I was barefooted, as my socks had worn through on the march. Beside me marched Dennis Darden, a Washington man, who knew every foot of the locality through which we were passing. Carefully we worked our way down our line till we were the last two in the ranks, for we had arranged to strike down the guards on either side of us, when we reached a certain alley, and make a dash for freedom. I figured on smashing my guard in the face with the horsehide boots and pulling his musket down over his back before he could empty its contents into my bosom. I made up my mind to make a better run than I made two days previously. Just before we got to the alley some of Darden's friends, learning of his capture, rode along the line of march and brought up in the rear, following at our heels, and offering cigars. Dennis turned pale and whispered to me that any attempt to escape would involve his friends, who would be arrested and possibly shot as accomplices in our escape.

About sunset we reached the Old Capitol prison, at the southeast corner of First and A streets, almost opposite the Senate Chamber. I was assigned, with thirty-six others, to a room in the front of the building overlooking the Capitol of the United States, with the gilded statue of Liberty on the dome. She stood against the winter sky and beckoned me to the freedom that she has since given; but in '64, I spent long days and weary nights at my grated window, wondering what particular significance that golden goddess with hand outstretched had for me. She looked awfully inviting, but I could not accept.

There was not much in prison life that interested me. What I was most concerned about was how to escape. I racked my brain for some brilliant idea by which I could bid *adieu* to everything north of Loudoun County, Virginia. One night, while exercising in the narrow yard in which we were permitted to move about, I watched the scavengers who came every twenty-four hours to clean out the prison. It occurred to me that I might make a deal with one of these men to escape in their cart. I arranged to give one of them a five-dollar gold piece, provided he would help me out. He was a former slave of a friend of mine in Virginia. He was willing enough, but offered the objection that I was a white man, while the scavengers were negroes. I told him I would take care of that part.

That night I burned a big cork, and in the shadow of the exercising yard I blackened my face like a minstrel, sauntered up to the scavengers' carts. The two men, anxious that I should play my part in a natural and easy manner, handed me their shovels, and ordered me to hustle around lively and show what stuff I was made of. I had no choice but to shovel garbage, and I put in half an hour of the hardest work of my life. The perspiration mixed with the burnt cork, and I looked more like a coal heaver than a Washington *coon*. Nevertheless, when the work was done, I jumped on the cart and we drove indif-

Lt.-Col. Chapman.   John Puryear.   Lt. Ben. Palmer.
Lt. Ed. Thompson.   Charley Dear.   Syd. Ferguson.

On the porch of the house in which General Stoughton was captured in 1863, in Fairfax Co. Va. Taken at a reunion in 1904

ferently towards the exit. We passed the post and it looked as; if we would get away. At the outer gate, however, a figure stepped out of the shadow and a well rounded Irish-American voice remarked, "Git down from that and go back to your quarthers: two of yez nagers come in, and three of yez is thrying to go out." I crept back humbly to my grated quarters.

Within a week I had another plan. It contemplated making an exit in the contract baker's wagon which came into the prison yard every day to deliver bread. One morning when conditions seemed to be about right, I jumped into the wagon, worked my way under a stack of warm, white loaves, and snuggled down in the flour dust, waiting for my baker coachman to come out and drive me away.

One of my large feet protruded from the bread pile and was discovered by one of the guard, who dragged me from my friendly loaves, wild with rage, much as a butcher pulls a side of beef from an ice-box. I was promptly marched off to the guard house and advised, privately, that my next attempt at rambling would be met with something calculated to keep me in for an indefinite period.

I was obliged to resort to these expedients because at that time the usual methods of escape had been worked to death. One of our men found a guard who for a consideration agreed to let him escape through a window under which he was on duty. The prisoner sawed through the iron bars of his window, made a rope from his bed clothes, and with infinite caution at the appointed hour, slid slowly down to what he imagined was freedom. Just as his feet touched the pavement and the thrill of liberty began to fill his soul, a bayonet driven by the friendly guard, pierced his back and passed through his heart. The guard was rewarded with a sergeantcy. A well-deserved promotion, perhaps.

The confinement was beginning to wear on me. While the food and the treatment were in every way satisfactory, I felt an intense longing to go back to Virginia, where the fighting and raiding and hurrahing were going on, and where I had friends, relations and countrymen. All my efforts to escape safely had come to naught it seemed I was destined to remain in prison until the Federal Government saw fit to turn me loose. Nevertheless, I stuck to the principles of eternal vigilance and watched the game as it went on around me.

In the daily life of the prison I observed a short, black-haired man, a member of the hospital staff, who passed in and out of the main entrance thrice a day. I found out that he took his meals outside, and that he was never challenged by the guards. The thought occurred to me that I might surreptitiously take his place. Upon reflection, however, I observed that he was short and stumpy, about forty and black-haired, while I was a tall, rakish, clipper-built blonde of eighteen; that I wore gray, while he wore blue; that he was out while I was in. Nevertheless I made up my mind to take one more chance, for life or death. This hospital steward's insignia consisted of a strip of green about two inches wide, bordered with faded yellow braid. In the centre of the strip was a faded figure of Mercury with a serpent coiled around the staff of the wand, with spreading wings on top. This figure was also in yellow or gold. I never got close enough to inspect the design carefully, but I had a pretty correct idea of its general characteristics. He wore one on either arm.

I had written an appealing, and probably exaggerated letter to my aunt, Mrs. Margaret E. Sangster, in New York, I described prison life so graphically that she sent me a generous supply of good gold coin with which to relieve the hardships I depicted. Sometimes I think that if novelists could spend a few years in jail, they could turn out literature that would have an irresistible appeal to their readers' hearts.

With a portion of the money sent by my aunt, I proceeded to mould myself into a hospital steward. My first purchase was a blue blouse from a Yankee prisoner who was in for jumping the bounty for the seventeenth time, as he informed me. To this day my aunt has never forgiven me for using her loyal gold to bribe a northern soldier, even though he was a bounty jumper. But I consoled myself with the reflection that I needed the liberty and that, if one of my name were ever to accomplish anything in a military way and make it famous, she must contribute her share to it, since she was a Munson.

The next step in the scheme was to trade my gray trousers for a pair of dark-coloured ones which, at a pinch, and in the evening, might be taken for good northern blue. Then came the rub; where was I to get the green strips so necessary for the strips on the arms? How could I find the yellow to make the figure of Mercury? I was in distress.

After cogitating over the matter I recollected that some of the southern uniforms contained a piece of green cloth sewed inside of the gray, or rather I thought I recollected it. How was I to get at these treasures? Only by ripping the coats or pockets open. Whereupon for the next week when my comrades were asleep, I got up, ripped their coats open, and prospected for two strips of green cloth, holding the garments up to the moonlight. Failing in my quest, I sewed up the rents, and passed on to the next coat. I was obliged to work slowly and noiselessly, and as I failed again I abandoned the attempt.

A fortnight passed uneventfully and my determination began to reassert itself. My one object in life now was to find something green, but oddly enough it was the one colour which seemed to have disappeared from the face of the world. Even the trees, rattling their bare branches in the winter winds, had lost their leaves, and the emerald hope was realised only in my dreams.

One afternoon I wandered into the sutler's shop, and while dealing with him my eyes fell upon a green pasteboard box on one of the upper shelves. Luck of all luck; it was the exact shade I had been seeking for the past month. I began to tremble with excitement. Did the sutler notice my emotion? No. I began to talk about needing a box to keep my valuables in. "That one up there on the shelf will do," I ventured, pointing to the green treasure.

"You can have it, young fellow," said the sutler, reaching up and pulling the box down from its position with the tip of his finger, "but you need not be afraid of burglars around here." He laughed at his joke and tossed the box into my hands. I hurried away to my quarters. Ye gods! but I was happy.

That night I got up cautiously and, with nothing to see by but the light that flickered through the grated window, proceeded to cut strips of the proper dimensions from the green box. I had scarcely cut into the paper before I discovered that the body of the box was yellow straw board of a dull old-gold colour that would easily pass muster for the one of Mercury and the coiled serpent. I almost broke into cheers. I found that, by trimming the edge of each strip of its superficial green layer, a nice yellow border was to be had.

When I had fastened the two strips of the proper length so that they would encircle my arms at the biceps, I went carefully to work on a crude outline of the figure of Mercury and the serpent. Michael Angelo never worked so hard over drawings as I did over these. Perhaps he had never experienced such inspiration as that under which I laboured. After what seemed an interminable time I completed the outline drawing and peeled the green layers off the cardboard, exposing the precious yellow golden tint underneath. Then I drew on my blue blouse, pinned the green badges of office on either arm and stood fearful and furtive in the silence, the prison hospital steward. Then the gray light of morning crept in upon me. Thinking of my two clumsy efforts at deception I felt a great fear rising in my heart that perhaps failure was to be the end, and that the golden goddess on the dome of the Capitol might beckon to me in vain.

Loud snores broke from one of the sleepers, stirring me from my reverie. I whisked the blouse off, tucked it under my bunk in the farthest corner and crept into bed. I could not sleep, for there passed in review before me scenes of the fight at Dranesville, Chapman and Richards leading their divisions, John Puryear dashing madly among the Yankees. Captain Montjoy singing his happy songs to the morning, and Colonel Mosby standing with his hands at his back, gazing across the Potomac towards Washington, I wanted to be with the Command. As the memories of the past two years rushed upon me, I felt my chin quiver and found myself swallowing a big lump in my cheerless rebel throat.

In the morning I took Dennis Darden into my confidence. He belonged to my company and I knew he could be trusted. The prevalence of spies in all the prisons made me cautious, which accounts for my reticence during the preparatory work. Before the war Darden had been in the secret service department of the government, and I knew he could instruct me what to do if I succeeded in making my escape. He did not take kindly to the plan and advised me against making the attempt. He urged that every step in my path was fraught with danger, and that if detected I was a dead boy. He reminded me that the reserve force had orders to kill the next man trying to escape, and that the Potomac was impassable in winter. He wound up, however, by giving me the names and addresses of several people in Washington to whom I could go for help if I ran the gauntlet and got away alive.

The prison rules permitted only two men to leave any one room and enter the yard at the same time, except for meals, and Darden therefore agreed to accompany me to the enclosure after dark. I did not dare to put on my blouse in the room occupied by my comrades; not that I mistrusted them, but I feared indiscretion of some kind. For that reason Dennis was the only man who shared my hopes and fears.

There was a little interval of time between the last of twilight and the lighting of the prison candles in our rooms, and these were the saddest moments out of the twenty-four hours that made up the day. It was then that we used to think of home, and many a wan face turned to some friendly shadows, while silent tears trickled down the cold cheeks of stern soldiers. I have seen plenty of brave met cry, and to this day I do not like the late twilight when I am alone.

It was at this hour that I changed my gray coat for the blue blouse. Picking up Tom Love's overcoat to hide the precious green insignia, I beckoned to Dennis Darden to follow me, and passed through the building to the yard, with Dennis at my side, our nervous hands grasped tightly in what was to be a farewell grip.

The sentries, believing that we were simply *en route* for our evening's exercise, passed along without comment. We trod the cold floor both ready to "burst out crying." I wish he were alive today so I could once again press the faithful old hand that clung to mine as a father's clings to his son's.

When we got into the shadow of the yard I took off Tom Love's overcoat and gave it to Dennis to carry up stairs. He felt at his throat as if his collar was choking him and, turning, walked back without looking at me again.

I watched him cross the yard and disappear in the shadows at the other end of the enclosure.

Suddenly a great and overpowering dread of the first sentry came over me and I stood as if petrified for at least a minute. Then the old longing for liberty came back and, I marched, numb with uncertainty, up to the main doors leading into the long hall through which I must pass to freedom. The sentry made no protest and, with that for a first success, I threw out my chest and held my arms so that the insignia of the hospital steward were prominently displayed. I passed all the inner guards unchallenged, and stepped by the night relief force just being formed in the hall, finally reaching the outer door of the prison, which was opened for me and held by the man on post.

A blast of cold, fresh, free air smote me in the face. A man on horseback with his cloak wrapped around him, cantered by on the hard pavement; lights glittering from the houses in the distance reached out and splashed on my green badges. The sentry bowed familiarly to me, and in three more steps I passed through the gates that had held me prisoner and heard them jangle and rattle as they closed behind me. The sharp click of the bolt in the big lock sounded like a pistol shot as it slipped into place. Involuntarily I contracted all my muscles, literally shrank myself up like a boy about to receive the paternal shingle, and crossed the street with a wildly beating heart, but free! free! free!

Dennis Darden hurried back to my former quarters, took our friend Captain Babcock by the arm and, leading him to the grated window, pointed to the figure sauntering across the street in the direction of the Goddess of Liberty looming on the Capitol dome. Then he whispered:

"There goes John Munson home."

CHAPTER 15

I Escape

Now that I was actually out of prison and free to proceed whither I willed, the difficulties of the situation began to present themselves. Where could I go that a Southerner was sure of protection and assistance? I had the names Dennis Darden gave me; names of people supposed to be sympathizers; but the novelty of the situation was too much for me and I began to feel like the guilty who flee when no man pursueth. Although I had been a resident of Washington for three months, I had kept strictly indoors and was not in the least familiar with the streets and the people. All of a sudden I bethought myself of the green insignia on my arms. I wrenched them from my blouse and tore them into bits, tossing the fragments into the Capitol grounds. They fell in a green shower and lay scintillating in the reflections from the gas lamps that lined the thoroughfare. I fled from them precipitately, ever fearful that the fat, dark, hospital steward would come sauntering along and see me playing his part.

Among the names supplied by Darden was that of a woman who kept a fashionable boarding house. I decided to call on her first and after considerable difficulty I found her residence. A young darky answered the bell.

"Yes sah, de Missus is in, but I don't reckon you can see her jess at dis hour. You name sah, if you please?"

At that moment the lady happened to come down stairs and to the door where I was standing. In a low voice I told her Dennis Darden had sent me to her, but before I could proceed, she said with considerable excitement, though well controlled:

"Never heard of him! Who is he? You must have made a mistake, young man."

I was heartbroken.

"George," she said presently, turning to the darky, "go upstairs and close the back window. There is a draught in the hall." The servant disappeared.

"Quick, my boy, what can I do for you? Yes, I know Dennis Darden well."

She drew me into the warm hall with motherly tenderness. "Do you want money? here it is," and she pressed me to take it. The roll of bills she offered me made me think this was another greenback raid. "I don't want your money," I replied," I have enough for my wants; I want you to conceal me somewhere. Can you hide me for a day or two, or just for tonight? If you can only catch on to my situation at present, I am on the run."

I said all of this in a good deal of a hurry, and in just as much of a hurry she said,

"Impossible! I am suspected of being a Southern sympathizer; this house is watched by spies, and Colonel Billy Wood at the Old Capitol will have his detectives here as soon as he finds out you have escaped. I will tell you where to go."

She gave me another address. The servant was returning and I bowed myself out, while she protested in a low voice that she had never heard of Dennis Darden and did not want to.

By midnight I had visited four "Southern Sympathizers" who protested hatred of everything south of the line. I cannot say in justice that I blamed them for giving me the cold shoulder, as Washington was full of detectives and spies engaged in ferreting out residents who were suspected of treasonable tendencies. It was a dangerous thing to display any anti-Union leanings in those days.

An exception to my general turning down was in the case of Dennis's old mother and sister, whom I called on after I left the boarding house landlady, but I only stopped for a moment to tell them about their son and brother, for I knew theirs would be one of the first houses to be searched. They welcomed me and would have had me stay and hide, but I knew that it would endanger them, and I moved on.

I wandered around the back streets in a sort of panic, ducking behind trees and sneaking into shadows every time a pedestrian or horseman came into view. I thought every soldier was after me, as the roll call was sure to disclose my absence.

The last address in my possession was that of a sporting man of the name of Lunsford. He ran a gambling hall down town, and his place was generally filled with army officers playing *faro* and roulette. I hesitated about going there, because of its popularity among the Union officers. Nevertheless, about midnight I decided to take the gambler's chance myself, and entered the place boldly. It literally swarmed with Federal uniforms, but by this time I was too desperate or perhaps too indifferent to care much what happened. I called Lunsford aside when he was pointed out to me, and told him my story, explaining how I had been turned down four times that night.

"Serves you right," he answered; "you should have come to me first. Did not Dennis tell you I could be depended on? Confound you, this idiotic delay may cost you your liberty."

At this greeting all my fears left me, and the world seemed to be mine, especially when he added cheerfully, "Better get some grub into you, and prepare to light out of Washington before daybreak. How is old Dennis? Does he want anything?" With that he hustled me into the back room where I satisfied myself at the guests' table, taking care of a meal that was by far the best and largest I had eaten since my capture.

After I had eaten, Lunsford called in his manager, told him to run the place until it was time to close up, and together we set out for Georgetown. I wanted to walk, so that if necessary I could break into a sprint, but he insisted on riding, and somewhere he got a cab and we drove into Georgetown about two o'clock in the morning. He took me to a little family hotel called "The White House," kept by a Frenchman named Tony Rodier, and instructed him to hide me until I could be safely started in the direction of Loudoun county. Lunsford thereupon bade me a warm goodbye, and after offering to share his roll with me if I was out of funds, drove back to Washington.

That was the last I saw of the brave and generous fellow, but I wrote to him after the war expressing my appreciation.

I remained most of the time in a room in the attic, as my host did not care to have visible a guest whose character was likely to be questioned at any moment. On the fourth day I had about concluded to strike out after dark and make my way back to the Command as best I could. But in the meantime Madame Rodier had arranged with a country market man that I was to leave the town with him, passing as his son; the idea being to get me outside of the picket limits and turn me loose in the open to go it alone. I did not realise then that it was infinitely harder to escape from Washington through the almost countless pickets than to get out of the Old Capitol prison. Madame Rodier told the countryman that it would be a pleasure for her to annihilate him if he failed in his mission. Evidently the farmer was impressed, for he displayed evident signs of fear; so much so, in fact, that the hotel man's wife had to supply him with courage in the form of a bottle of brandy. The effect was instantaneous and we departed for the rural districts in fine feather.

About two miles outside of the city limits the last of the pickets we had to pass held us up and wanted to know where the farmer had "dug up" the boy, meaning me. An argument ensued, but the farmer protested stoutly that I had come in with him, and that I was sleeping among the vegetables when he entered the lines. The guard looked incredulous, and then to try and trip the old fellow, asked if he did not have something to drink. My "father" insisted that he never took a drink in his life and, after a brief parley, we were permitted to proceed. When we came to the first turn in the road where we were hidden from the soldiers, the old fellow drew out his bottle and took a long pull at the contents, saying to me, "Sonny, if you was as badly scared just now as I am you'd be mighty glad to take a swig out of that bottle, young as you is."

For several days and nights after the garden-truck man set me down, several miles outside of Georgetown, I was kept busy dodging pickets and straggling troopers, and keeping out of the way of strangers, to say nothing of the extreme difficulty of getting enough to eat. I gradually made my way north-westward, not far from the Potomac at any time, and at length I began to feel that my prospect for reaching the stamping ground of the Rangers was improving.

Just about sunset on the seventh day I was set down from a stage coach in the little towns of Poolesville, in Montgomery county, Maryland, pretty tired, but hopeful, for I had caught a glimpse of the Blue Ridge Mountains that afternoon and made up my mind to reach their friendly shelter or know why. I was looking rather seedy for my clothes had seen hard usage of late and they were not new when I got them. I found a soldier in Poolesville who was doing cavalry duty in the neighbourhood. He was a Federal trooper and seemed to be a decent sort of fellow. I inquired of him the way to a certain house near the Potomac river, a house occupied by a "friend" to whom I had been directed. He advised me to keep away from the river, saying the Federal pickets might mistake me for a rebel and shoot me. I insisted on going, however, and he offered to let me walk beside his horse while he rode out into the country, promising to start me right when we got to a certain fork in the road.

It was a bitter cold night and the patches of snow lay white and shimmering along the fields on the highway. Before us, covered with frost and ice, was the winding road, sometimes in the open white light of the moon, and at other times heavy with the shadows of trees. My guide was rather a talkative person and under the influence of his chatting I began to warm up to the trip.

Once when we were passing along a frozen stretch of the road I reached out and grabbed a pistol holster from the trooper's saddle, in an effort to support myself. The instant my fingers touched the leather a thought flashed through my mind. Why not capture him? Never had a man such a chance as this. He had everything that I lacked; a good horse, a carbine, two pistols, and a warm coat. I withdrew my hand from the holster and trudged along. The idea began to appeal to me. I recalled the time when my Captain, Billy Smith, of Mosby's Command, while being led off captive by the enemy, pulled his captor down by the wrist, dealt him a blow in the face, dragged him to the ground; how he took his pistols, mounted into the empty saddle, and galloped back to the Command, cheering his own prowess.

It would be a very simple matter to haul that Federal trooper to the earth, and the idea that the colonel would approve of it if I told him of it, was a consideration not to be overlooked. I did not want to execute the manoeuvre in a hasty and bungling manner, so I set about studying the conditions more closely. I recollect how, in my conversation, I made many gestures, all of which were calculated to bring my hands more closely in touch with the rider's boots, his revolver holsters, his stirrup, and such other important things as were likely to come in for a share in the mix-up. Once I put my hand over on the stirrup casually, just to see how far his foot went into the slot. At that particular moment the trooper had slipped his boot almost out of the stirrup and I could have then and there carried out my plan with little risk to myself. I glanced up in his face just to see if there could be any possible suspicion in his eyes, intending to raid him when we struck the shadow of the next tree. Just then he spoke.

"If you are tired, comrade, I will walk and let you ride a spell. I guess it must be pretty hard jogging along these frozen roads."

When we separated a little farther up the road and I shook his hand, I hoped that the genuine warmth with which I grasped it might compensate for my thoughts such a short time before. I stood there alone, watching him melt into the landscape, and the sane thought presented itself to me that the river was frozen over, making a horse unnecessary, and a prisoner would have been an awful handicap to me. There is no fool like a fool looking for a fight.

I found my way to the house I was in search of and spent that night and the next day under a dry and hospitable roof, changing my clothes for warmer garments. When I finally went down to the river's bank, under cover of darkness, I heard voices and hid behind a pile of rocks. A trio of Federal soldiers passed so near me that I heard their voices. The amusing part of it was that they were holding an animated conversation about Mosby and his captivating tactics. I gathered from what I overheard that the Command had been raising no end of trouble during my absence.

After the Yankees passed I made for the river rapidly, and found it completely frozen over, as had been reported. A bad storm was blowing up, however, and I could hear the ice crackling and humming ominously. The snow began to lose its crispness and I knew that a thaw was about to set in. This gave me another reason, an excellent one, for getting across to the soil of Virginia, and I made tracks over the frozen bosom of the old Potomac, like a timber wolf loping back home. All the way I could hear the ice sheet humming and warping under my feet. A blinding wind from the southeast was eating into the ice hummocks, and I felt the moisture coming through my boots. The thaw was on without a doubt.

At every few steps my feet slipped on the rough lumps and I fell sprawling on my face, only to lie quiet for a moment, and gaze up and down the river and try to find out if I was discovered by the pickets stationed along its banks. I could see their fires for miles both ways, and my overwrought nerves made the noise of each stumble and fall appear to me like explosions of a mine. I could almost imagine the guards could hear me grunt and groan. The ice broke up and the river opened two hours after I crossed.

I landed a few miles below Leesburg and tramped into that town about ten o'clock at night. On the way I heard the sound of horses, and dropped down behind a clump of bushes to hide. They proved to be a raiding party of Yankees returning from our country to their camp in Fairfax. I spent the night at a friend's house in Leesburg and another raiding party came into town during the night and searched the house. I began to think getting out of prison was easy compared with dodging raiders. The next day I walked out to West Aldrich's home, a few miles from town, and he gave me a lift as far as Upperville, the town near which I had been captured nearly three months before, and where a meeting of the Command was being held when I reached there.

I walked in on my old comrades like a spectre, for some of them had heard that I had died in prison of smallpox. I had much to tell them of the boys I had left behind and much to listen to about the adventures and experiences of those that were safe. The burden of my advice was, "Don't get caught, for it is hard to get back."

Colonel Mosby had not yet returned to the Command from his severe wound received late in December at Lake's house and, as the men were not particularly busy "annoying the enemy," I was given an indefinite leave of absence and went home to Richmond.

My first questions were, when I reached Upperville, about my horses, especially of the mare who got me captured by refusing to take the stiff stone wall. Until then I did not know what had become of her. I learned that my old comrade, Emory Pitts, had taken care of all my animals in my absence and, when I went into the stable where they were munching their oats, two of them, old "Champ" and the mare "Annie," stopped eating and whinnied their recognition and welcome. Maybe it was silly and boyish, but I could not help it; I hugged both of them and cried just a little bit.

When at home in Richmond, I walked in on my mother, who had also heard that sickness had carried me away in a northern prison, there was a convulsive reunion. When my father came in that evening and asked the threadbare question, "Heard anything more about John?" the fact that I was hiding behind the door did not deceive him as to the meaning of the expression on my mother's face.

Well, somehow or other I got out from behind the door and fell into my father s arms like a helpless child, and for a while there was a triple crying and hugging and laughing. Truly it was worth a short term in prison to be part of such a family reunion.

It may be interesting to know what happened in the Old Capitol prison after my departure. Within half an hour following my exit, the superintendent and his guard made their nightly rounds and called the roll. It was then discovered I was missing. Search was made in every conceivable spot, even up the chimney and in the sewer. Careful investigations were resorted to and after several days it was discovered that the bounty jumper had sold me his blue blouse. As a punishment he was sent to the Dry Tortugas. All the rest of the prisoners were handcuffed in pairs and sent up to Fort Warren in Boston Harbour, where they were kept till the summer of 1865.

I should have mentioned before that Mosby's men were not exchanged during the latter part of the war, and the only way to get home was to go home. I believe now, after forty years have passed, that the life of the old Partisan Command was what lured me back and made me take the chances one must take for liberty. I was fully repaid when, amid the stirring scenes of my soldier life, I heard again the old familiar order:

"Mount your horse, Munson, and come along with me."

CHAPTER 16

Trying for Big Game

About the middle of August, 1864, I don't recall just the date, but I believe it was the 15th, Major "Dolly" Richards's squad killed Lieutenant Walker of the First United States Cavalry. I have referred to it previously. In one of Walker's pockets the boys found a miniature likeness of his bride, with her name and the date of her marriage inscribed on it. Watkins of our Command gave it to a lady nearby, and asked her to see that it was sent through the lines, in safety, to that waiting bride. I hope she got it. I don't like to think of the incident.

Walker's horse was a splendid animal, and when his master was killed the poor, frightened creature dashed away toward the camps. Willie Martin chased him, but finding he could not overtake him, yelled to a Yankee soldier standing in the way to catch and hold him, which he did and, when Martin rode up, he told the man to get on the horse and "come along." It looked like a rather ungrateful way of paying him for doing a favour. The boys presented the horse to Major Richards. One of the men went through Walker's pockets and got five hundred dollars in greenbacks.

Lieutenant Alfred Glasscock took fifteen men to the Valley about this time to annoy Sheridan. He was raiding near Kernstown with his little squad of fifteen men when he saw a company of cavalry approaching. His men wore rubber *ponchos* to keep off the rain. He could not distinguish the number of the enemy approaching, owing to a bend in the road, but told his men it was no time to run for, if there were too many of them, he would pass on by and trust to luck not to be discovered, but if there were not too many he would attack them and demand their surrender. He said:

"Now, boys, I am going to show you how to capture Yankees in the regular Mosby style."

As the commands approached each other, the Yankee said to Glasscock: "Hello, boys, I thought you were rebs." Glasscock smilingly told him not to be worried on that account, and as he rode on past the company his fifteen men scattered along the line from front to rear and, at a signal from Glasscock, every man presented a cocked pistol. The entire crowd surrendered, and not a shot was fired. We captured thirty men and their horses, and no record of their disappearance was left behind. It may have reached Sheridan's ears and "annoyed" him, or he may have heard that his men deserted in a body, or that the ghosts had spirited them away; but, whatever report of the disappearance of one of his cavalry companies was made to him, if any was, could not have added much to his cheerfulness.

Mosby had such confidence in the ability of his officers that he permitted them frequently to lay out their own work, or rather the details of it He would send an officer to the Valley, for instance, and tell him to find something to do around Winchester, while another one would be told to go with a few men to the neighbourhood of Charlestown or some other point. Hardly a day passed from the first of August, 1864, till midwinter, that some of our men were not troubling Sheridan. Some time toward the middle or last of August, Major Richards tried to capture Sheridan, and but for a simple accident, it might have been accomplished. The game was at least worth the candle.

He took a dozen of Company B and crept stealthily toward the sleeping army, encountering a picket who was captured silently. He then marched into the camp of the Nineteenth New York, but the soldiers were scattered so thickly on the ground that he could not ride through them. He had to retrace his steps and get in some other way. In passing a sentinel, Willie Martin, in a spirit of fun, spoke to him in a commanding voice, and told him to hold his gun properly, saying: "That is no way for a soldier to stand on duty." The man at once assumed a soldierly position and our boys had a quiet laugh at his expense.

Wherever Richards turned the sleeping soldiers were so thick he could make no progress among them, nor could he get the information he wanted about the location of headquarters, even though he woke some of the men to ask them. He turned to the pike once more, hoping to get from some of the men moving, the location of General Sheridan. He captured a man and took him along, hoping to extract something valuable from him, but not letting the fellow know he

Mosby and a group of Baltimore Guerillas in 1865

was a prisoner. He found him quite communicative and learned that he had just passed unchallenged through the sleeping army. Major "Dolly" proposed to do the same thing and to stop at the first officer's quarters and wake an officer up.

He and his little squad were in the heart of Sheridan's entire army, and were comparatively just as safe as if they had been in their beds at home. They were really safer. When he thought success was about to crown his bold effort, the man who was with him realised that he was in a hornet's nest of guerrillas and, dashing away from them in his fright, began yelling at the top of his voice, as he rushed into an infantry camp:

"Wake up! the rebels are on you! Wake up!"

Richards knew at once the game was spoiled, and galloped away for safety outside the lines of the camp, bringing out all but one of his men, and he turned up safely the next day. Outside of the camp he captured a few stragglers near Castleman's, to compensate him in a slight degree for his failure to get the general, who was destined to become in story, the hero of the twenty-mile ride; but, to counteract this petty success, he lost one of the brightest, and gamest, and the best boys that ever followed his Command into the fray.

On the way home Lieutenant Willie Martin was accidentally shot and killed by one of our own men who was riding at his side. He was buried in Upperville on the 21st of the month. Death had snatched away another one of our shining marks, and left a vacant place that seemed never to be filled. There were men and boys among us who had become so prominent by their individual bravery that when they left us we did not know who to stand up in their gaps, and so we left the gaps open. Willie Martin was one of them.

In the fight at Mount Zion Church a little more than a month previously, this boy had charged up among the Second Massachusetts men, and got so closely wedged among them that they clubbed him into insensibility with their carbines, as he was too close to them to be shot with safety to themselves. Company E was organised on July 28, 1864, and Willie Martin was named by Mosby as its second lieutenant, an appointment, like all the rest he made, for gallantry. Three weeks later with his two little modest strips on his collar, the insignia of the promotion he was so proud of and which he so justly deserved, they laid him to rest forever.

In May, 1864, Richards, with fifteen men, crossed the Shenandoah River at Berry's Ferry to find out what was "doing." We struck the

Valley pike near Newtown early in the morning and picked up quite a number of stragglers during the day. Late in the evening he sent the prisoners back, and taking ten men, went into Newtown to get information.

At first the people would not believe we were Confederates, but we at last convinced them, and found there were no Federal troops at 2 o'clock p. m. on that day. Richards determined to raid Winchester. It commenced to rain about night and the darkness was very dense. We were riding in single file on the side of the pike.

On the old Kernstown battlefield we heard the enemy coming up the pike. Richards immediately halted his men and gave orders for no one to say anything, as he would do the talking, saying that, if it was a small detachment, he would try and capture them, and if it was a large body we would pass on.

We again started down the road, and after going a short distance we were halted by the challenge: "Who comes there?" Richards answered, "First New York," as he knew that it was with Sigel, for we had captured some men from it that day. They answered:

"All right, we are the Twenty-First boys, come on advance guard of the regiment guarding wagon trains."

The officer in command of the detachment asked where we were going, and Richards replied:

"Couriers on the way to Martinsburg to telegraph that Sigel had whipped the rebels and gone on up the Valley."

The Twenty-First gave three cheers, and Richards told them to hold fast as his business was urgent, and we had to go on. As he reached the rear of the detachment he stopped, and the men turned on the Yankees and demanded their surrender. They were in the act of surrendering when some one fired a shot. I think that one of our boy's nerves gave way and he fired. The fight then became a *mêlée*, both sides hallooing and cursing. The regiment that was guarding the train charged on us and we left. Charley Dear was shot through the side.

Speaking of Charley Dear, the following contribution from him will prove interesting, I am certain. I offer it entire, and take this opportunity to thank him for it.

On January 30, 1865, Major Richards started from Bloomfield, with thirty men, to raid the Baltimore & Ohio Railroad. We reached the railroad running from Harper's Ferry to Winchester about midnight, and found that road so heavily guarded by infantry, and patrolled by cavalry every half hour, that we could not accomplish anything.

Richards determined not to be outdone, and sent part of his men off with John Russell, and kept about fifteen men with him. He endeavoured again to cross the railroad but failed, and then called Jim Wiltshire and me to him, and told us to go and bring him a prisoner, and be certain to bring one before we returned.

The weather was cold and the snow was on the ground; the moon was shining bright. Wiltshire and I moved quietly up the railroad and soon met two men who asked us where we were going. We answered, "The Twelfth Pennsylvania, sent out to see what had become of you fellows, as you had stayed beyond your time," We were then right up to them, and covered them with our pistols, and told them to keep quiet and go with us, which they did. We took them to Major Richards, who after a talk with them of a few minutes, called Wiltshire and me to him, and told us to take the prisoners aside, separate them and demand the countersign, which we did, with a six-shooter at their heads. They gave it to us but, when we compared notes, the word did not come up right; we tried it again, with the pistols cocked this time, and pressed against their heads, but with no idea of shooting them. It was very persuasive this time, and when we again compared notes they had agreed, as they had given us the same word: the countersign was "Dry."

Charley Wiltshire, Will Shepard, Jim Wiltshire and I were sent down the railroad to see if the word would work, which it did, and the boys brought in four more prisoners.

After this it was clear sailing. After talking with the prisoners Richards determined to pay our respects to the guard-house of the Twelfth Pennsylvania Cavalry. The reason we went to the guard-house was we heard there was a prisoner there, Charley Aisquith, who was from the Second Virginia Infantry.

Richards sent back the prisoners and kept with him nine men. As we approached the camp all was quiet; they little dreaming that the Mosby men were there. The interior guard halted us and Charley Wiltshire gave them, "Patrol," and riding up to him, asked him if he wanted the countersign. He said "No."

Wiltshire shoved a pistol in his face and told him to keep quiet and, putting him behind one of the men, we rode quietly through the camp to the guard house, making the prisoner show us where the guard house was, with a man riding beside him with a pistol at his head telling him to remain quiet. The camp was laid out in streets, with stables on one side, where we could see the fine horses; the front of it was open, sentinels walking their beat in front; cabins on the other side covered with canvas; all asleep.

We rode straight to the guard house and, as we arrived there, a soldier had just come out to replenish the fire in front of the guard tent. Charley Wiltshire jumped off his horse and captured him and Jim Wiltshire also dismounted to see if the Charlestown boy was in there. Jim Wiltshire walked to the door of the tent, pulled up the flap and he and I looked in to see if Aisquith was inside. He was not. If he had been Jim Wiltshire was going in after him. The soldiers were lying side by side, asleep, little thinking that two of Mosby's men were looking in upon them.

Joe Bryan and Joe Gibson were also dismounted, holding their horses, and the rest of the boys commenced cutting loose the horses around the guard tent, ready to take a hand in the fray. Bartlett Bolling, seeing a sentinel standing near looking on, rode up to him and demanded his surrender. The soldier replied with a shot, and that broke up the fun.

We did not go out as quietly as we went in; the boys made it lively for them, giving the Mosby yell as we rode out, firing down through the tops of cabins, as they were covered with canvas. We were going out at a dead run and Hearn was riding a very fine race mare, and his bit broke. She went through the camp fairly flying, and he called to Major Richards, "For God's sake catch my mare, or I'll go to hell."

Richards replied,

"I have been expecting you to travel that road for some time."

We got out safely with eight horses and, as we came through Charlestown, the enemy opened a fusillade on us from both sides of the street, from the old court house and the jail. It did no harm.

We raised pandemonium in the camp, as bugles were blowing and men shooting in every direction. I think Reno did not sleep so quietly after that.

CHAPTER 17

The Sutler

Mosby's men had a decided weakness for Yankee sutlers, and though few of these capitalists were captured during the latter part of the war, the traditions of the Command about them were so fascinating, when related by the older members, that it kept all the men constantly on the lookout for them.

I remember an occasion once, in October, 1864, when we saw a covered wagon going down the pike in the Valley, guarded by a few men only. When the men caught sight of it there was a cry of joy from a hundred throats.

"A sutler at last!"

And away a lot of us dashed for it, though a big force of the enemy was in sight. We overtook it and only succeeded in getting the driver to stop his team when we began firing into him. He was so near his men he thought he could reach them. When we finally hauled him up we found, instead of a sutler, that the wagon contained only a General (Duffie) and two other officers. Some of the men who did not go to church regularly gave way to a species of profanity. It was an awful disappointment. We did not need any generals, but we wanted good things, such as the sutler's wagon always carried, and we wanted them badly.

While the boys were chasing the wagon they were telling each other what they intended choosing when they got into the goods. One boy said to another, "If you get hold of a pair of number seven high boots, save 'em for me, and I'll give you some of the flannel shirts I get, and don't forget to save me some figs and candy, and some cigars." When that boy saw General Duffie he almost cried.

In the early months of the Command's history the capture of sutlers was as common as the capture of soldiers. They seemed to swarm in Fairfax County, and they travelled around without guards for, up to the time Mosby went into the country, there had been no necessity for protection. They were safe to go where they chose. On nearly all the early raids a sutler would be numbered among the spoils, and the average army sutler was not to be despised. He was a travelling retail general store, with a saloon attachment, sometimes, and sometimes a bakery and confectionery to boot There was never any effort to divide his goods equally among the captors: each man pitched in and took what pleased his fancy, and whatever he took was his own. The men frequently exchanged with each other after the raid, things that each did not want, for others they did want.

I recollect we raided some sutlers one night, and the supply of stuff they had was simply bewildering. It was in the early autumn of 1863, September 16th, and they were located near Warrenton. I do not know how many of them were interested in the outfit, but there was a small building filled with goods, and there were several wagon loads outside. These wagons were standing in front of the house, and the horses were haltered to the wagon tongues. I dismounted and climbed into the back of one wagon, and found it loaded two-thirds of the way up to the roof of the cover. A large buffalo robe was spread over the goods and two men were lying asleep on it. They had been playing cards by candle light, for the unlit candle in their candle-stick and a deck of cards, were lying between the men on the robe.

I woke one of them out of a sound sleep and told him Mosby's men were all around him, and I wanted his pocket-book before I went any further. He cursed me and told me to "clear out" as he was tired of being held up by a lot of camp bums calling themselves Mosby's men. I tried to convince him I was in earnest, but I gathered from his growing warmth that his own men had been trying in the past to rob him, and he proposed to put a stop to it. Fearing he might get up suddenly and knock me out of the wagon (he was lying down all this time), I slipped my pistol out carefully and slid its cold barrel along his upper lip and held it there. The change was instantaneous. He wilted and began handing out his valuables, and when he had given me everything detachable which he had, I turned him out and told him to sprint for his life.

As I did not care to open and look into his big boxes and packages, I secured the robe and fastened it to my saddle and went into the house where our men were plundering. I had never seen quite as interesting a collection of sutler's goods before. These fellows actually had everything we could possibly have wanted, and I never saw such a busy lot of men as ours. It was a regular bargain counter crowd, scrambling and surging and crowding to get the best of everything. The men would eat and drink a little of everything that came within their grasp. Think of a mixture in a human stomach of sardines and raisins, cakes and claret wine, cheese, figs, beer, chocolates, pickled onions, champagne, oysters, more cheese, jelly, and Hostetter's Bitters—but where would I ever stop if I tried to mention everything? Well, this is just about the collection most of the men consumed and the order of its consumption. When every man had filled a big sack with useful things, and his stomach with what he was pleased to think "nice things," we set fire to the building and wagons and started away.

One man, Sewell Williams, in the midst of all the bewildering variety, was so dazzled that he only filled his sack with cigars and playing cards, and the strange part of it was that he neither smoked nor played cards. As soon as we started off every man went to Williams and got one or more cigars and began to smoke up, whether he had ever smoked before or not. The result was that smoking, and the outraging of the guerrilla stomachs caused by the fluids and solids recently introduced into them, brought on an illness which extended down the entire line, and Mosby's Command never appeared so abjectly miserable and helpless in all its career. One good healthy Yankee could have taken them all that night, and if he had promised to cure them of violent sick stomach they would all have been glad to go.

Among the personal property of the sutler who yielded up his all at my armed request, was a big pocket-book containing his accounts and papers. When it first fell into my hands I fancied I had the fellow's roll and I hastened to investigate it only to find papers. Among them were a lot of requisitions from army officers for supplies and delicacies which he had filled in Baltimore, and was delivering when we found him. The sutlers had printed blanks which the officers would fill out and sign, and these became vouchers later for their pay when the goods were purchased and brought to camp. My sutler seemed to have a very select trade among the officers, for his orders called for champagne, brandy, whiskey, high-grade canned and bottled goods, in fact all sorts of delicacies and necessities, and he had filled and checked up all his orders, and we got his goods.

A short time after this raid I was in Richmond for a day or two, and at my father's office, which was a sort of rendezvous for officers on leave, especially for Louisianans and Marylanders, who could not get to their homes. The morning of my arrival there I found the office pretty well filled with these officers, and among them General Pickett and old Colonel Fred, Skinner. I took out my sutler's requisitions and read them to the officers, who listened with bated breath to the fairy story I was reciting. I wound up by saying:

"Now, gentlemen, you've heard me tell you of all these good things, and I'll add that we captured everyone of them and consumed them, and it is quite a common occurrence for us to do the same thing."

If you will only think that at that time a grand dinner in Richmond consisted of bacon and corn bread, you can appreciate the heartlessness of my conduct. Old Colonel Skinner swore he would resign at once and join our Command. For the rest of my stay in my father's office I believe I was disliked by every hungry officer in the room.

Very near the close of the war, I believe it was only a few days before Lee surrendered, John Russell and I were on a scout in the Valley, when we saw a man walking with two ladies near the camps of the Union army. We galloped over to him and found he was a sutler who was taking a little stroll outside of his lines with two of his best girls. When we pounced on him the girls broke away from him with little screams, and we each took hold of one of his wrists and, keeping him between us, galloped back to where we started from, our sutler running along to keep his arms from being pulled out of their sockets.

As we ran I reached down on my side of him and took his watch and chain out of his pocket, very carefully, while John Russell reached down on his side and got his pocket-book. Then I slipped his ring gently off his finger while John as gently slipped his scarf-pin out of his tie. By the time we had finished running him we had finished searching him. We were only searching him. Then we discovered that his coat and trousers and boots, being all of fashionable style and good quality, would be very acceptable to a couple of young country fellows we knew, so we relieved him of these also. We left him his undershirt, drawers, socks and a red cravat.

Then we turned him loose and told him to go back to camp, suggesting that he hurry up. He started off on a run, and we could see him until he got inside his lines for, in his efforts to avoid the two girls, he skirted around among the hills and valleys for a mile or so; we could see those little white legs trotting along faster than they had ever carried him before. If either of those girls saw him stripped as we left him, he never got one of them for his wife.

General Augur thought to catch Mosby at one time by sending

one of his detectives, named Pardon Worsely, to our country in the guise of a sutler. He came with a wagon load of fine stuff and had his wife with him. He said she was his wife, and we did not ask to see his marriage certificate. As soon as he got into our country he was promptly captured, but he begged the men to take him before Mosby and let him tell his story, which he did. He said he had slipped through the lines with his load, believing we would be glad to protect him and buy his goods from him, if he would promise to fill our orders for anything we wanted at fair prices. It sounded very nice, but Mosby looked him over very carefully and sized him up correctly. He told Worsely he had caught too many sutlers to be caught by one, but that he would protect him if he would fill our orders and make no effort to do any funny business.

Worsely saw a fine opening for making a lot of money by fooling General Augur, and for some time we enjoyed an open express line to the North. I suppose Augur caught on in time and put our transportation line out of business.

Among the things I ordered Worsely to bring me was a big doll baby for a little girl relative at home. Worsely made me pay him twenty dollars in gold for it. I suppose he got it for five, but it was as big as a real young baby, and when it arrived in Richmond people from all parts of the city came to see it, for there had not been a new doll baby in Richmond since the war began.

I also got him to buy me cloth for a fine suit of clothes and, in fact, a general outfit of finery for which he made me pay regular blackmail prices, but I made him pay me a good stiff price for a big box of chewing tobacco and in that way I got even with him. Colonel Mosby got old Worsely to bring him a sack of coffee from the North, and I believe he had some of that coffee on hand when the war ended.

On July 13, 1863, Mosby, with twenty-seven men with him in Fairfax County, captured twenty-nine loaded sutler's wagons, about one hundred prisoners and nearly one hundred and fifty horses. He brought his captures out safely as far as Aldie on the turnpike, when he was overtaken by Colonel Lowell with two hundred men of the Second Massachusetts Cavalry, and nearly all the prisoners, with all the wagons and horses, were recaptured. If the boys could only have got home safely with those twenty-nine loaded wagons we could have opened a big department store in Mosby's confederacy.

On October 11, 1863, about forty of us, under Mosby, were on a raid and scouting trip in Fairfax County, on the pike a few miles from

Alexandria. We had lain hidden in the thick pines all the day before, because the Yankees were all around us, and constantly on the move along the roads. Mosby took Walter Whaley with him and hid in the bushes where he could see the pike, and Captain Smith made me go with him a little farther up the road, where we got another hiding place on the pike.

A body of two hundred and fifty cavalry came along, which for obvious reasons we did not attack. They were the escort of a long train of wagons, and we preferred wagons to large bodies of cavalry, so we waited for the wagons. Mosby and Whaley rode out from their hiding place and cut out a few of the last wagons of the train and had them driven into the woods, while Captain Smith and I picked up a straggling wagon in the extreme end of the train and gathered it into the common fund. It proved to be a gold mine, and the Waldorf-Astoria never spread before its guests a more enjoyable feast than we consumed that morning. All sorts of eatables and drinkables, all sorts of wearing apparel and useful and ornamental things and, best of all in our opinion, nearly two hundred pairs of cavalry boots. We simply revelled in riches out of that unfortunate sutler's supplies.

A man named Dunham, living in that part of the country, had been down to Alexandria with his wife trying to buy supplies, but was refused the privilege; they were on their way back to their home, in their empty wagon, when they were brought into our camp at the time we were in the midst of enjoying the sutler's goods. We listened to their hard-luck story and amply recompensed them for their fruitless trip by loading up their wagon with something of the entire supply we had appropriated. I thought our men were past-masters in the art of handling sutlers' goods, but Dunham and his wife made us ashamed. It was their first experience, but they did not require any teaching from us. They got a sample of everything.

On several occasions when we captured sutlers and soldiers on the same raid and opened up the sutler's goods for distribution among our men, we always invited the prisoners to pitch in and help themselves. It was amusing to see the fiendish delight with which the boys in blue would go through their natural enemy. They always looked upon their own sutlers as robbers, and they never got a chance to get even with their foe except on occasions of this sort.

Mosby sent a party of us into Maryland in the summer of 1864, under Lieutenant Joe Nelson, and our objective point was Adamstown, on the Baltimore & Ohio Railroad. When we galloped into the little town we were on the lookout for sutlers' stores more than for soldiers and, spying a rather attractive store, the boys dismounted and began appropriating the stock. The owner was frantic in his objections to our robbing him, claiming to be a good Southerner, and rushed around among the men begging and threatening by turns. We paid no attention to him, and when we filled our sacks with plunder of all sorts and were about to mount, Joe Nelson came in and ordered every man to give back whatever he had taken or pay for it, saying we had no right to rob a good Southerner. I had my doubts about the man's loyalty to Jeff. Davis, and also had my mind firmly made up to carry back with me at all hazards my carefully selected assortment of merchandise, which I considered worth several hundred dollars.

I was enough of a soldier however to obey the orders of my superior officer, so I gave the merchant five dollars in Confederate money and, without waiting for the change, or for his receipt, rode south. One of our boys who had taken a lot of the man's hats paid for them by leaving his own. We started back home after doing all the damage we could and recrossed the Potomac near the mouth of the Monocacy River, but not before we had to whip about fifty Federals stationed there to cut us off. They thought they had us in a trap, but Joe Nelson and Harry Hatcher, each with a part of our little Command, charged them from different directions and killed four of them and captured a dozen more. We charged and scattered another crowd at the river and captured six of them. Our only casualty was the wounding of Johnny Alexander, who on that occasion, as on all others, never knew when to stop fighting. We brought him out safely.

When we rejoined Mosby he asked some of the men, not me, where the captured good things were and was told Joe Nelson had prohibited the men from bringing any away because the store keeper was a good rebel sympathizer. Mosby said he gave no such order, and that we ought to have taken everything in the store, for the man was one of the worst Yankees in Maryland. My conscience was at once eased and I rather regretted parting with my five dollar Confederate bill, though just at that time it would have only bought me one good cigar in Richmond.

CHAPTER 18

The Celebrated Greenback Raid

In reading these recollections, I would suggest that the reader should keep in sight the fact that our mission was to "annoy the enemy." How we did it, when we did it, and where we did it, were left to our own ingenuity and application, the whole idea being to make the Federal Army uncomfortable.

One of our modes of annoyance was to tear up part of the railroad track and stop a train. If the officers and the men had anything valuable about their persons, we annoyed them also; but it was the enemy in general, the great and glorious United States Government, that our little body of men were trying to worry and destroy piecemeal. A pretty big undertaking, wasn't it?

I suppose that if General Sheridan had been asked what he considered the greatest piece of annoyance introduced into his campaign in the Valley of Virginia in 1864, by Mosby's men, he would have cited what was known as the "greenback raid," for it annoys any officer to lose all his pay roll at one fell swoop, especially when it summed hundreds of thousands of dollars. Sheridan did not lack opportunity for comparing our different grades of annoyance, for while he was campaigning that summer and autumn in the Valley of Virginia we took good pains to let him know we were around. He had not been in the saddle but a few days when we swept down on one of his big wagon trains and cleaned it off the face of the earth.

In many respects the greenback raid was as sensational as any event for which we were responsible. It brought to our Southern friends an idea of suddenly acquired wealth beyond the dreams of avarice for, at the time it occurred, our Confederate money was getting very low in purchasing ability, and a greenback note seemed to them as big and as green as a wheat field in May. In fact most of them had never seen a

165

greenback and none of them had ever owned one.

To the average Northern man it was a blow at the pocket of his government, and a Northern man does not like a blow at his pocket. He makes his money generally by his brains, and he does not like to see it slip away from him for lack of precaution. To say the least it was an annoyance and that is just the thing we wanted it to be. It came about in this way:

On the twelfth of October, 1864, Colonel Mosby took eighty of our Command over to the Valley to operate in Sheridan's rear. They crossed the Shenandoah River in the night and arrived on the Valley turnpike the next day in time to pick up some stray prisoners, coming and going. As nothing of special interest developed during the day, except their occasional captures, the colonel moved the Command at dusk towards the Baltimore & Ohio Railroad, and halted before midnight immediately on the line of the railroad about eight or ten miles west of Harper's Ferry. A detail of men began ripping up the tracks with the idea of derailing a train from Washington. The colonel had selected a deep cut in the rood as the most likely place to derail a flyer, figuring that the high embankment would protect the train from toppling over and becoming a total wreck. He was always considerate of non-combatants, no matter how actively we might be engaged in annoying the enemy.

After tearing up the rails the horses were taken back from the immediate line of vision of the track and the men partly concealed themselves and waited for a train to round the curve.

It was one of those cold autumnal nights that always seem colder in the South than anywhere else, and the boys needed something to warm their blood. Let me say here, while I am speaking of warming blood, that there was not a more temperate body of men in the army than Mosby's. Although there were a number of distilleries scattered through our country, and home-made whiskey could be had for the asking, I very rarely saw one of our men who drank it, and I never saw a drunken Mosby man in all my army life. Mosby would not tolerate drunkenness, and the fact was that no man among us could afford to muddle his brain with drink, for he needed his wits all the time. Lots of our men carried captured canteens but they did not contain whiskey.

Shortly after midnight the whistle of the engine was heard, and in a few minutes she came snorting along at full speed. The men hugged the ground a little closer and stopped breathing, waiting for

COLONEL MOSBY AND GROUP OF RICHMOND MEN.

Taken in 1865.

1 COL. JOHN S. MOSBY.
2 N. V. RANDOLPH
3 SERGT. A. G. BABCOCK
4 LT. JOHN W. PURYEAR
5 LT. FRANK RAHM
8 O. L. BUTLER.
9 CHAS. QUARLES.
10 —— NOEL.
11 I. A. GENTRY.
14 TOM THROOP.
15 SERGT. R. H. PARROT.
16 LT. W. B. PALMER.
17 LEE HOWISON.

the crunch of the wheels in the sand and gravel, and the fight that might have to follow if the soldiers were aboard.

Nearer she thundered. Every man put out a restraining hand to hold his neighbour down. There was a flash of yellow light in the deep cut, and with a snort that was almost human the engine and entire train proceeded to rush off the track and turn over against the side of the cut on the side of the curve, where it brought up jangling and groaning. The engineer knew that the rails had been purposely removed, and throwing his throttle to dead centre, stopped. A volume of steam escaping from the exhaust filled the air with a white cloud, out of which our men began dropping on the train from the bank above. The conductor stepped from the train, waved his lantern and said:

"All right, gentlemen, the train is yours."

Jim Wiltshire, Charley Dear and West Aldrich climbed into a car, emitting the Mosby yell and howled, "Surrender" to the whole crowd.

A soldier at the far end of the car drew his pistol and before he had a chance to use it Charley Dear dropped him in his tracks. He and West Aldrich rushed up to a group of five officers and demanded their surrender. Two of the group bore the rank of major, and one of them held in his hand a bag to which he clung as if he wanted to fight for it; and his associates advised giving it up and surrendering.

The persistence with which the officers adhered to the bag and tin box, supplied excellent evidence of their worth, and Charley Dear and Aldrich insisted on taking possession of officers and luggage. They took the party to Colonel Mosby who was busy giving orders. Before they reached him with their prize somebody told somebody else that somebody had said the bag and box contained greenbacks, and that the two captured majors were Ruggles and Moore, paymasters of Sheridan's army.

They confirmed the rumour and admitted that they carried the pay for the army.

The booty was immediately passed over to four of our boys, Grogan, Wiltshire, Dear and Aldrich, with instructions to fly across the Shenandoah River and the Blue Ridge mountains into Loudoun county, and to there await the coming of Colonel Mosby and the Command.

In the meantime the rest of the boys were taking charge of things generally. The ten cars of which the train was made up were rapidly emptied; the civilians separated from the soldiers, and a torch was ap-

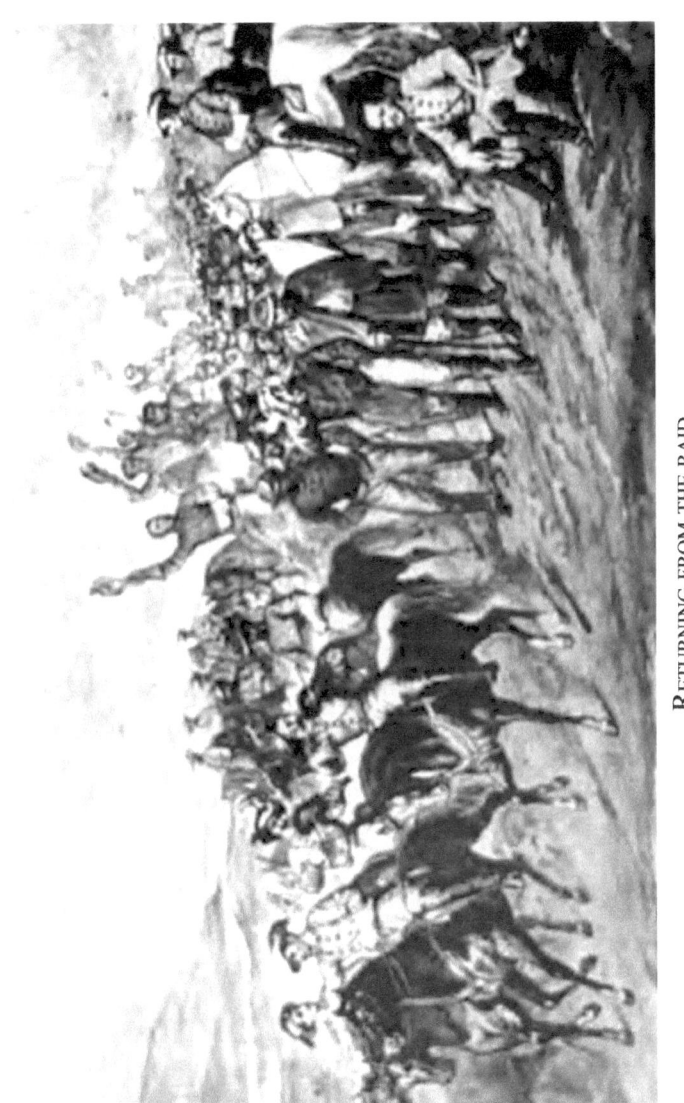

Returning from the Raid

plied to the rolling stock of the Baltimore & Ohio Railroad. A lot of foreigners aboard who could not speak English were only induced to leave the cars when the fire was well started.

In the midst of the excitement Jim Wiltshire was seen escorting a handsome lady away from the burning train. His gallantry was never under eclipse. It was said when she reached the colonel she threw herself, figuratively speaking, into his arms, crying,

"Oh save me, save me. Colonel Mosby, my husband is a Mason."

She then tried, dramatically, to swoon, and the colonel replied, "I can't help that, but you shan't be harmed, notwithstanding," and had her escorted back to the group of civilians, no doubt by the gallant Wiltshire, himself a Mason.

Quite a collection of prisoners was got together for the homeward march; tender goodbyes were spoken, much more tender on the part of the Rangers than the forsaken civilians and, with the sparks flaring into the black sky and the prisoners hanging their dejected heads, the little column vanished as silently as it had come, fading away into the autumnal night, once only, halting and looking back at the group clustered around the burning cars.

The whole thing, while it was almost a bloodless affair, had its element of tragedy and some humour as well. While the colonel sat on his horse, looking at the confusion of the burning train, Monroe Heiskell, a grandson of President Monroe, brought a prisoner to him who had been captured by Charley Dear. The man had on a foreign uniform, or rather part of it, and spoke broken English. He had explained to Heiskell that Mosby's men had taken from him, in addition to everything of value which he possessed, a very highly prized ring, an heirloom, which he hoped could be restored to him. Charley did not take his ring: he only took his overcoat and gave it to Jim Wiltshire.

Mosby inquired where he was from, what uniform he wore, and learned that the man was formerly an officer in the Austrian army and that his acquaintance with American life was necessarily brief, inasmuch as he just arrived. What he wanted most, however, was to recover that family ring.

"What the devil did you want to come over here to fight us for?" asked the colonel.

"I come to learn de tactics," he answered.

"Well, that's part of them," replied Colonel Mosby, gathering up his reins and trotting away. Before his departure, however, he asked

Heiskell to try and recover the officer's ring and restore it to him, which was done, and the student of tactics was admonished to look out for himself in the future. Heiskell also handed his prisoner some money, advising that he would find it of service to him when he got into Libby prison in Richmond, to which he was soon to be headed under guard. Not long afterwards the Austrian halted Heiskell as he passed by with wailing and lamentation, and said,

"De poys haf robbed me again."

This was more tactics.

In the meantime Mosby's financial committee was hurrying into Loudoun county with the treasure-laden box and bag. It was said that one of the four men, Charley Grogan, had a fall in the darkness, and dropped his package, which burst open and let the money out on the ground, and that, when the others returned to help him gather it up and save it, he waved them away with the remark that a few thousand dollars made no difference as there must be millions of it still left.

Close on the heels of the three men followed the rest of the Command. The plunder bearers were overtaken at the appointed spot and a balance sheet was struck, with the result that the treasury was found to contain one hundred and seventy thousand dollars in crisp new greenbacks, issued by the government which it was our duty and our pleasure to annoy.

The money was divided then and there, each of the men who were on the raid receiving twenty-one hundred dollars. Not a cent of this money went to Colonel Mosby. He paid his own way during the whole of his Partisan Ranger career out of his private means, buying his own horses and uniforms and everything he had. It was one of his delicate notions of honour, and his men respected him for it. Officers of other commands who took captured articles lost not only the good opinion but the respect of their men.

Fancy the feelings of other members of the Command who were on other raids at the time, or who remained at home! No raid, no greenbacks: that was the rule. To share the spoils, a man had to share the danger and be at the capture. At the very time of the Greenback raid Captain William H. Chapman had a part of the Command on a raid in Maryland, about eighty in all, burning boats on the Chesapeake & Ohio Canal, capturing horses and mules, cutting telegraph wires and making himself disagreeable generally. On his return towards the Potomac River his men were attacked by the enemy under Captain Grubb, of Cole's Battalion, but Chapman whipped him severely and captured a number of his men and horses without the loss of a man of his own command.

If one will stop to think of the effect these raids had on the powers in Washington, the full purpose of "annoying the enemy" will be understood and appreciated. We plied our industrious calling over a radius of at least one hundred miles, at one and the same time, from one base. It was necessary for the Federal troops to guard every wagon train, railroad bridge and camp with enough active and efficient men to prevent Mosby from using his three hundred raiders in one of his destructive rushes at any hour of the night or day. Thousands of soldiers were kept from service at the front because of Mosby's activity. General Grant at one time reported that seventeen thousand of his men were engaged in keeping Mosby from attacking his weak points, and thus away from active service on the firing line. Finally it was not safe to send despatches by a courier unless a regiment was sent along to guard him.

Mosby frequently divided his men into small detachments, each under a competent officer, and sent them out in different directions with instructions to hit a head whenever they found it exposed; and, through his excellent judgment of men, he had surrounded himself with officers for the different companies in whom he could place implicit confidence in carrying out his orders. The men were supposed to choose their own officers for elections, but it was merely a little agreeable fiction on their part.

Mosby knew what sort of men could do his bidding intelligently and when an election was held the slate was already prepared and the men went through the hollow form of voting. He knew his business better than we knew ours. If it had been left to us to choose our captains and lieutenants, some good looking fellow with big blue eyes would win over a cool, headed, seasoned soldier every time. What did we know or care for military talent? The boy with the dash and the merry song for us.

Washington, always with its ear towards the seat of war, would suddenly hear that a steeping camp near Winchester had been beaten up and a hundred men and horses captured, with the usual number of killed and wounded; that a wagon train near Fairfax Court House had been stopped, the wagons burned and the horses and mules driven off; that a railroad train in Maryland and been thrown from the track and a lot of prisoners taken and property destroyed; that a picket post on the Potomac River had been surprised and the men killed; that a

Lieutenant-Colonel William H. Chapman in 1865.

raiding party had been seen not many miles from Washington. All this cheerful news would come in on the same day. Wasn't it reasonable that official nerves should be somewhat unstrung?

It was Mosby's business to keep this thing up, giving as much variety to the program as possible. His mind was constantly at work devising new phases of the entertainment, besides keeping Lee and Stuart informed of every significant move of the enemy, using his own judgment as to the importance of each incident as it occurred. He could not afford to make any mistakes.

The effect of the greenback raid was electrical. Every telegraph wire between Washington and the front was kept hot with messages. From the most remote points there came back echoes of that midnight haul. Paymasters wired to Washington for instructions how to proceed or where to hide their funds. For instance Paymaster Ladd telegraphed from Martinsburg as follows:

> I have my funds in the parlour of the United States hotel here guarded by a regiment. I shall make no move until I can do so with safety and, in the meantime, await orders from you.

The war department wired to General L. Thomas, who was at Wheeling with six regiments of negro soldiers, on his way to Washington, that the Secretary of War thought it unsafe to come by the way of the Baltimore & Ohio, because of Mosby's liability to attack other points on the line; and suggested that he should take some other route. Every general or commanding officer within reach contributed his version of the story, and Washington was smothered with telegraphic advice. Orders were sent broadcast to "overtake the guerrillas and capture them." Troops started out from a dozen points some in the right direction, in wild pursuit. There was a great hullabaloo everywhere; but in the quiet of a little Loudoun County village, undisturbed by any fear of interruption. Uncle Sam's crisp greenbacks were handed around equally, and liberally, among eighty of his grateful and admiring friends, and the incident was closed.

Chapter 19

Glimpses of Guerrilla Life

While the Federals were at work in the autumn of 1864, rebuilding the Manassas Gap Railroad and incidentally occupying the best part of Mosby's Confederacy, much to our disgust, Lieutenant Ed.. Thomson with about thirty men rode over to the neighbourhood of Salem, now called Marshall, and stopped in a little ravine. Thomson wanted to draw the enemy out from the town so he could get at them on some sort of fair basis as to numbers, and he thought the best way to get them out was to go in town or send in and invite them out by firing into them. He asked for three volunteers to undertake the rather risky job, and Louis Powell, Tom Benton Shipley, of Baltimore, and Bowie of the Northern Neck, stepped to the front before others could answer. They were first class men, always ready for any duty, and game.

Poor Powell ran amuck after the war and paid with his life for his mistake. While in our Command he boarded with a Mr. Payne, and in some unaccountable way, certainly in a moment of temporary insanity or mistaken loyalty to the South, he joined in the assassination of President Lincoln, taking the name of his old host, Mr. Payne, and making the name a disgrace for the many well-born, well-bred people of our country who bore it, until they found his name was Powell. It was he who attacked and stabbed Mr. Seward, the night that Booth killed the president. I have never heard how he became one of that crowd of crazed conspirators, but I have always held that it was the original purpose of Booth and his associates to try and kidnap Mr. Lincoln, and perhaps other prominent officials, and get them across the upper Potomac and into our part of the county, and hide them in the mountains until terms for their release could be made with the authorities at Washington. If Powell suggested it I would not be surprised, for he was always keyed up for any new sensation. When he left our Command to go to Washington he became a deserter, and our connection with him ceased.

But to our story. Powell and Shipley and Bowie galloped into Salem and fired on the pickets, while Thomson and his men were concealed in the bushes, watching for the enemy to come out, and ready to signal to John Puryear to charge them, with Thomson in the rear, as they passed. Our men got them in a lane between Utterback's and Shumate's and killed, wounded, and captured all but one of them. The man who escaped was chased by Thomson and John Dulin for a mile to Tom Rector's gate, where they killed his horse, not intentionally, while he jumped the fence and got away.

When Thomson got back to his men they gathered all the prisoners together, many of them wounded, and the road was filled with their dead and dying. The prisoners were sent out to Gordonsville, and Thomson got a promise from the Misses Mountjoy to care for the wounded. He turned over one of the wounded men to a Mr. Wm. A. Morgan, a gentleman who lived in that locality, and the kindness bestowed on the man was well repaid by the protection given him by Colonel Gallop, commander of the regiment at Salem to whom Thomson had applied for a surgeon and nurse for the wounded men. Colonel Gallop complimented Thomson for his kindness.

It is not necessary to say what John Puryear did that day. He was supposed to be in Command of a part of our men, but he forgot all about that when the fight opened and, as he dashed along that lane where everybody was crowded, he mowed them down. We captured about seventy-five men and their horses and did not lose a man.

I never knew of any sham that could fool Mosby. No sham soldier could do it for a minute. Many people within the Confederate lines never saw a grain of real coffee after the second year of the war, and in its stead they drank decoctions of roasted peanuts, or beans, or sweet potatoes, or almost anything that would look black, and taste burnt. Mosby would not drink a drop of any such sham coffee, and he could distinguish the slightest adulterated article from the real bean.

As we were always inside the enemy's lines, there were many of the people who managed in some way to get a little coffee now and then. Those at whose homes the colonel occasionally called to pay a short visit or take a meal, and who were so fortunate as to have a supply of coffee, would always see to it that he had a cup of the real stuff, no matter what the rest of us had to drink.

In order to insure his supply he sent North by a sutler and bought a sack of it and divided it around among his friends, as geographically equal as possible. He reserved a small portion for emergencies, and at times carried a little bag of it in his saddle pocket when he went on a raid. I do not believe the colonel ever drank a glass of whiskey in his life.

When I asked some of the members of our Command to let me have a few of their recollections to add to mine, I got a reply from Fred Hipkins, who is a broker living in New York.

He said that he remembered "once upon a time"' when he and I were with the colonel on a scout in the Valley of Virginia, and the colonel wanted a cup of coffee badly. Taking a little bag of the roasted article from his saddle pocket he gave it to me and told me to ride to Mrs. ——'s not far from where we were hidden in the woods, and get her to make a cup of it for him. As I started away he told me not to let her make it unless she had some sugar to sweeten it with. When sufficient time had elapsed as he thought for the proper brewing of the beverage he and Fred Hipkins followed me to Mrs. ——'s and on entering found an elaborate breakfast prepared at my request, consisting of fried chicken, ham and eggs, hot biscuits, flannel cakes, honey, and peaches and cream.

The lady served us bountifully and poured a cup of steaming hot coffee, for the colonel, remarking as she handed it to him gracefully, "I am awfully sorry, Colonel Mosby, but I have not a lump of sugar in the house." Hipkins says the colonel stopped short as if he had been stricken, and turning sharply on me said, "I thought I told you distinctly not to have my coffee made if you could not get some sugar to sweeten it." He ignored the chicken, and the ham and eggs, and the cakes, and everything else on the groaning board and only thought of his coffee. What effect his disappointment had on our hostess I do not know, but the absence of the sugar did not interfere with the healthy appetites of the colonel's two scouts.

Captain "Bill" Kennon was a polished, highly educated, well-bred gentleman who was a conspicuous member of our Command. He was somewhat of an adventurer and free lance, and had served with Walker, in his Nicaragua filibustering expedition, a few years before the war. He was a delightful man to talk to, or rather to listen to, for he was the most picturesque liar, in a harmless way, that I ever knew. Colonel Mosby always enjoyed "Bill's" romancing, and the captain never wearied of contributing to his and our amusement and amazement. He was not in the least coarse in his conversation, but he sometimes indulged in a little well selected profanity. It was refreshing to hear him when he used his full repertoire.

On one occasion he was riding along a road in Orange County near General Stuart's camp, when he was overtaken by an army chaplain who picked up a conversation with him. Captain "Bill" was not long in discovering his chance acquaintance's calling and controlled his profane tendencies far longer than he was accustomed to. Finally the reverend gentleman asked Captain Bill what part of the army he belonged to, and the captain said he was chaplain for Mosby's Command. In great surprise the stranger asked:

"Don't you find them a hard crowd, Brother Kennon?"

The captain was at the end of his rope, and replied: "Yes, my brother, a damned hard crowd."

He was quite a lady's man, and as he was a very handsome, as well as a fascinating man, his company was sought by the gentler sex and much enjoyed.

In the early part of these recollections I said in speaking of our men in a general way that we did not know anything about bugle calls. I forgot about Brewer. Brewer said he knew all about them and none of us dared contradict him, for we had no way to prove he was lying. But there were a lot of us youngsters who doubted Brewer's assertion and we concentrated our efforts for several months after Brewer came to us with his musical bravado, on the capture of a Yankee bugler with his instrument. While we were looking for that bugler, I believe we would have scorned to capture a sutler's wagon, so intent were we on humiliating poor little Brewer. At last we were rewarded. In a fight one day with a raiding party some one of our anti-Brewer crowd spied a bugler at the head of the column. Like the followers of Robert the Bruce, King of Scotland, when his heart, encased in a silver casket, was thrown far into the ranks of the enemy, they followed it with the cry, "The heart, the Bruce's heart," there arose on the wind in that charge of ours the wild cry, "The bugler, the bugler," and we dashed after that poor non-combatant and smothered him before he could perform "one blast upon his bugle horn."

We tore his bugle from him, and did not even take his pocketbook; no doubt some of the pro-Brewer men saw to that later. As soon as we could find Brewer the bugle was thrust into his hand and he was told to "blow her," which he proceeded to do very skilfully, much to our surprise and disgust. The truth of this story compels me to say, however, that Brewer at once became a hero, among our little crowd who had been inclined to belittle him. Brewer assumed at once the position of Mosby's bugler, as much to our joy and amusement as his first performance had been to our surprise, for we made him blow whenever we met him.

Two or three weeks after Brewer was equipped with his new toy we went on a raid into Fairfax County. He and two or three others stopped at a farmhouse to get a good meal, while the Command went ahead; and about a mile down the road we ran into the Yankees unexpectedly, had a rattling hot fight, which, like lots of others, lasted only a few minutes, gathered the prisoners together and started back up the road and when half way back to the house where Brewer had stopped, we met him galloping down on us full tilt, his bugle to his lips, blowing the "charge," with all the power in his lungs. I do not know whether I ever laid eyes on Brewer again: in fact I do not know if I would have acknowledged his acquaintance after such an unpardonable failure to make himself and our Command famous. I took the thing to heart, for my idol had fallen.

This was the first and last bugle and bugler we ever had, and we tried to forget it.

Our Command never numbered over three hundred and fifty men available for active service at any one time, but probably not a day passed from the time Mosby arrived in Northern Virginia, in February, 1863, with his original detail of fifteen men until after Lee's surrender, that some of the men were not raiding and scouting somewhere. There was no idle time for us. We never went into winter quarters.

During our career of a little over two years death was making its unceasing subtractions. In that time we had seventy of our best men killed and nearly one hundred wounded. We had nine of our commissioned officers killed, and nineteen of them were seriously wounded. Colonel Mosby himself was honey-combed with bullets. He was severely wounded in a fight at Goodin's tavern August 24th, 1863. On the 15th of September, 1864, he was wounded not far from Centerville in Fairfax County. He had two men, Tom Love and Guy Broadwater, with him, when they ran into five of the Thirteenth New York cavalry who had been sent out to head him off. He was shot in the groin but kept his saddle and whipped the men. That bullet is in him yet.

On his way back he stopped at a house on the roadside and had his wound dressed, the old lady of the house assisting. Ten days after, he passed that same house on a raid to Fairfax and woke the old lady up to ask some questions. She opened her window and asked who it was.

"It's Colonel Mosby; don't you remember me?" he answered.

"Oh no it aint? Colonel Mosby was here ten days ago badly wounded. I wouldn't believe you unless I saw the wound."

"You're as bad as Thomas who doubted his Lord," the colonel answered, "but I can't stop now to show you my wound."

On the 21st of December, 1864, he was again dangerously wounded at Lud Lake's house. The bullet went into the left side of his body and was cut out of the right side. He closely escaped peritonitis. All his wounds were at close range. There is a belt of wounds around his waist. Dr. W. L. Dunn was the surgeon of our Command at the time the colonel received all his wounds, and attended him.

One of our best men, Ned. Hurst, was wounded seven times, twice in one fight. He was one of the original fifteen men who started out with Mosby, and he came pretty nearly being in all the fights of the Command, for he was often in his saddle when he ought to have been in bed. He thought he was safer in his saddle.

Dr. Jim Wiltshire wrote to me recently, charging me not to mention Ned Hurst without saying that he killed at least one hundred men during his Partisan Ranger career. One night we had a fight at White Post in the Valley, and we were all pretty well mixed up in the darkness. I dropped my pistol down on a man at my side, and was about to pull the trigger, when a gentle old voice said softly,

"Don't make a fool of yourself Johnny: it's me."

And I recognised Ned's voice.

Another of our men, John Ballard, lost his leg in a fight in June, 1863, and the following winter he got hold of a second-hand artificial leg somewhere and kept up the fighting until the war ended; but in a fight in the Valley one day he broke it, and somebody after that gave him the false leg of Colonel Dahlgreen, of the Union Army, who was killed near Richmond on his celebrated raid.; Our little Command in two years lost more men killed, wounded and captured, and more officers killed and wounded, than any full cavalry regiment during the entire four years of the war, and we were in more fights, big and little, during our two years of existence, than any cavalry or infantry regiment in the army. Our loss in killed and wounded in nearly every fight was much less, proportionately to the number of men on both sides, than the enemy's, but in a few engagements our dead and wounded outnumbered theirs.

At Harper's Ferry we had eight men killed in a fight, eight of the bravest and best men in our Command, or in the Southern army. Captain William Smith of my company, D, and Lieutenant Tom Turner of Company A were of the number, men on whom Mosby relied under all circumstances.

Frank Stringfellow was a scout for General Stuart who, with a detail of about a dozen men, operated in our section of the country for a short time in the winter of 1863-4. He was trusted by General Stuart and was a brave, untiring, valuable man. He informed Mosby of the condition of the camp at Harper's Ferry early in January, 1864, and, on the night of the 9th of that month, acting on his information, verified by Mosby, we attacked a camp with one hundred of our men. Major Cole and his Maryland battalion of cavalry were camped on the mountain-side of Loudoun Heights in winter quarters, with heavy re-enforcements of infantry nearby. The night was bitterly cold, and the march in single file up the frozen mountainside was a reminder of Washington at Valley Forge. Mosby had laid his plans carefully for a successful blow at the enemy and, if Stringfellow had not blundered. Cole's Command would have been wiped from the face of the earth.

Every condition was favourable for the accomplishment of a brilliant night attack and victory, and Mosby rarely failed to carry out his plans. As a compliment to Stringfellow, Mosby ordered him to surround the Headquarters building and capture Cole and his officers, while our Command attacked and captured the camp.

We reached the rear of the camp and found everything favourable for our purpose; within one or two hundred yards of the camp Stringfellow was sent ahead on his mission, and we followed slowly in order to give him time to do his part. Suddenly and without warning, Stringfellow and his men came charging and yelling and firing into the camp, having made no effort or attempt to catch Cole or the other officers.

Mosby then charged, mistaking them for the enemy. The noise had aroused Cole and his men, and they met us with a deadly fire from their protected position in their camp. Our attack was so impetuous that they were driven into the surrounding woods, but they continued to pour their deadly fire into us and, as String fellow's blunder had thrown us and our plans into confusion, and as the nearby infantry would soon be on us, we retreated in good order, bringing out our prisoners and horses safely, but leaving our dead and some of the wounded on the field. While the fight lasted it was terrific, for both sides were in deadly desperation, but they outnumbered us two to one, and we had to retreat. We killed five of Cole's men, wounded seventeen, and captured and brought out six prisoners and about sixty horses. Our loss was four killed and seven wounded, four of the latter dying in a few days. We lost only one man taken prisoner.

Ordinarily the result of this fight would be considered in our favour. Nevertheless, we always looked upon it as a little Waterloo, for the men we lost seemed to us worth more than all Cole's Battalion.

Chapter 20

"The Chief"

I have referred frequently to Mr. Blackwell in preceding chapters, but I have not given any particulars of the man as we knew him. About the time I met Mosby by appointment at Blackwell's, in the summer of 1863, there was only a slight acquaintance between the two men. I don't believe to this day Colonel Mosby could give any special reason why he began going to Blackwell's after our meeting there, but it is a fact that, unintentionally or unconsciously, the men began to call the place Mosby's Headquarters. In fact he could be found there oftener than at any other place in "Mosby's Confederacy "when he was not in the saddle.

If our men wanted to see him or wanted to hear of him they naturally drifted to Blackwell's and if he was not there they generally learned something about him. I am inclined to believe he was attracted largely by the personality of Mr. Blackwell. The man was attractive, as well as unique; and he was loyal. There was nothing about his house or his farm to draw one to it, for the dwelling was so small that the few of us who made it our home completely filled it. There were only five rooms in it and they were little rooms, but the warmth of welcome there was enough to have filled a baronial castle.

The little dining-room could accommodate, on a pinch, about eight people at table; and I never knew the day that a second or third relay of visitors was not entertained at the board. Joe Blackwell never let a man go away from his house uninvited to break bread with him, and all invitations were accepted. How he kept his head above water I do not know, for his farm did not produce a thing but grass and not much of that. His place was too much of a storm centre to admit of any farming, and, as the negroes had nearly all gone North, Blackwell's field force was reduced to one gentleman from Limerick, Ireland, Mr.

Lat Ryan, who was totally unable, physically, to cope with the problem of successful farming. Most of Lat's time was spent in fussing with Colonel Mosby's old negro, Aaron, who was always boss wherever he was living, and who ordered Lat around all day and every day. I managed to keep on Lat's good side by occasionally stocking him with tobacco, or a flask of newly, distilled corn nectar, from some mountain still, but if my contributions were too far apart I was sure to hear from him in some disrespectful remark reflecting on my generosity or my bravery; and sometimes, when old Aaron had been rubbing Lat's fur backwards for a day or two, I came in for dire threats of losing my horses in the next Yankee raid, by his refusal to run off to the mountains with them.

Mr. Blackwell sometimes found fault with Lat and threatened to discharge him, but would promptly relent when he remembered that Lat was the only available farm-hand, white or black, in the county. All the negroes had run off and all the white men were soldiers except Lat, and he would gladly have been in the army if the authorities would have accepted him; but on examination he was found to be badly crippled in both legs and both feet; nearly all his teeth were gone (and teeth counted during the war, for cartridges were made of paper and had to be torn), his hands were twisted and curled up with rheumatism; both eyes were dim at certain stages of the moon (Aaron said he was moon-eyed) and he was hard of hearing when you asked him to do anything. In fact he was a sick man from a military standpoint, and was only waiting for the war to close and the Manassas Gap Railroad to resume operations, so he could get a job as flag man at the crossing nearby, a duty he had performed before the war.

But, if men were lacking on the Blackwell farm, their absence was more than made up by a force of women who did all the domestic work. The old yellow cook made biscuits and loaf bread and corn pudding that would make your lips smack, and the house maids were kept on a trot from the kitchen to the house during the three meals each day. Mr. Blackwell showed his pleasure in having the colonel and the men around him and, little by little, he took upon himself a military importance which the colonel encouraged and when, one day, he was addressed by Johnny Edmonds and me as "Chief," his place in the Command was settled.

From that moment everybody addressed him as "Chief," and he swelled, fairly swelled, with importance. He was colossal of stature, anyway, but the newly acquired title simply inflated him till he appeared to weigh about four hundred. He began wearing a gaudy uniform of gray, though he had never served a day in the army, and his boots were Wellingtonian. Steel spurs jangled on his heels and a brace of revolvers never left his belt except when he went to bed. He bought a splendid horse to ride and got a complete military equipment. He strutted around his domain with infinitely more pomposity than any general in either army and, from discussing our raids, he in time began criticising them; before the war ended he wanted to command us.

There was a question as to who was the more afraid of being captured, he or old Aaron, but he was always the first to get away when the report of the Yankees came. He bragged so much about his valour and his military ability, that we finally badgered him into going on a raid with us, and that came near being his undoing. We held out the inducement of plunder to him, and he fell. We took him on the Point of Rocks raid, July 4, 1864, and as he approached nearer and nearer to the Potomac, and the boys pictured to him the splendours of a sutler's store and the glory of capturing it, his enthusiasm rose to its highest, and he was frantic for the attack.

Scrambling across the river at the imminent risk of drowning, he finally emerged soaking wet, and started with the rest of us in a gallop to attack the post. Just then a volley was poured into us from the men in the works, and the "Chief" broke down. He had not expected any fighting, for we told him there never was any fighting when sutlers were captured. At the first report of the guns he checked up his horse with a jerk, and began bemoaning his unhappy fate.

"Oh, my Lord, why did I ever come on this damned raid, to have my brains shot out? Why did I make a damned fool of myself just for a few yards of calico and a new pair of boots? Why didn't I stay in my own comfortable home and let the damned guerrillas do their own fighting and robbing? Ah! will I ever see my family again? No! No! No! I am a dead man sure! How can I get away from these infernal Yankees that have been after me for a year or more? Oh! if the Lord will only forgive me this time I promise never to make an ass of myself again! If I ever get back home again I'll stay there the balance of my life!"

But the "Chief" forgot all his woes very soon afterwards. In a few days all his bravado returned and he swore he never enjoyed anything so much as the raid on Point of Rocks; in fact he said we never would have taken the place but for him. For two or three months we all humoured him in his conceit and praised his valour, and I really believe

A RICHMOND GROUP IN 1865
Lt. Ben. Palmer.   Walter Gosden
John W. Munson. Tom Booker.   Sergt. Babcock.

we might have induced him to go with us on another raid, but the Yankees came up to our country and settled on us for awhile and soon after their arrival they burned the "Chief's" little home and all his farm buildings, and drove him and his family away, to seek shelter elsewhere; and the happy years of our experience at Mosby's Headquarters were to become only a memory.

Few of us ever saw the chief again during the war, but Colonel Mosby got an appointment for him in the government service some years afterwards, which he held for a number of years. He and the colonel kept up their friendly relations until a short while ago.

As I write these lines I hear from a friend in Virginia that the old chief has just died. I am truly sorry to hear it, for I never had a more unselfish friend.

CHAPTER 21

The Colonel's Serious Wounding

The little god of love captured some of our best men during the war and held them more securely than the Yankees did. There is no record of any escapes from his imprisonment, nor of any attempt at escape. Among the good men he got hold of and held onto were Colonel Chapman, Lieutenant Fount Beattie, and Ordnance-Sergeant Jake Lavinder. The latter was married on December 21st, 1864, at Mr. Blackwell's home, or rather the place he was living at after his own home had been burned. Colonel Mosby attended the wedding, the bride being a sister of Mrs. Blackwell and of Johnny Edmonds and, like all the rest of her family, great favourites of Mosby.

Word came during the festivities that a raiding party was in the neighbourhood and Colonel Mosby and Tom Love started out to look for the raiders, and if necessary to gather our men together to attack them. Near Rectortown he saw them going into camp for the night, as he supposed, and rode as far as Lud Lake's where they stopped for supper, tying their horses to the front fence. The house was surrounded by Yankees before the colonel was aware of it, and one of them shot him through a window of the room where he was at supper. The raiding party, which was a detachment of the Thirteenth and Sixteenth New York, under Major Frazer, had not gone into camp at Rectortown as Mosby supposed, but had only stopped for awhile and then resumed the march to their camp, passing by Lake's house on the way. Mosby had thrown his hat and cape and overcoat to one side when he went into Lake's house, and when the Yankees rushed into the house they captured these articles.

Seeing the colonel lying on the floor desperately wounded, they examined him and left him to die. He had hidden his uniform coat when he fell and there was nothing to indicate his rank. The members of Lake's family and Tom Love "disowned" him, saying they thought he was a lieutenant in some Virginia regiment.

As soon as the enemy left, taking Tom Love with them, the colonel had Mr. Lake remove him in an ox cart to a farm a few miles away, where he remained a few days and was then taken to his father's home near Lynchburg.

The bullet had entered one side of his body and passed around the abdomen; it was cut out of the opposite side, and he did not entirely recover from the wound until some time in the following February. It was the worst jolt of many he got during the war, and but for his splendid physical condition it might have put an end to him.

Colonel Mosby's brother, William, who was our adjutant, had about half a dozen men with him on the day when he ran into this raiding party, but had to get out at double quick. The Yankees were too many for "our Billy." In the retreat a boy named Cocke was thrown from his horse and would have been captured but for Hugh McIlhaney who caught him by the arm and lifted him up behind on his horse, fighting the pursuers all the time to keep them off. They crowded Hugh closely and drove him to a fence which he tried to jump, but the load was too much for his horse and he and Cocke were captured.

Although the Yankees had Colonel Mosby's overcoat, cape, hat and hip boots to identify him by, they did not find out who it was they had wounded for several days, and then searching parties of hundreds of men were sent to our country to find him, but the bird had flown away. Our boys who were captured the day he was shot swore like gentlemen that they did not know this man, though they gladly admitted they themselves were Mosby's men.

General Sheridan reported to General Stevenson on December 29th that he had very satisfactory evidence that Mosby was mortally wounded. On the 31st, in a despatch to Emery he said:

> I have no news to report except the death of Mosby. He died from his wounds at Charlottesville.

Major Frazer, who commanded the raiding party that shot Mosby, reported on December 31st to Colonel Gamble that he examined personally the man's wounds and pronounced them mortal; that he was in a hurry to return, as he was behind time, having been skirmishing all the afternoon with the enemy ("the enemy" consisted of Billy Mosby, Johnny Foster, Hugh McIlhaney, Willie Cocke and two or three others), that all his officers saw the wounded man and none of them had the slightest idea it was Mosby; that when he went into camp an orderly brought him the captured hat and he at once knew it was a field officer's, and tried hard to make the prisoners tell him who the man was; and that on returning from a scout for information that day, December 31st, he was unable to say the wounded man was Colonel Mosby.

Colonel Gamble endorsed the report as follows:

> I exceedingly regret that any such blunder was made. I have given orders that all wounded officers and men of the enemy be brought in, although I thought any officer ought to have brains and common sense enough to do so without an order.

Sheridan, in his report of December 27th, said:

> They fired at Mosby and some of his men through the windows, wounding Mosby in the abdomen.

My own opinion is that, if some of our men who had chances to shoot Sheridan and Custer and Hancock and others as they sat at night in their tents, had committed such a murderous attack as Frazer's men did on Mosby there would have been a mighty outcry. But then it did not matter what manner was employed to kill the "Guerrilla Chief," so long as he was killed.

Last year I called on a lady in New York, at Colonel Mosby's request, and identified the hat which was captured forty years before. It had been treasured as a valuable war relic all those years. She sent the hat to the colonel, and I believe it is now in the museum in Washington with other war curiosities.

CHAPTER 22

The Guerrillas' Last Fight

Within a very few days of the final winding up of our career as Partisan Rangers, or to be accurate, on the 30th day of March, 1865, there occurred a disastrous little fight. There was in our Command a young fellow from the Valley of Virginia, Charley Wiltshire, who, like his brother Jim, was one of the blue hen's chickens. He had served honourably in the regular Confederate Army, before he joined our Command, and had been seriously wounded several times in hard fights; in fact he was on crutches when he came to us, having been honourably discharged for disability. He began his guerrilla tactics when he should have been in the hospital. He was not long idle after he became a Mosby man, and in his first "mix-up" he broke his crutch over a Federal soldier's head. A sabre would not have been half as effectual. Mosby thought very highly of him and told him late in the month of March, 1865, that he intended making him a lieutenant in the new Company H which was soon to be organised.

On March 30, he told Charley to take a few men on a scout into the valley around Berryville, and with George Murray Gill, Bartlett Bolling, John Orrick, and Bob Eastham, he crossed the Shenandoah River beyond Snickers' Gap. Bolling and Eastham were told by Charley to stop at a house on the roadside to get some information, while the others rode on and caught sight of two Yankees at Mr. Bonham's house running towards the barn. Charley and his two companions dashed off after the two Federals who were inside the barn for protection. Charley galloped up to the door and leaning over his horse's neck, so as to reach as far as possible into the barn, he fired, and was immediately shot from within the building.

Several shots rang out from inside this "fort," and Gill and Orrick fell, the latter thrown from his horse. One of the Federals fired through a door and the other through a window. When all three of our men were down the Federals dashed out and made a run for their horses. One of them, who proved to be Lieutenant Eugene Ferris of the Thirtieth Massachusetts, caught Charley Wiltshire's horse and mounted it, shooting at the dying boy who was lying on the ground and who had raised on his elbow to shoot at Ferris. Then, ordering the other man who was his orderly to follow him, they galloped away at top speed towards their camp nearby.

When the firing began, Bartlett Bolling and Bob Eastham rushed to the house at top speed and met Ferris and his man leaving on a run. Ferris shot Bolling in the breast as he passed but did not entirely disable him, and he and Eastham started in pursuit of the two flying men, overtaking them before they reached their pickets. Orrick recovered sufficiently to join them in the chase, which ended when they reached their camp. Bolling, wounded as he was, dragged the orderly from his horse and captured him, while Eastham fired at Ferris and began to club him from his horse, but Ferris on the captured horse got away, still chased by Bolling and Orrick.

When the race was over and they rode back to Bonham's house, they found Charley Wiltshire and George Gill desperately wounded and being cared for by the ladies. Charley was later removed to Mr. Gilbert's and died there April 6. George Gill managed to go as far as the mountains on his way back to our country, but had to stop and in a very few days died, breathing thanks with his expiring breath for the privilege of giving his young life to his country.

Mr. John Gill of Baltimore, who was then attached to General Fitzhugh Lee's staff, was in our country scouting, and had gone on several raids with our men. George Murray Gill was his cousin, and John Gill was at his death bed and gave him Christian burial on the mountainside. The body of our gallant Maryland boy now rests in Green Mount Cemetery in Baltimore.

For his part in this affair Lieutenant Ferris received from the Secretary of War a medal of honour for his distinguished gallantry in the face of the enemy.

Dr. Lawrence Wilson, of the pension office in Washington, formerly of the Seventh Ohio Infantry, First Brigade, Second Division, Twelfth and Twentieth Army Corps, read an account of this fight, in a book written in 1867 by Major John Scott. The doctor only saw the book thirty years later and, being attracted by the story, he wrote to some of the participants and then applied to the Secretary of War. The medal resulted.

The last record of our defeat is, by a singular irony of fate, the record of our last fight, a fight that took place on the 10th of April, 1865, one day after Lee's surrender at Appomattox. We did not know of that event at the time, but possibly the fight would have taken place just the same if we had known it. The Eighth Illinois Cavalry was our adversary on this occasion, as it had been so frequently for two years preceding. We had tested their mettle and felt their bullets sufficiently to have a proper respect for them. These men would fight at the drop of a hat, and we knew it meant bloodshed whenever we came together.

On the 9th of April Captain George Baylor of Mosby's Command was put in charge of Company H, which had been organised but a few days before, and was composed almost entirely of recent recruits to the Command. With him was a part of old Company D, and his mission was to raid the Federal communications in Fairfax County and capture a wagon train; incidentally to win his spurs. Every newly elected captain was given the chance to show what stuff he was made of Baylor had come to us with a fine reputation won in the regular army, but that did not signify that he would make a good captain of Mosby's men, and so he was turned loose on his own responsibility, "to do something."

Lieutenant Ed. Thomson acted as guide for the party. The wagon train which it was supposed Baylor would find hauling wood, had been withdrawn; possibly the authorities had heard of the projected raid, and he was returning with his men. He stopped at Arundel's farm for rest and feed, and the men dismounted. Baylor did not put out a picket, and suddenly out of nowhere that Eighth Illinois crowd burst on him and his men, bringing confusion with them.

The Mosby men, unprepared for the attack and many of them unarmed, broke for cover. One of Baylor's boys, J. D. Shewalter, now a lawyer in Colorado Springs, acted as rear guard during the entire retreat of several miles. He was riding a horse that would not run, insisting on trotting the whole distance and, as all the rest of our men were sprinting, he was left in the rear.

The Federal commander called on him early in the engagement to surrender and the boy was willing to do so, but that trotting horse of his would not let him. Some of the older members of the Command made an effort to check the stampede, fighting their pursuers, in a way, as they ran, but their efforts were in vain. Among them were Captain

Baylor, Joe Bryan, Ed. Thomson, Charley Dear, Jim Wiltshire, Frank Carter, Walter Gosden, and a few others. Bryan and Wiltshire saw one of their men. Sergeant Mohler, trying to escape on foot. His horse had been shot, and they rode up on each side of him and, taking hold of his wrists, galloped along with him until he overtook a riderless horse which he mounted; but he was captured shortly afterwards. He always declared that if he had been allowed to proceed under his own steam he would have got away.

Walter Gosden checked up his horse to help a man that was down. Shewalter saw the danger of stopping then and called out to him to save himself. Just then the bullets were flying pretty fast and Shewalter began using a very select brand of profanity which Gosden thought was emanating from one of his Yankee pursuers; as each new expression escaped Shewalter's lips, Gosden's spurs went deeper into the sides of his horse and, without looking around to see who was cursing, he fired his pistols back recklessly but harmlessly at close intervals, till both were empty and Gosden was almost dead from exhaustion.

Our loss was one man wounded and four taken prisoners; the enemy's loss was four men wounded and a number of horses killed. The chase was kept up as far as Wolf Run Shoals near the old Bull Run battlefield. Jim Wiltshire and Frank Carter fired the last shots in the affair and shot the last man.

Charley Dear made his will the night before this fight, and among his legatees was Joe Bryan, who was to fall heir to some new socks which Charley had come in possession of, and of which he was very proud. During the fight Charley was thrown from his horse and rolled over and over into a gulch, with his horse following a close second. Joe could not help thinking of the priceless socks that were so soon to be his. The unfortunate Ranger turned up next day, however, safe and sound, and the new socks did not change hands.

This was the last fight and the last whipping of Mosby's Command. Colonel Mosby was not in it, but every man wished he had been, for a different story would have been told. Once before, on the 29th of October, 1864, a newly elected captain, trying to win his spurs, had run into the Eighth Illinois Cavalry and got a thrashing. There seemed to be a fatality in pitting a new captain of our Command against Farnsworth's old Eighth.

The foregoing are some of the most memorable fights in which the enemy got away with us. I have not undertaken to record all our disasters; as I said, I am not writing its history. Now that I look back

JOHN S. MOSBY
At the Conclusion of the Civil War, in the
Uniform of a Confederate Colonel.

over it all, and review the memories of those eventful years, I cannot help thinking that the defeats we occasionally suffered did as much as our victories, if not more, to cement us closely together in those days, and to make us feel tenderly towards each other now that we are old.

In this, our last affair, some of the first and some of the last to join the Command fought side by side, and such was the influence of the "Mosby men of record" upon the newcomers, that the latter sprang, full-fledged, into the booted and spurred Ranger the instant he touched elbows with the former on a raid or in a fight. After the first division of the spoils of a successful raid all guerrillas looked alike to me.

Usually a young fellow who joined Mosby's Command came to him with romantic ideas of the Partisan Ranger's existence. It was something vague in his mind. He was ever on the look-out for its secrets and its inner workings. He took his lessons from some one or more old models, but he learned the first day of his enlistment that he must keep awake and fight. These were the two important first lessons. In a hand-to-hand fight one day in the latter part of 1864, a young fellow who had just joined the Command the day before found himself rather bewildered by the surging, yelling, fighting crowd all around him and, turning to Harry Hatcher, one of the old veterans, said in an innocent, schoolboy way,

"How can I tell who are our men and who are the Yankees?"

"Damn the difference," Harry replied, "pitch in and shoot anything."

Just then an Eighth Illinois pistol was poked under the boy's nose, but it was not quick enough, for Harry's lesson had been learned when it was given, and a Yankee saddle was emptied.

That Mosby imparted the spirit of courage and daring to his soldiers is undoubted. I have cited many instances to show what a wonderful influence his presence in our Command had over the men who came from so many parts of the South to join him.

Every member of the battalion did something worthy of record, and I had hoped to be able to speak of it. None of the officers or men were ever idle. What I have written is a mere chapter of our story. The little personal incidents, the individual scouts and fights, the daily experiences of each man, these are what would have proven most satisfactory in a book about Mosby's men, but I could not remember a tenth of it all, and I must leave what is unwritten to some other, who will write the story as cheerfully and as lovingly as I have written my share.

Chapter 23

The Beginning of the End

There came the time at last when Mosby's men had to stop their raiding and fighting. Four years of the bitterest conflict, four years of hardship, weariness, privation and horror, had made the soldiers of both armies weary of war. We of the Partisan Rangers had had little more than two years of it on our own account and, although our Command had more of the poetry and romance in its history than fell to the regulars, we had begun to feel some of the weariness, the exhaustion and the satiety that invariably come to an army, with bloodshed; to the victors as well as to the defeated.

So far as its physical well-being was concerned, Mosby's Command had never been in better condition than when Lee surrendered at Appomattox. Every man in the saddle was a seasoned Ranger, better equipped, better prepared in every way to continue fighting, than any of the cavalry in the regular army.

Gradually the undesirable element had been weeded out; the drones in the hive had been eliminated by a process which was practically the survival of the fittest; the unruly element, whenever it showed itself, was hustled off under guard to the regular army, and a series of unusual achievements had filled the Command with an overwhelming desire to precipitate measures that looked towards a continuance of the struggle.

That we were in magnificent shape to perform our best work there is no possible doubt; but the general relaxation that came along the line after Appomattox doubtless communicated some of its depression to us and, while we resisted its influence, we became, as did all concerned, its unconscious victims.

We had cast off our old horses for new; as each individual pocketbook swelled, a better horse was added to the already good private stud. Each man's equipment was better after every raid; a new suit of buff and gold-embroidered gray was ordered from the local tailor or the underground road from the North. Our arms were the best to be had, and the entire Command, reaping the fruits of war, found itself equipped in paraphernalia of the finest. Many of the men had exchanged the ordinary raw-hide covered McClellan saddles of the private soldier, for the more elaborate, brass-trimmed, enamel leather saddles of the commissioned officer.

Naturally we came to the conclusion that the entire Southern Army was sufficiently equipped, and our hopes were lifted in proportion to the success we met on the raids we made.

It seemed to most of us that the cause for which we stood was soon to be won and that the long winter through which we had passed was to offer us full compensation in the shape of victory.

Our last fight, which I have just described, was fought by some of the best-dressed, best-mounted, and best-equipped men in the army. The last shots fired were fired by two of our young lieutenants, Jim Wiltshire and Frank Carter, mere boys, who were dandies in their gorgeous attire.

Suddenly Richmond fell. General Lee surrendered at Appomattox, and the curtain of war was rung down on the last act

Mosby's Men, as I have previously related, did not know of the surrender, when, on the following day, we went into battle with the Eighth Illinois. I sometimes feel sure that, if we had known it was to be the last fight of our career, every man of us would have died rather than suffer the defeat that followed.

One may imagine the effect that Lee's surrender had upon the Partisan Rangers, although the tidings did not reach us until several days afterward. The Northern forces in the Valley of Virginia were commanded by General Hancock, who, under the date of April 10th issued a circular addressed to the citizens in the neighbourhood of his lines, urging their co-operation in the immediate restoration of peace. He told them, however, that Colonel Mosby, the Partisan Ranger, was not included in the terms of surrender.

On the same day, General Grant informed Mr. Stanton, the Secretary of War, that he thought all the fragments of the army of Northern Virginia would come in and surrender under the terms given to General Lee. He added that he "wished Hancock would try it with Mosby."

On the same date, April 10th. General Hallock, however, in sending on to Hancock the Secretary of War's Order to have the correspondence between Grant and Lee printed and circulated, closed his communication with this positive sentence:

> The guerrilla chief, Mosby, will not be paroled.

General Augur also issued a circular in which he styled Mosby "an outlaw," stating that he would not be paroled under any circumstances. It will be seen that there was considerable confusion as to Mosby's exact status.

On April 11th General C. H. Morgan, Chief of Staff to General Hancock, addressed the following letter to Colonel Mosby:

> Headquarters Middle Military Division,
> April 11th, 1865.
>
> Colonel John S. Mosby, Commanding Partisans.
>
> Colonel: I am directed by Major-General Hancock to enclose to you copies of letters which passed between Generals Grant and Lee on the occasion of the surrender of the Army of Northern Virginia. Major-General Hancock is authorised to receive the surrender of the forces under your Command on the same conditions offered to General Lee, and will send an officer of equal rank with yourself to meet you at any point and time you may designate, convenient to the lines, for the purpose of arranging details, should you conclude to be governed by the example of General Lee.
>
> Very respectfully.
> Your obedient servant,
> C. H. Morgan,
> Brevet Brigadier-General, and Chief of Staff.

The reader will observe that General Morgan did not ask Colonel Mosby to surrender himself, but "the forces under his command."

On the following day, April 12th, General Hancock notified General Hallock that he had sent a communication to Mosby offering to receive the surrender of his Command, and added:

> It is quite as likely that Mosby will disband as that he will surrender, as all his men have fine horses and are generally armed with two pistols only. They will not give up these things, I presume, as long as they can escape. I will employ the cavalry force here in hunting them down.

Three days later, April 15th, Colonel Mosby sent his reply to General Hancock, acknowledging the receipt of General Morgan's letter of the 11th, concluding as follows:

> As yet I have no notice through any other source of the fact concerning the surrender of the Army of Northern Virginia, nor, in my opinion, has the emergency yet arisen which would justify the surrender of my Command. With no disposition, however, to cause the useless effusion of blood or to inflict on a war-worn population any unnecessary distress, I am ready to agree to a suspension of hostilities for a short time in order to enable me to communicate with my own authorities, or until I can obtain sufficient intelligence to determine my further action. Should you accede to this proposition I am ready to meet any person you may designate to arrange the terms of an armistice.

This communication was sent to General Hancock through the hands of Lieutenant-Colonel Chapman, Captain Walter Frankland, Adjutant William H. Mosby, and Dr. A, Monteiro, of our Command, and was delivered to the general in person.

General Hancock sent a prompt reply, agreeing to cease hostilities until the following Tuesday at noon. On the same day, April 16th. General Hancock received from General Hallock a notice that General Grant authorised him to "give Colonel Mosby and his Command the same terms as those agreed upon by General Lee."

On the 18th, Colonel Mosby met a number of the Rangers at Paris, in Fauquier County, and proceeded with them to Millwood in the Shenandoah Valley, where he met, by appointment. General George H. Chapman and his officers. Colonel Mosby, having as yet received no news from headquarters, asked for an extension of time.

The truce was extended to the 20th, with a conditional ten days further truce if approved by General Hancock.

On the 19th, General Hancock wrote to Colonel Mosby informing him that the truce would end at noon the next day, and would not be renewed. On the same day Hancock notified Hallock of what he had done.

Promptly at noon on the 20th, Colonel Mosby, with twenty of his men, walked into one of the rooms of the little brick building in Millwood, near Winchester, where the Northern officers were waiting for his decision. The colonel was informed that General Hancock refused to extend the truce any longer than that hour and, as Mosby refused to surrender, the Federal commander said to him:

The truce is ended. We can have no further intercourse under its terms.

He looked the colonel square in the eyes when he said it and both men appreciated the serious import of the moment. This was the first time that Mosby had come, face to face, with so critical and peculiar a situation without instantly acting. Anything approaching it in the past had meant bloodshed. To add to the suspense, one of our men, a rough diamond named John Hearn, who had remained outside among the soldiers and had got up an impromptu horse race with one of them, discovered, at the end of his half-mile dash, that a regiment of cavalry was drawn up near the little town, hidden behind a clump of trees. Instantly he dashed back to where Mosby was and bolted into the room where the conference was being held, shouting in a voice so loud that all assembled could hear him:

"Colonel, the d——d Yankees have got you in a trap: there is a thousand of them hid in the woods right here."

Mosby looked squarely at his informant.

"Let's fight 'em, Colonel," he continued coming to Mosby's side. "We can whip 'em."

Up to that moment the conference had been dignified, although unusual. At the conclusion of the trooper's dramatic announcement, Mosby, who had been seated during the conversation, rose to his feet and placed his hand on his revolver.

"If," he said slowly, keeping his eye on the group of Federal officers, "the truce no longer protects us, we are at your mercy; but we shall protect ourselves."

Followed by his twenty men, all ready to draw their weapons at the signal, Mosby strode from the room.

If, at that critical moment some hot-headed Partisan had made any move towards trouble, or a hammer of a six-shooter had clicked in cocking, that tavern room would have developed a catastrophe that Dodge City, or Abilene, in the palmiest days of the old cattle trail, could not have equalled.

The handful of Rangers filed out in breathless silence, Mosby at their head. Each man mounted his horse without molestation and they galloped down the turnpike to the Shenandoah River. Plunging across it, full tilt, they rode over the Blue Ridge Mountains, into our own "Mosby's Confederacy," their arms in their holsters and chagrin in their hearts.

Chapter 24

The Rangers Disband

There is not room here to recount all that we did and all that we felt that night. The outlook for the morrow was gloomy. Failure of the cause for which we had fought made the chilly winds of early spring seem colder and the drizzle from the trees all the drearier. Colonel Mosby, like the rest of us, showed plainly that his heart was heavy. The blow had fallen with awful force and, though little was said, the gloomy faces of the Partisans told how tumultuous were the thoughts surging amid the memories of past achievements. Many of us slept in strange beds, or in none at all, that night, for we felt that we were to be henceforth wanderers. In the morning, after very brief preparations. Colonel Mosby, who was at Glen Welby, the home of Major Richard Henry Carter, in Fauquier county, asked for paper and writing material, and then and there penned his farewell address to those of the Partisan Rangers who had gone through the war at his side; to those who loved him as men love their fathers, their brothers, and their kin.

By previous arrangement the whole Command, or as many as could be mustered, met on that morning at Salem, and by noon the line of faithful followers was drawn up to hear his parting words. No sadder ceremony ever occurred in the life of that little band of men and, as Mosby rode along the line, looking each man in the face, it was plain that his heart was breaking.

The document that the colonel had prepared earlier that morning was read to each squadron. From the original draft, now in possession of Mr. Frank R. Pemberton of New York City, I herewith quote the historic address in full:

Fauquier County, April 21, 1865.
Soldiers: I have summoned you together for the last time. The

visions we have cherished of a free and independent country have vanished, and that country is now the spoil of the conqueror. I disband your organisation in preference to surrendering it to our enemies. I am no longer your commander. After an association of more than two eventful years, I part from you with a just pride in the fame of your achievements and a grateful recollection of your generous kindness to myself. And at this moment of bidding you a final *adieu*, accept the assurance of my unchanging confidence and regard.

Farewell.

John S. Mosby.

I submit this as one of the most genuine expressions of regret that was ever penned, and it is small wonder that Mosby afterward said:

When writing I had some of the feelings of Boabdil when he took his last look at the Alhambra.

It isn't possible for me to write an adequate description of the scene that followed. Each of those present was so occupied with his personal griefs and regrets that the full effect of the occasion did not present itself. Singly and in groups, the participants in this saddest of farewells, Mosby's men, gave way to their feelings in a manner that requires no description. Strong men, who had laughed in the face of the gravest dangers and smiled at the pains of grievous wounds, walked apart to weep. Colonel Mosby, with his hat off, stood at the side of the road, receiving the clutch of friendly hands, and bestowing brave words on the men with whom he had fought for the lost cause. The wild excitement of the past two years, the crash of pistols and carbines, the yell of victory, and the fever of battle were all ended now. To many of those men that parting was their first sorrow.

Colonel Mosby told them frankly that they could do whatever they chose; that if they went to General Hancock they could get their paroles and be protected in their homes; that he did not intend to surrender, but would go South, possibly to connect with General Johnston's army.

In little groups the men dispersed to meet next day under Lieutenant-Colonel Chapman and proceed to the Valley of Virginia, there to surrender. Mosby was left with a handful of boys who preferred to remain at his side, to follow him blindly wherever he chose to lead them, to become Knights Errant in a new Crusade.

There were only about a half dozen boys in this remnant of Par-

Fauquier Co: April 21st/1865.

Soldiers—

I have summoned you together for the last time. The vision we cherished of a free and independent country has vanished, and the country is now the spoil of a conqueror.

I disband your organization in preference to surrendering to our enemies. I am no longer your commander. After an association of more than two eventful years, I part from you with a just pride in the fame of your achievements, and grateful recollections of your generous kindness to myself. And now, at this moment of bidding you a final adieu, accept the assurance of my unchanging confidence and regard. Farewell!

Jno. S. Mosby
Colonel

FACSIMILE OF MOSBY'S FAREWELL ADDRESS.

tisan Rangers who were with Mosby at the last, and I was one of the number.

We started South with more, but only this little group got as far as the neighbourhood of Richmond. Colonel Mosby sent Coley Jordan and me into the city to discover the situation and report to him the next day at a point a few miles west of the city, on the James River. I went to the old Jeff Davis mansion, which was then occupied by Federal officers, and ascertained that we could raid them successfully at night, capture the whole crowd and get out of the town with them. I then inspected the officers' stables which were on Franklin street, where I found we could take every horse in the stable and the few guards who were on duty.

After getting all the information I wanted on which to base one of the most audacious and sensational and destructive forays of our career, I rode back in the night and reported to the colonel, who had got tired of waiting for my return and thought that I had fallen by the wayside to the pleadings of my parents to remain at home. He turned to Ben Palmer and said:

"Ben, if Munson don't come back tomorrow, I want you to go into Richmond, but don't go near your father."

While I was gone a canal boat came along from the city with some officers aboard. Ben Palmer, at Mosby's request, went down to the canal to get the news and was given a copy of a Richmond paper which contained an account of Johnston's surrender. Ben waited all night on the roadside for me, and I turned up promptly the next morning. But when I reported to Mosby he said,

"Too late! It would be murder and highway robbery now. We are soldiers, not highwaymen."

Our new-born crusade had come to a sudden end. The war was actually over.

It has always been some satisfaction to me to know that I performed, as well as I could, the last order for service ever given by my colonel to any man in his Command; and, as I had done duty as marker of the cavalry company which performed the first active service of the war in Virginia, and as this trip to Richmond was one of the last active services of a Confederate soldier in the State, I congratulate myself that I saw the race from start to finish.

Mosby bade the four or five of us an affectionate farewell and, in company with Ben Palmer, rode away towards his home in Lynchburg. About two months later he took his parole.

The day he left us he and Ben Palmer stopped at a farmhouse for dinner. He did not tell who he was, and the old farmer, unable to control a natural curiosity, asked him his name. Mosby told him, and the old man said:

"Colonel, where is your Command?"

Turning around and pointing to Ben he said,

"There it stands! That is all that is left of it."

No truer, braver, or better soldier in all the South, or all the North, ever unbuckled his weapons and laid them down for peace, than John S. Mosby, Commander of the Partisan Rangers of Virginia.

"Mosby's Men" became a memory. They scattered far and wide, each to take his place in the busy world; each to contribute his share towards the development and progress of the reunited country over which we fought so long and bitterly: each to try and make his presence felt in the new scheme of things. That the great majority of them have proven worthy of the confidence Colonel Mosby reposed in them, is attested by their lives today. They and their children are scattered throughout the land in all walks of life, adorning the professions, the arts, the sciences and the trades.

Thirty years after the Civil War, John H. Alexander of Leesburg, Virginia, one of the foremost members of the Command, issued a call for a re-union of the survivors to be held in Alexandria, Virginia. In response, there came about one hundred and fifty of the Rangers, Colonel Mosby among them. Many speeches were made by prominent ex-officers of the Confederate Army, but most impressive of all was that of our old commander. I quote it in full, for I think no more graceful or appropriate reunion speech was ever made at a gathering of soldiers.

Colonel Mosby's Speech.

Comrades: When, on April 21st, 1865, I told you that I was no longer your commander, and bade you, what we then considered, a long and perhaps eternal farewell, the most hopeful among us could not reasonably have expected ever to have witnessed a scene like this. Nearly thirty years have passed away and we meet once more on the banks of the Potomac, in sight of the Capitol, not in hostile array, but as citizens of a great and united country. Gunboats no longer patrol the river; there are no picket guards on the banks to challenge our crossing.

Your presence here this evening recalls our last parting. I see the line drawn up to hear read the last order I ever gave you. I see the moistened eyes and quivering lips. I hear the command to break ranks. I feel the grasp of the hands and see the tears on the cheeks of men who had dared death so long that it had lost it's terror. And I know now, as I knew then, that each heart suffered with mine the agony of the Titan in his resignation to fate.

The rock, the vulture, and the chain.
All that the proud can feel of pain.

I miss among you the faces of some who were present that day, but who have since passed over the Great River. Memory brings back the image of many of that glorious band who then slept in the red burial of war. Modern scepticism has destroyed one of the most beautiful creations of Epic ages, the belief that the spirits of dead warriors met daily in the halls of Walhalla, and there around the festive board recounted the deeds they did in the other world. For this evening, at least, let us adopt the ancient superstition, if superstition it be. It may seem presumptuous in me, but a man who belonged to my Command may be forgiven for thinking that, in that assembly of heroes, when the feast of the wild boar is spread, Smith and Turner, Montjoy and Glasscock, Fox and Whitescarver, and all their comrades, will not be unnoticed in the mighty throng.

I shall make no particular allusion to the part you played in the great tragedy of war. Our personal associations were so intimate that it would not become me to do so. But, standing here as I do, amid the wreck of perished hopes, this much at least I can say—that in all the vicissitudes of fortune and all the trials of life, I have never ceased to feel, as I told you at parting, a just pride in the fame of your achievements, and a grateful recollection of your generous kindness to myself. I remember—and may my right arm wither if I ever forget—how, when the mournful tidings came from Appomattox that "Young Harry Percy's spur was cold," you stood with unshaken fidelity to the last, and never quit my side until I told you to go.

A great poet of antiquity said, as descriptive of the Romans, that *they changed their sky but not their hearts*. While I lived in far Cathay, my heart, untraveled, dwelt among the people in whose defence I had shed my blood. In the solitude of exile it was a solace to hear that my name was sometimes mentioned by them with expressions of good will. Nothing that concerns the honour and welfare of Virginia can ever be indifferent to me.

I wish that life's descending shadows had fallen upon me in the midst of friends and the scenes I loved best. But destiny not my will compels me to abide far away on the shore of that sea where the god of gladness sheds his parting smile. I must soon say to you farewell, a word that must be and hath been. I shall carry back to my home by the Golden Gate proud recollections of this evening, and I shall still feel, as I have always felt, that life cannot afford a more bitter cup than the one I drained when we parted at Salem, nor any higher reward of ambition than that I received as commander of the Forty-Third Virginia Battalion of Cavalry.

Mosby's Men

Contents

Preface	215
A General View of Mosby's Men	217
Securing a Mount	231
My First Raid	236
The Guard Hill Raid	244
In Fairfax County	250
The Point of Rocks Raid	259
The Mount Zion Fight	267
The Adamstown Raid	273
The Greenback Raid	278
The Blazer Fight	287
The Fight at Dulany's	296
Drawing Lots For Life	304
A Lively Ride Before Breakfast	311
The Hamilton Fight	314
A Pair Of Scouts	320
My Boy Frank	327
Eulogy of Rev. Sydnor G. Ferguson a Typical Mosby Man	330

To
The
Confederate Cavalryman

Preface

This book does not purport to be a history of Mosby's Command, in the sense of being a full and accurate account of its operations. It is a narrative of what the writer saw of the men and their doings, as they impressed him at the time and as his memory reproduces them now. Many of their exploits—perhaps their finest performances—he neither participated in nor saw. When he has had occasion to refer to incidents outside of his personal knowledge, it is indicated. The extent and character of his information is also indicated.

It is very rarely that two men see the same thing in exactly the same way; and of all subjects upon which eyewitnesses differ, it seems that upon a fight—a battle—there is the most frequent and pronounced variance. So it is quite probable that some of our comrades may remember certain occurrences differently from the way I remember them. All that the writer claims is that they are here reproduced with absolute fidelity to his memory of them and there is nothing between the lids of this book which, in that sense, is not strictly true. He has in no instance consciously lapsed into fiction or coloured an incident in the faintest degree. In these pages the reader has *Mosby's Men* exactly as the writer had the privilege of knowing them, and as he now understands them, after a lifetime's observation of men and things.

J. W. FOSTER
CAPTAIN COMPANY A

CHAPTER 1

A General View of Mosby's Men

My friend and comrade, Joseph Bryan, of Company D, now of the *Richmond Times-Dispatch*, used to say that he never indulged in war reminiscences except to auditors who had themselves had experiences, because he feared that his reputation for veracity would not stand the strain. If he, who is recognised as the very soul of truth, albeit he is vested with the liberty which is accorded to newspaper men, should feel such sensitiveness, I may well hesitate to commit myself to posterity in the following pages.

The grounds of my apprehensions are, that actions which were natural and mere matters of course under conditions which then prevailed, would be impossible now; and, viewed from the standpoint of these "piping times of peace," they seem fantastic and incredible. It is hard to get the right perspective on them, and make due allowance for difference in times and circumstances. The great poet advised—

If you would view fair Melrose right,
Go view it by the pale moon's light."

And so, there is a certain light—sentimental, artificial, if you choose—with which either narrator or hearer must invest these scenes of long ago if one would see the deeds and the actors just as they were. To those of us whose experiences cover that period memory brings back "*the tender grace of the days that are dead.*" We must trust those of the rising generation to imagine that atmosphere of romance and chivalry which then pervaded the land, and in which only were possible the deeds which I shall attempt to recount.

The part which Mosby and his men played in the great war between the States was interesting, striking, and in many respects picturesque. Of the brilliancy and value of their achievements I leave the historian to speak; and he will find abundance of material for his work stored up for him by their enemies in the *Records of the Rebellion*. I shall attempt to present to you merely some pictures of the partisans in every-day life; showing how they lived and their relation to the people among whom they lived, the things they did and how they did them; so that you may judge what manner of men these were who have gained for themselves a peculiar place in history and song and story.

Of course my first object is to entertain you, and I have culled from quite a mass of material just those things which I think will please you most. At the same time, I hope to present the facts so as to lead you to true conceptions of my old companions in arms, and to vindicate them from the unjust charges under which they have rested in some quarters, of being a band of ruffians and desperadoes. I confess that I had some such opinion of them myself, and when I left my home in the Shenandoah Valley in the spring of 1864 it was with the purpose of enlisting in the Black Horse Cavalry, among whom I had many friends. But as I passed through Mosby's Confederacy I tarried among these bold spirits, and "the hearts that they bore and the tales that they told" won me to their side. Of all the years that have come to me, the one which I rode with them brought to me the most of which I am proud.

Rough riders they were, as indeed they had need to be. For three or four hundred men to preserve their organisation for years in an open country within fifty miles of their enemy's great capital, and escape capture by the armies which surrounded them and constantly traversed their territory; for them to dispose themselves so as to be at any given time, to all intents and purposes, at every point on a circle about them, and keep forty thousand of their enemies back from the front actively and anxiously engaged in watching them: all this required pretty lively equestrian exercise. The most active among them had several horses apiece, and their only respite from the saddle for days and days would be at the bivouac and short halts on the march. Fifty miles a day was no unusual ride; and I have known them to make infinitely better time than that, for short distances—under the pressure of circumstances.

The same party that prowled with Underwood among the Federal camps in Fairfax one night, would be galloping with Russell among Sheridan's wagon trains in the Valley before the rising of the second sun. The scout that crouched in the spray of the Great Falls and assured himself that "all's quiet along the Potomac tonight," tomorrow would dream of home and loved ones on a grassy bank while the Shenandoah lulled him with her murmurings to her kindred stars.

Desperate fighters some of them were; but this, too, was largely of necessity. Real hard fighting was often the only alternative to disaster.

> *Some there were "who loved the bounding*
> *Of barbed steeds that bore them to the fray";*
> *The grim, tense hush, the war cry sounding,*
> *The headlong charge, the dark mêlée;*

... but I believe that none of them pursued fighting as a healthful recreation. While waiting in position for a fight, I have known the best of them to sicken and tremble with nervousness, caused not so much I think by fears for themselves as anxiety about the work that was before them. "Killing men is a painful business," and to sit quietly in cold blood and contemplate it is a fearsome thing. But at the first shot fired one could see the whole line brace itself, and with the wild hurrah that sounded a charge the thin veneering over men's native savagery would crack and burst. There is no thrill like that which strains the soul in the onward rush of battle; no ecstasy on earth like that with which one sees the foe shiver, break, and run. Of course men lost their company manners in the crush and tug of a hand-to-hand fight, and human life was cheap. I believe Ben Palmer was the only man of whom I ever heard who could preserve the amenities to the point of killing a foe with apologies for his rudeness, and going through a captive in the graceful form of a request for "whatever surplus Federal funds he might have about his person."

In the delirium bred by the pistol crack and the smell of powder smoke and the sight of blood, I've seen the gentlest men do desperate deeds—things of which they were incapable in their civilized condition. Let brave men judge each other about these matters.

I believe, too, that Mosby's men often affected dare-deviltry, for the same reason that some folks nowadays assume honesty—it was the best policy. We banked heavily on the maxim that *"the boldest front oftenest wins the fight,"* and all of our tactics were pervaded by a distinct calculation of the awful odds there are usually in favour of the fellow who is hunting for a fight. The presumption is that he is fixed for it. So, when one was to come off we always sought the initiative, not only because that gave us the choice of time and position, but for the stronger reason, as dear old Harry Hatcher used to put it, "Boys, everything depends upon getting the bulge on 'em." We acted under

David Harum's version of the Golden Rule, "*Do unto the other fellow as he would do unto you—and do it first.*"

If a charge was to be made we did not go into it in serried ranks and with orderly approach as if to impress the enemy with our awful dignity; but each man realised that the shorter the time from the start to the finish the less the danger was, and would clap spurs to his horse, often throw the bridle rein on its neck, and with pistol in each hand bend every energy to getting there, and making himself as numerous and influential as possible on the way. Of course nothing ever resisted such onsets—not even infantry behind a fence, as at Rectortown, nor dismounted cavalry in a blockhouse, as at Warrenton Junction. An infantryman captured in such a charge was asked what made them break. "Why," he said, "you fellows came so quick we hadn't time to think, and besides, if we had shot the men off, the crazy horses would have run over us."

The story went that Colonel Mosby called Lieutenant Hatcher to book for making that charge, but the brave, bluff fellow's defence was, "Well, Colonel, you told me to make a demonstration to get them from behind that fence, and if that didn't mean charge 'em, I don't know what it did mean." You see, such operations were against all tactics, and the very insanity of the thing—apparent or real, I've never determined which—insured its success; and I think this was true of many things that the Rangers did.

Major Forbes complained bitterly of our "irregular" treatment of his crack California battalion. He had formed his well-appointed thoroughly disciplined veterans in magnificent battle array on a hill in an open field and awaited our attack with all the confidence of the proficient commander of an invincible machine. *His* program was that we should charge him in front up the hill in solid column and receive the volleys from his drilled platoons, a procedure the exigencies demanded and the books authorized. But we were not out illustrating Hardee's tactics that afternoon, and our helter-skelter race for his front put our killers into his ranks and we got down to smashing his beautiful machine before it was in working order. The major insisted with tears in his eyes, that this was "unprofessional." Well, maybe it was.

The truth is, we were an undisciplined lot. During the twelve months of my service I learned but four commands—fall in and count-off by fours, march, close up, and charge. There was another movement with which we were not altogether unfamiliar, an order technically known as the "skedaddle," but I never heard the command given. The Rangers seemed to know instinctively when that movement was appropriate, and never waited for the word; and I want to tell you that this is a highly strategic movement which I have never known to be appreciatively discussed by any military critic. You see when the Yankees broke they would always run in a bunch, and all we had to do was to follow and pick them up. For instance, out of the California battalion of three hundred which we broke up at Mount Zion, only five or six escaped. When we routed Blazer's hundred and fifty at Myerston only two, according to the War Records, ever reported for duty. But when we found it necessary to leave the scene of action, each man worked out his own salvation and "struck for home and fireside" by his own particular path. We dissolved like the mist "before their wery eyes wisibly" and left them nothing to follow.

Perhaps the successful execution of these movements, or any execution save utter demoralisation, was possible only with men of our peculiar training. When not under the immediate command of the officers, each man was his own commander, commissary, quartermaster and everything else. He was dependent upon his own resources for supplies and his own wits for safety. In the enemy's country, too, such a life made him watchful, alert, and self-reliant. It developed in the men a strong individuality which made them feel personally responsible for results, and made them more than mere automata to be manoeuvred by commands of officers. They seldom lost their heads, and when thrown upon their own resources were usually equal to the emergency.

These same conditions also demanded that the men should be expert in the use of their weapons. Uncle Sam's ordnance department supplied them abundantly with ammunition and much of it was consumed in target practice. This deadly aptness with the revolver not only reacted on our men and gave them nerve and self-confidence, but it increased their efficiency and formidability to a degree that one can scarcely appreciate until he stops to think about it. It is one thing to shoot for the purpose of making smoke and noise, to shoot at random, or automatically in volleys; it is an awfully different thing to shoot to kill. Believe me, a calm, cool "dead-shot" behind a Colt's revolver or a Spencer repeating rifle has more moral force than a Gatling gun. The average soldier has an unconquerable prejudice against a pistol which he knows is going to hit somebody when it goes off, and he just will not go to meet it. You must reckon with this characteristic when you undertake to account for some of the exploits of Mosby's men, for it was an important one.

It will explain the extraordinarily large number of the enemy killed and wounded as compared with the number of prisoners taken (a fact which has been urged as proof of our brutality), and it will enable you to understand how small squads of Rangers over and over again discomfited, or at least stood off, large bodies of men, even regiments. A half dozen such "dead-shots" across a narrow defile, especially if their number were not positively discovered, could hold up a road full of Federals almost indefinitely. Allow, too, for the Federal soldier's mortal dread of decoys and ambuscades, of which he often had bitter experience, and you will appreciate the following story of how one lone ranger held up a whole regiment on an open turnpike, in broad daylight; how he caused them to advance upon him in regular line of battle with skirmishers deployed, and finally rode away from them, more or less at his ease.

This young fellow was convalescing from a wound, and had so far recovered that one spring morning his "*fancy lightly turned to thoughts of love*" and he rode down the turnpike from Middleburg to Dover to call on some ladies. Our command had gone down the same road the day before on a raid into Fairfax, and he had reason to believe that he was the only military body in the neighbourhood. So, when he raised on a swell in the road to a plateau about two hundred yards long and saw a file of horsemen ride on to it at the other end, there was a moment of mutual surprise. His first thought was that it was the vanguard of our own command returning; but he instinctively halted and drew his revolver. When the four horsemen dashed toward him, yelling and shooting, and others came rushing into sight, he took in the situation. He knew that a long, hard chase was before him. But as he turned his horse for the start he concluded he would offer a suggestion to his pursuers not to crowd him too unceremoniously. He lingered a moment until they came within pistol range, and fired.

One of them fell to the ground, and the other three, recognising the force of his argument and yielding to that prejudice which I have mentioned, promptly jerked up their horses. As the ranger galloped down the hill again and for a moment disappeared from the sight of the enemy, he recollected that his horse had cast a shoe and realised that a race on the metallic road was almost hopeless of escape. He determined to take the chances of turning into a lane which opened ahead of him, but rode for a distance of several hundred yards at an acute angle with the pike, which brought him in some degree nearer toward the enemy. As he sped across this space, sure enough, he got a broadside from a squad of *carbineers* who had gathered on the plateau, but safely reached the turn in the road and a hollow alongside of some woods. With a sense of safety came the determination not to leave until he ascertained something more about the number and character of the raiders. Thereupon, he rode on a hill in an adjoining field and saw the road filling with Yankees. His reappearance elicited the attention of the long-range gunners, and, with a shout and a wave of his hand, he retired to another convenient body of woods.

All these movements, perfectly guiltless of such design, evidently convinced the Federals that he was a decoy and that the woods were full of Mosby's men. In a short while he had the distinction of being approached by a full regiment of Federal cavalry in magnificent battle line, with banners flying, and preceded by a line of skirmishers. But this was more honour than he was looking for that morning, and, under cover of the woods, he retired to surroundings more in accord with his modesty. But it has been one of the regrets of his life, he assures me, that he could not remain near enough to hear the remarks of his friends, the enemy, when they reached the woods and found no more serious engagement awaiting them than to frighten the birds from the bushes.

But it is time that I give you some sort of a personal introduction to the men in whose company you are asked to spend a while. They were, for the most part, young men in the very flush and prime of youth. Many of them were beardless boys, whose looks were far more suggestive of the nursery than of the war-path, and I fear that not all of them were model Sunday-school boys, either. Most of them had run away from their homes to join Mosby, and I recollect that the thing which pleased them most was their chieftain's commendation of them when asked what in the world he did with such children.

"Why," he replied, "they are the best soldiers I have. They haven't sense enough to know danger when they see it, and will fight anything I tell them to."

But these boys were, in a very material sense, veterans before they joined the command. Reared upon the border, they had passed the most impressionable time of life amid the scenes which attended the flooding and ebbing of the tide of war about their homes. They had become familiar with war in its darkest phases, and acquainted with the enemy in his strongest and weakest points. Armies had marched and countermarched about them; battles had been fought around them;

their homes had been pillaged and burnt before their eyes; scouts and spies and deserters were their familiars; they had become experts in running pickets, and securing and conveying secret information. In short, they had learned a whole lot of things which are not down in the standard books on the culture of youth, but which admirably fitted them for partisan warfare. Not a few of them had already made tests of their qualifications, and presented themselves for enlistment already mounted and equipped with the fruits of their experiments. I recall that my own charger—a spanking fine one—was a more or less voluntary contribution from Uncle Sam. I had the distinguished honour of riding him through the streets of Warrenton with General Torbert and his staff about dusk one evening. By sunrise the next morning we were in Mosby's Confederacy.

A large number of our command were veterans from the Regular Army who had either served out the term of their enlistment or had become disabled for that service, and many of them had already distinguished themselves in that field. Most of our earliest officers were men from the army who, upon some occasion of service with him, had attracted Colonel Mosby's attention by their bearing, and he had secured their transfer to him by promoting them to officers. On the other hand, many of our privates had been officers in the army; high-spirited fellows who chafed under the monotony of army life and were attracted by stories of our adventures to resign their commissions and join our ranks. And so it happened that captains were about as plentiful in our command as colonels are now in civil life. I recall two captains, Kennon and Dee Shane, from the celebrated Louisiana Tigers, who joined us as privates upon the extinction of that regiment. One can hardly estimate the benefits which the discipline and experience of this class of men brought to our band of amateur soldiers.

Then, too, we had some grim old sires who had neared or passed their third score year, and whom the merciless laws of war relegated to their homes. But the ruthless hands of those who knew no laws had made their homes only dark spots of desolation, or had put upon them some deep affront that set on fire even the sluggish blood of age. These were men who had some grievous wrongs to avenge, and their implacable and unwavering hate furnished a kind of conservatism to the younger and, perhaps, more erratic spirits.

Altogether, it was peculiarly adapted material which Providence sent to our brilliant young leader; and his wonderful genius manifested itself as much in understanding and handling his men as in recognising and rising to the opportunities which came to him. He knew each man personally, and seemed to read him at a glance and ascertain exactly what sort of fellow he was and exactly what use to make of him. He mingled with his men, rode with them, slept with them and fought side by side with them. Few members of the command had a longer list of wounds and captures than himself, and fewer still perhaps were responsible for more personal execution. His care against needlessly exposing them; his great skill in securing them every possible advantage; his cool, quiet courage and the almost unvarying success of every enterprise which he personally conducted secured the perfect confidence of his men. His ready sympathy with them, which in hours of relaxation or in times of suffering revealed his big and tender heart, inspired them with an affection for him which has survived the vicissitudes of the years and is no less strong now because mellowed by the rays of life's setting sun.

It has been flippantly said, "The command was held together by the cohesive power of spoils." The truth is that it was gathered, held together and shaped for its destiny by the personality of its leader. Those whom he failed to impress, and in this sense magnetise,—in other words, those who failed to respond to his personal influence,— he simply sent back to the regular service. Between his command proper and himself there was a perfect rapport, and they delighted in working together. I think the most potent inspiration to honest service and gallant action was the knowledge that each man's standing was accurately known by our commander, and the ambition to hold his esteem amounted to a passionate devotion.

One of his veterans holds no prouder memory than that of having been spoken of by Mosby as "one of my best men." At the same time he was absolutely imperious, and no one cared to provoke the second time his trenchant disapproval. It is claimed that he had officers who were nearly, if not quite, equal to himself, and to whom the honour of many of his achievements belongs. If it be true, there is not one of them who will not proudly claim that his gracious chieftain discovered and developed him. The truth is that Mosby conceived a plan of warfare, sought and found a favourable theatre, attracted and made the most of suitable men, and with them worked out his conception to glorious results.

We differed from the Arabs in that we had no tents to fold when we "*silently stole away,*" and no place to put them if we had them. The establishment of a camp would have been immediately reported to

F. H. Rahm
Forty-Third Battalion Virginia Cavalry

our enemies; and to have kept the command together at one place for twenty-four hours would have been tempting annihilation. When on raids the skies or spreading trees were our canopies and the green heath, or a rock pile, or even a snow' bank our acceptable couches. When it rained we usually let it rain, and spent no anxiety except to keep our powder dry, likewise our tobacco.

When off raids we boarded about at farmhouses, two or three of us, and sometimes half a dozen at one place. Our homes were known to Colonel Mosby, and generally to each other. When a meet was desired, one which had not already been appointed at the last disbanding, word of the time and place would be sent to one house and the men who were there would bear it to others, from whom it would pass on with promptness and certainty. In this way a hundred men could easily be rendezvoused in a few hours; or certain numbers gathered at different points at the same time for simultaneous sorties; and in a comparatively short time the whole command could be massed at a given point. This gave a mystery and weirdness to our operations which were not without effect on the enemy. And this is how it happened that after one of his successful "skedaddles" Mosby was recorded in the War Records as driven from the country one day, and the next day reported as "dealing damnation around the land" in a half dozen different places.

That was a pleasant fiction, that story about our being "featherbed soldiers." The men slept in old huts or shacks hidden away in the woods or in rock breaks and fence corners. The greatest hardship of the service that I can recall was spending a cold winter evening in the cheer of a glowing fire and brighter eyes and at bedtime riding a mile or more away to chilling couches on the lee side of a big rock, or at best snuggled up under a straw rick. A fire would have been a beacon to guide a band of raiders to our side. Those who let their luxurious tastes get the better of their discretion usually rolled out of their downy beds on to bunks in a Yankee prison. Indeed, the most righteous in this regard were often scarcely saved. I have even yet a vivid sense of an exhilarating "eye opener" to which I was treated one morning on arising from my dewy couch beside a stone fence, when I discovered that a column of Federals had marched along the other side during the night.

As to the commissary. We would start on a raid with a few sandwiches in our haversacks, a supply which usually lasted over the first night out. After that we were dependent upon the generosity of the people along our line of march, and adopted a method which, from the character of the rations most frequently secured, was technically known as "pie-rooting." But the results of this were very precarious, and confined to those who were most energetic and pushing. The majority of us had to tighten up our pistol belts and turn for comfort to the inevitable pipe. And oh, that pipe!

> *How oft do I sit in the light of my firewood*
> *And call back those scenes from the long vanished years,*
> *While I breathe through my Powhatan, Meerschaum or Briarwood*
> *The breath of the weed that soothes while it cheers!*
>
> *But, ah me, in spite of my utmost endeavour*
> *With Pride of Virginia, Lone Jack or Bob White,*
> *I can never call back the dear lost flavour*
> *Of the pipe that I smoked on the march in the night:*
> *The old wooden pipe, the battered burnt pipe,*
> *The pipe that I smoked on the march in the night.*
>
> *I may dream in the clouds of a fragrant Havana*
> *When roses and dew drops smile back at the moon,*
> *And the breezes that float up from vale and savannah*
> *Are laden with perfume of hay newly mown.*
> *But in vain do I long for that subtle aroma*
> *That pulsed through my senses in throbs of delight—*
> *The pungent, pervading, ineffable scent, from a*
> *Pipe that was smoked on the march in the night:*
> *An old wooden pipe, a cracked clay pipe,*
> *Any old pipe on the march in the night.*

But at our homes we fared verily on the riches of the land. The loyal, generous people of Fauquier and Loudoun opened their hearts as well as their homes to us. A genuine affection inspired the many little offices which softened the roughness of a soldier's life, and it was with an actual sense of defending home and loved ones that more than one Ranger laid down his life on the threshold of his host. When we started on raids farewells were spoken with moistened eyes and in broken words, and the soldier knew that if he were brought back on a bloody bier there would be gentle hands to lay him to his rest, and some quivering lip to "kiss him for his mother."

This constant recurrence to the amenities of social life kept the soldier to his best, and always under the inspiration of *noblesse oblige*. The influences of home life were about him. His standing and deportment as a soldier were public property, and his sensitiveness to what those among whom he lived thought of him did more to urge him to gallant deeds than did even the *esprit de corps*, which indeed was very high. None understood this better than Colonel Mosby, and he took care that each man's excellences should be duly reported where they would do the most good. The women of Mosby's Confederacy were the divinities to whom the Rangers were always true; and the chorus to their favourite battle song was,

At home bright eyes are sparkling for us,
We will defend them to the last.

And right here I wish to put on record a fact which I have frequently stated in public, and it has never been gainsaid. It speaks volumes and volumes for Mosby's men. Notwithstanding their admission to the very inner circle of their entertainers' homes; notwithstanding the relaxation of rigid forms which necessarily obtained, and the consequent freedom of social intercourse; although many of them were far from their homes and the influences which usually restrained men—never have I heard of a single instance of the betrayal by one of them of a too-confiding woman's trust.

But I must continue to use the plural when I speak of each man's "divinities." If it is not good grammar, it is true—like Ben Jonson's poetry that didn't rhyme. The fact is that the boys were guilty of considerable laxity (or perhaps I should say liberality) in the matter of sweethearts. Their devotion to the sex was too ardent and profound to be exhausted by a single object, and they could not be absolutely loyal to Katie Wells and Gentle Annie both. The most that I can claim for a real Mosby man is that he could be perfectly "happy with either dear charmer, with t'other dear charmer away"—and this seemed to satisfy each in her turn.

Indeed, they were just as much sinned against as sinning in this regard. The dear girls took their liberties too. For instance: After the Greenback raid, the boys were pretty flush. Among other means which two of them took to get the good of their money before they died, they sent across the Potomac for engagement rings for their best girls. Now it happened that they sent by the same blockade-runner and he brought back two handsome bands which were exact "twinses." In due course and with all proper ceremony they were set as seals to the pure and endless love which they were intended to symbolize. The swains soon made an unexpected call together upon a certain lady, and you can imagine the satisfaction with which they discovered both rings on the same finger. Some embarrassment arose in the adjustment of relations, but as neither fellow could identify his property, the girl remained mistress of the situation and of the rings.

One *belle* of the Confederacy, a girl "of a provident mind," thought to hedge against the casualties of war by placing her bets, so to speak, judiciously around—some in Mosby's command, and some in different branches of the regular service. She played to great luck, and, after the surrender claimants for her heart and hand turned up from various directions. I happened to be at one of her levees (as a spectator) and could not but admire the skill with which she met the embarrassing situation and made each one happy in the assurance that he was the favourite. However, one of those accidents which will happen, betrayed the truth. Whereupon her victims held a caucus and unanimously passed a resolution that she was too smart for domestic purposes. I recall another pair of *belles* who were twins, and as much alike as the two rings which I mentioned. They studied uniformity in dress and manners and played many pranks on the boys. Like those babes in *Pinafore*, they would get mixed up in a way that was utterly bewildering, and I have seriously doubted sometimes if they knew themselves apart.

It was no uncommon thing for a Ranger to make an engagement with one which would be kept by the other, no less to his satisfaction because he didn't know the difference. And I have heard of their swapping escorts back and forth so often on a certain occasion that they themselves lost the run of the identities. One dashing young fellow of Company D fell in love with them. He didn't intend to love but one—but it amounted to the same thing as loving two. Finally he paid his addresses, and they were accepted, more or less. At his next call he was received by the sister, whichever one that was; and when he essayed to take matters up where he had left off—well, he met with some discouragement. But when the other one was called in and denied "the soft impeachment" the situation became serious. So he determined to transfer his affections to another object, possibly less attractive but more easy of identification.

And now we turn to sterner scenes.

CHAPTER 2

Securing a Mount

During the summer of 1863 the Federal troops occupied Warrenton, Va. The camps of the Sixth Corps dotted the hills about the town, and General Sedgwick had his headquarters in what was then the John Smith house at the western end of Winchester street.

Just north of the town and scarcely beyond the camps was a long, narrow meadow. On one side a thin strip of woods separated it from the Centerville turnpike; on the other side a high hill hid it from the town and the neighbouring camps, and at the lower end it was skirted by a large body of pines. Down the middle of it ran a bold stream of water on its way to Cedar Run, a mile away.

On the Cedar Run bottoms the pasturage was rich and in those times free to such of the town cows as had not been "confiscated." We were so fortunate as to have one at our house, and it seemed that my mission in life just then was to look after her. There were four or five other lads who were dedicated to the same high calling. I recollect Frank and Lytt Helm, Will Saunders and Frank Jennings as being in the party. And we surely did have grand times herding cows on Cedar Run that summer. We practiced soldiering, camping, raiding, running pickets, surprising camps, and such amusements as imaginative boys, imbued with the spirit of war and turned loose to themselves, would naturally run into. What we couldn't do we dreamed of, and vied with each other in concocting wild adventures and describing the things that we might do.

The bubbles we blew under the old elms on the grassy bank may not have stood the tests of high art, but they were immensely fascinating. I wonder if they all did dissolve into air, *"and left no wreck behind"*? I sometimes fancy that Mosby afterward reaped some fruits from the spirit and education which we helped each other acquire those summer days. For every one of us, I believe, subsequently joined his command.

One beautiful afternoon I started from town to join my friends down on the creek. When I reached the meadow I saw a number of soldiers at the brook bathing themselves and washing out their clothes. Their horses had been turned loose, without saddle and bridles, to luxuriate on the rich herbage while the owners sought the next thing to godliness.

I stepped in the woods by the roadside and watched the scene. There were things about the bathers and their doings to interest a boy; but what most impressed me was their absorption in themselves. The horses seemed to have drifted out of their attention altogether, and one of them, especially, became the object of my intense interest. He had wandered some distance below his fellows, and I noticed that he was a spanking fine one. How the curved lines of beauty in him were brought out against the green! How his dark brown coat glistened in the sunlight! My heart went out after that horse with a yearning; he stirred in me all that spirit of adventure which I had been cultivating at the cow-camp. He certainly was worth some risk—indeed, that element in the case appealed to me irresistibly, as I thought of what the boys would say if I should succeed in "acquiring" him.

The ethics of the matter did not bother me in the least. Indeed, I do not recollect that they rose out of my sub-consciousness. Doubtless the question was fought out there, and it was downed in its incipiency by the knowledge of how many things the Yankees had taken from me and my people. Besides, if I were not then a combatant in actual service, I would become one as soon as I connected myself with that horse; and I was anticipating my rights very slightly.

He was near enough for me to see that he had on a halter, the strap of which was tied around one of his fore ankles, so as to keep him from running. I moved through the woods until I came within perhaps a hundred yards from him. I then fell upon my hands and knees, and even a little lower sometimes, into the high grass, and wormed my way to him. A few soothing words kept him quiet while I untied the halter strap from his foot. In the same posture as before, I slowly led him to the brook. While he stood beside the bank and drank, I jumped upon his back, and with a few bounds we were within the shades of the pine woods beyond.

I do not think that any of the soldiers saw us. As I glanced over my shoulder toward them, I observed nothing to indicate that they were interested in us at all. They doubtless assumed that it was just someone who was crossing the meadow. What they thought when they came to round up their stock and found the brown gelding missing, was another story, a story which some of them may tell.

I hitched him away down in the pines, near a stream of water, and kept him there for a week. Each day I stole away from the cow-camp to carry him a bundle of grass and give him water, and cultivate him. I spent hours in rubbing and petting him; and you may believe that we became fast friends. In the solitude of those pines an attachment was formed which was, I think, a solace to both of us on many a weary night-march, and a comfort in hours of deadly peril.

But his nature demanded something more substantial than caresses; and one drink of water a day and only such grass as I could pack to him surreptitiously, scarcely met his needs. I saw that his beautiful form was pitifully shrinking, and noticed something more plaintive than regret in the wistful looks with which he would part with me. I had to get him to more satisfactory quarters. How to do it was, you must admit, a pretty serious proposition to a sixteen year old boy, under my conditions.

Well, of course I laid awake at nights over it. I thought of little else through the day. Thought and nerve and imagination were at highest tension to devise a way to save that horse.

One day I heard my aunt, Mrs. Sowers, say that she was anxious to visit Middleburg, a village some twenty miles north of Warrenton. She had an ambulance and one horse; what she lacked was another horse and a driver. She was staying at Mrs. Spilman's, near General Sedgwick's headquarters, and he had established quite friendly relations with the family. Here was my chance.

I took her into my confidence, and it was arranged that she should secure the necessary pass from General Sedgwick, and I would do the rest. Inasmuch as the weather was warm and travelling in the early morning so much more pleasant, I insisted that we should start sometime before daybreak. My real object was to pass through the pickets while it was still too dark for them to see the U. S. brand on my horse.

Our cow was not brought up that evening. Instead, I rode out on the Centerville pike about dusk on a bareback horse, with only a halter to control him. My plan was to sneak him into my aunt's stable in the twilight. As I reached the pike a squad of cavalry was halted there. My heart went down to where my boots ought to have been.

Ned Hurst
Company A

But they evidently took me for some hanger-on to a cavalry camp or an officers' mess, and paid no attention except to chaff me as I rode quietly past them.

The court-house at Warrenton stands on a high hill facing the Centerville pike, and in front of it sweeps Winchester street, the main street of the town, leading to General Sedgwick's headquarters and my aunt's house. At the foot of the hill an alley turns at an acute angle out of the pike, up a steep and rough way to Winchester street. When I reached this alley I was shocked to find a Yankee sentinel there. He promptly ordered me to halt. But I could not, as he saw for himself. My horse shied from him up the alley. I pulled hard on the halter strap and called him vociferously to stop; but he seemed to pay more attention to my off heel which was hammering his flanks, and before the sentinel and I could come to an understanding we had gotten so far from him that that "incident was closed."

But I butted into another one when I reached the top of the hill. The old residents of that period will recollect how General Torbert, with his staff, used to make dress parade through town every evening. Just as I landed into Winchester street, the gorgeous parade was passing. 'Tis true that I did not add much style to the procession, but, with the impudence of a boy, I fell in behind and nobody objected. I did myself the honour of riding with General Torbert's staff through the streets of Warrenton, as far as the gate into Conway Grove, through which I quietly dropped, and stabled my steed. He surely got a good feed that night.

We started out of town betimes the next morning, according to program, and by high noon drove into the capital of Mosby's Confederacy.

I don't know what sort of a record my horse had made under the Stars and Stripes; but he did make a dandy partisan ranger.

CHAPTER 3

My First Raid

In my initiation into partisan warfare I think I took more than one degree. At any rate, my first raid gave me several characteristic experiences. About thirty-five or forty of us met at Hooper's blacksmith shop near Middleburg one bright April morning in 1864. After our horses' feet had received necessary attention from that master of the craft and such of our men as could assist him, we moved off to a retired farm-house, where we remained until afternoon. When the sun "got tangled in the grape vines," as the darkies used to describe that time of the day when the longed-for evening seemed to tarry, we moved out on the road toward Fairfax County where the Federal camps were located.

Mosby's men on the march always made a picturesque appearance; but the effect upon my boyish mind that afternoon was simply fascinating. As we moved along the dusty highway or made a short cut across the fields; over hill, through dale; now in the broad glare of the sun, now in the delicate shade of the woods just putting on their spring verdure—I sat silent on my horse, trying to shape the thousand emotions that crowded me. Sir Walter Scott's tales of border wars had been the food of my youthful imagination, and perhaps they stirred some of the old Moss-trooper's blood which slumbered in my veins. However it came about, my imagination was keenly active. Each man was a study to me as he passed or repassed me, now moving to the front, now dropping to the rear in the go-as-you-please march, or paused to crack a joke with the new recruit.

And a motley crew they were. There rode a boy whose pink and white cheeks were guiltless of down, and beside him an aged sire whose reverend gray locks, straggling from beneath his cocked hat, made pitiful protest against the companionship in which they found themselves. Side by side rode the planter's son and the overseer's boy; the banker dressed in soft officer's gray richly trimmed with gold lace, and the poor adventurer whose suit of Union blue betrayed his dependence upon "the spoils of the chase."

One spirit of devil-may-care hilarity seemed to possess them all. The merry song, the jovial laugh rang out along the line, jest and joke followed amusing anecdote; and now and then a group would bunch together to listen to some old veteran's tales of the regular service or of prison life. This was one of Jim Sinclair's specialties, and the colonel would often summon him to the front and call for some favourite yarns.

This levity struck me at first as being singularly out of place. Here rode these men on the most serious business that could engage human enterprise. But a few short hours, at most, were between them and the terrible charge, the deadly encounter and, for aught that any knew, death. Yet they rode on to it

Like some gudelie companie
To a midnight revelrie.

My young spirit soon caught the contagion, and I laughed with the loudest and jested with the merriest. Surely, soldiering with Mosby must be the jolliest life in the world!

As the shades of night fell "a change came over the spirit" of the entertainment. The jests were still bandied, but they seemed to be put with more delicacy; the tale was still told to eager listeners, but it was more fitted for a lady's bower. The songs that had rolled forth in quaint melody from knots here and there, or some solitary singer down the line, were hushed; and from the choir which had assembled at the head of the column there came floating back upon the night plaintive music inspired by thoughts of home. Soon all other sounds had ceased and every ear was set to catch the strains. I saw more than one tear glisten in the moonlight as the voices of those who awaited our coming home seemed to echo the words of the song, now sung with a pathos I never heard elsewhere, "*We shall meet but we shall miss him.*"

The song ceased, and a great sigh of relief seemed to go up from the body of moving men. Then a merry tune was struck, the chorus caught up along the line, and we were the same light-hearted fellows as before.

I recollect that we had just emerged from the shadows of a forest and entered an old field when the sounds in front hushed and the word came down the line,

"Silence! Pass it back."

My heart jumped into my throat. This began to look like business. Instinctively my hand sought my gun. A grim old ex-Louisiana Tiger, who rode by my side, saw the movement and said, "Pshaw! we're just getting in hearing of 'em. Don't be scared."

I felt that I had betrayed my greenness, and was properly subdued. Nothing was now heard but the tread of the horses on the hard crisp turf—suggesting to my mind "muffled drums and funeral marches," and there came solemn thoughts, and my martial enthusiasm died away.

Directly my attention was attracted by some sounds on my flank, and I looked to see several dusky forms galloping toward us over a hill.

"There they are!" I cried excitedly, and in a twinkle my revolver was out and cocked. Nick Skeldon's hand was on my arm with no gentle pressure, as he growled,

"Don't be such a tarnal fool. They are our scouts. What the devil did you leave your mammy for?"

The question was a pertinent one, that's a fact, and one that my own heart echoed with considerable unction.

The newcomers pushed to the front and made their communications to the colonel. At once our line of march was changed and we struck, at single file, down through the thickest, darkest, loneliest pine forest in all that dreary country. This move was not very reassuring to me. Every dark tale of ambuscade that I had ever heard recurred to me with a force which nothing but my surroundings could have given it. Nor did the weird wail of a whippoorwill, that every now and then came moaning up out of the pines, tend to soothe my nerves. But when the dismal hoot of an owl suddenly boomed out on the night, I well-nigh jumped from my saddle. At first I could not define the impression it made upon me. Ere long it was heard again, and just in front of us, as before. This time my fancy identified it, and I recognised in the hoarse "Whoo hoo" the signal of a Yankee vidette warning his fellows of our approach. And again and yet again, at seeming regular intervals and just in advance of us, the ominous croak was heard; and each time I felt more and more assured that the next interruption to the gloomy silence would be a volley from the bushes; and each time Nick's question repeated itself to me with increased force.

At length we reached a broom sedge meadow in which we dismounted and disposed ourselves to rest, letting the horses graze, *with* halters tied to our arms or legs, while the colonel went off with Bush Underwood to reconnoitre. He never took chances in matters of which he could make sure and, whenever practicable, personally verified the reports of his best scouts. Along toward morning he returned and roused us. A detail was left in charge of our horses, canteens, spurs, and everything that would jingle and make a noise, while the rest of us moved off in single file into the woods.

I shall never forget that grim and stealthy march. Creeping along through the deepest hollows and darkest shades; never a sound save the smothered tread of the men or the scream of a bird scared from its roost or the rustling through the bushes of some varmint aroused from its lair; moving awhile in one direction and then in another to avoid the videttes whom the colonel had located—we kept on slowly but surely approaching our prey. Stalking one's fellow-kind is a grisly sort of business.

The silent and monotonous movement had beguiled me into a half-dreaming state, when suddenly I was aroused by the coughing of a horse and looked to see a dark mass looming up in the centre of a small clearing that we had just reached. Fortunately, the horse's cough was a stubborn one, kept up for several minutes, and drowned the sound of our foot-falls as we circled half around the glade, still keeping the cover of the woods. Then it ceased and all was silent as the grave. I distinguished several horses out of the dark pile in front of us, and then took in the situation.

This was a Yankee picket post. Just then one of the men trod on a stick and it cracked beneath his foot. A quick voice called, "Who comes there?" and almost simultaneously with the challenge the sentinel fired his piece.

"Charge 'em, men!" the colonel cried. And there were shots and yells and running men and snorting horses and the odour of much brimstone, of one kind or another, and—well, that's pretty much all that I know about the fight. Out of a hazy uncertainty whether I was on my head or my heels, there comes to me the recollections that I started into the charge with the others; that I struck the limb of a tree and knocked my hat off; that I even stopped to pick it up (think of it!) and that as I started on a few straggling shots were winding up the affair. And then I realised what a record I had made. I thought it would never do in the world to say that I had passed through my first fight without firing a shot, so, directing my pistol to where I thought the enemy ought to be, I fired the last shot of the occasion.

The surprise had been so complete that there was no opportunity for resistance. Our men were in among the prostrate forms of the Yankees before they were fairly awake, and they assisted some of them to unwind from their blankets. None of them escaped except the sentinel, who must have dashed away into the darkness before his gun had fairly exploded. We supposed that there had been no casualties upon our side, until Welt Hatcher reported that he had come through the fight all right, because there wasn't any, but while he was standing on the bank after the thing was over "some d——d greenhorn behind him had let off his gun and shot him on the heel." I did not say a word.

We knew that if we lingered on the scene the man who had escaped would order something hotter than coffee for our breakfast. Therefore, hustling together the prisoners and their horses we hurried back to our own steeds and soon struck out for Loudoun without standing on the order of our going. When we reached the Little River turnpike about twelve miles below Aldie without any signs of pursuit we felt practically safe. Colonel Mosby now left us to seek at some friend's house a cup of "blockade coffee," and the nervous strain on the men being relaxed, we sauntered on up the road indulging in felicitations on our success. We had taken nearly a prisoner apiece, each with the most approved arms, and also a splendid lot of horses. Some of the boys had already effected trades for the latter, in which the proverbially sharp Yankee had hardly come out even.

For instance, Sam Alexander, a burly young Ranger carrying upward of two hundred pounds of weight to five and a half feet of length, had created much merriment on the march the day before by his impersonation of Sancho Panza on a diminutive mule. Today he had discovered that the captive sergeant "fairly doted on mules" and had generously exchanged his mule for the sergeant's handsome sorrel. Lieutenant Hunter was gratifying his next strongest passion to fighting by prancing along the highway upon a superb dappled gray for which he had negotiated his raid-worn hack. Alas, how soon was he to verify the Scripture about pride and a fall.

Nor were the barters confined to horses. My friend, Welt Hatcher, found a ready means of repairing the hole in his boot made by my ill-timed bullet, in a swap with a prisoner. And if he suspected me of being the author of his casualty, I am sure that I detected no malice in the beaming smile with which he called my attention to his new patent leather tops. In like manner, hats and even pants and coats changed owners, and if the material advantages were decidedly with the Rangers, I believe the prisoners scarcely regretted it, because of the excellent good humour with which their business successes inspired the captors. A striking illustration of the advantages of free trade!

It was a pity that the pleasant commerce should have been rudely interrupted, and a "change of the balance of trade" threatened, by a body of Yankee cavalry putting in an appearance in the pursuit of us. One of our men, who had stopped at a farmhouse for breakfast, was seen coming up the road at full speed, waving his hat and gesticulating. Lieutenant Hunter, ever alert, quickly straightened the boys out, hurried the prisoners and led-horses off up the road in charge of a detail, and made his disposition of the rest of us in anticipation of the news which our comrade was bringing. He reported the road full of Yankees close behind him. Indeed, the head of their column immediately hove in sight, about half a mile away. Now the proposition was, to hold them in check until those prisoners and horses could be gotten safely into the Bull Run Mountains, for Mosby's men were as energetic in securing their captures as they were enterprising in making them.

The country along there is broken—intersected by streams which are bridged only on the pike, accentuated by bold hills and interspersed with woods. After crossing Cub Run bridge the road climbs a hill for three or four hundred yards, and it was then skirted by woods nearly halfway down. Some half dozen of our men, of whom the writer was one, were found to have carbines and they were placed in charge of Lieutenant Hatcher in the woods next to the bridge. As the advance files of the Federals rode on to the bridge these *carbineers* galloped out into the road and opened on them. At the same time Hunter appeared on the hill-top in our rear, filling the road with his men as if preparing for a charge. This sudden appearance of opposition brought the Yankees to a quick halt, and some empty saddles at the bridge admonished them to get out of the range of those carbines.

While they were forming into line and deploying skirmishers we moved back to the hill-top, and taking station across the road just below the brow, we interested them while Hunter moved his men back to another position a mile or more up the road. When we *carbineers* retired on our main body it was not altogether a race. Every now and then one of us would wheel, and the angry spit of his carbine warned the pursuers not to straggle into a chase. This kept them in a solid body, which could move only as fast as their slowest horses. When one of them, better mounted than his fellows, ventured to let out his horse, one or the other of them soon caught a hot bullet.

We came up with Hunter's men mustering about the edge of a piece of woods; and his movements, not understood by them, and his number still being undiscovered, again gave the enemy pause. When they had formed their line and deployed their skirmishers for another advance on him, he once more retired under the cover of the pit-pat of our carbines. And so the thing kept up, with variations, until we reached Aldie. By this time we were satisfied that our detail with the prisoners was far away and our hard-earned assets safely banked in the mountain fastnesses, and we determined to give our pursuers a cordial farewell.

At Aldie the turnpike makes a sharp turn around a spur of the mountain and at once crosses Little River over one of those narrow stone bridges. The enemy would have to cross it four abreast. In a meadow just west of the stream Hunter formed his two dozen men; and as the vanguard of the Yankees bolted around the mountain and across the bridge, he charged them. They recoiled for a moment, but, being well closed up, their numbers simply crowded us out of that gorge in the mountain. Lieutenant Hunter's Yankee horse had fallen and thrown him; Lieutenant Nelson had been shot down in a desperate effort to remount him; Hatcher had been borne off from the front by the pressure of the crowd, and the boys, recognising the propriety of the "skedaddle" movement, melted away like the morning mist.

The Yankees, too, seemed to have had enough exercise of that kind for one morning, and marched back to Fairfax with their lone prisoner. Lieutenant Hunter. The loss of him and the wounding of Nelson made a considerable price we paid for our twenty odd prisoners, though they did have such fine horses.

When I met Colonel Mosby the next day he seemed inclined to find fault with us for "running from those Yankees." Possibly he would have managed things differently if he had been there; but, for my own part, I have always felt that I never left anything to be desired in the way of adventure as long as I stayed with Harry Hatcher.

The pursuing party was commanded by Major Alexander G. Davis, whose home was near Aldie, but who had been driven into the Federal service by mistreatment on account of his Northern birth and proclivities. He was a perfectly fearless man, and developed quite an interest in Mosby and his men. Some months after this he and the colonel met in a hand-to-hand fight and each was wounded desperately. He was quite a gracious old fellow and has talked with me more than once about this adventure. He told me that when the news of our capture of the picket post was brought into camp he called for volunteers to go after us. In response to the call he gathered tip more than two hundred of the most reliable and best mounted men in the camp, who went out on the chase in perfect assurance of bringing us back. He said that his great difficulty was in discovering our number and on that account he could not determine how to handle us. When I told him that there were less than thirty in the party that was opposing him, he politely said, "Well, I don't understand it at all"; but I felt that my standing for veracity, with him, was undergoing a strain.

CHAPTER 4

The Guard Hill Raid

About four miles north of Front Royal the turnpike from that place to Winchester passes over a high hill, thickly wooded. From a tradition that it was the site of an old fort for the protection of the early settlers of the Valley from the Indians, it has retained the name of Guard Hill. Here, in May, 1864, the Federals had posted a heavy picket, upon whom Colonel Mosby determined to make a call.

About a hundred of us assembled at Paris, a little village at the eastern base of the Blue Ridge, and crossing the mountain through Ashby's Gap we reached the Shenandoah River about nightfall. We found it so swollen by recent rains as to be past fording; and as swimming at night was impracticable, we retired to an old field on the mountain opposite Mount Carmel Church and put up for the night.

I well remember how that old field abounded in stones. Every fellow of us could have had a Jacob's pillow for his own, and doubtless did have visions, but not of angelic hosts. I recall how the horror of snakes kept me anxious all night, though, to tell the truth, I saw and heard of none. Speaking of snakes reminds me of something that has been a mystery to me since those days. Mosby's men often slept in such places as this, where the deadly rattler has his home; sometimes on the river bottoms, where the copperhead prevails; and habitually in fence corners or rock-breaks which the *moccasin* or black constrictor may be presumed to pre-empt, and yet I never heard of a Ranger being troubled by snakes of that variety.

The next morning we returned to the river and found it higher than the night before. But Colonel Mosby, who had crossed over in a skiff during the night and gone scouting ahead of us, had arranged to have such boats as could be found gathered at the ferry for use. With the half dozen *batteaux* which had been secured the men could soon

John H. Alexander
Company A

be put over, but the horses were troublesome. The river here is nearly two hundred yards wide, and being flushed the current was pretty strong. A horse, like a Kentucky colonel, does not take kindly to water. We would start with one or two trailing after the skiffs, to act as sort of bellwethers for the others, which we would drive in after them, and with much difficulty we got most of them over in this way. But some refused to be driven in at all, while others would turn and come back as soon as they struck the strong current. These had to be taken over by their riders in a swim from bank to bank. At this time I learned a trick about swimming horses which I often had occasion to utilize on subsequent trips to the Valley. If the stirrups are crossed over the saddle the feet of the rider will be brought so high that the tops of his cavalry boots will rise above the water, though it washes the horse's back. A man stooping in his stirrups with one hand on the saddle bow to steady himself and balance his horse, and the other drawing his rein gently to steady and guide his horse, can swim indefinitely without getting a thread wet.

A necessary condition is that he keep cool, for his horse gets his nerve from his master; and the result of his getting rattled will be that the horse will lose his balance and both will get a ducking. Barring a few such casualties, we all got safely across the Shenandoah that morning. Then we rested under the grand old trees on the river bank and in Mr. McCormick's lawn, while our horses browsed in a convenient meadow. The hospitable doors of his mansion, too, were thrown open, and many of the boys renewed or established pleasant relations with his four or five attractive daughters. And during the day all of us found our way to the dining-room, where a substantial luncheon was provided by these gracious folks and their neighbours who had learned of our presence. It was wonderful how these Valley people could always find something for Mosby's men to eat, even during that dark time when Sheridan had well-nigh made good his boast that "a crow that flew over the Valley would have to carry his rations with him."

Late in the afternoon a message came from Colonel Mosby, and we marched off by unfrequented byroads across the country toward Front Royal. Dark overtook us long before we reached a secluded glen at the foot of Guard Hill, where we found the colonel awaiting us. As soon as he assured himself that we all were in ship-shape he took Captain Sam Chapman and four or five others and went off to reconnoitre the picket and locate the videttes. It was while on this scout that he met with quite an interesting adventure, in which he exhibited his characteristic quick wit and nerve.

While he and his party were standing in front of a house on the pike, where he had stopped in quest of information, they saw in the starlight a squad of cavalry approaching from the direction of Winchester. This was the patrol on its rounds. When they got within hailing distance they stopped and inquired of our party who they were.

"Friends, with the countersign," Colonel Mosby replied, with the best Yankee twang that he could improvise.

"One of you advance, then, and give the countersign," was the response.

"No," said the colonel, "you are coming from the direction of the enemy. One of you advance."

This was a correct proposition, so one of them rode forward. When he came up the colonel said to him in a low, terribly distinct voice, as he levelled his revolver at him:

"Give the alarm, and you are a dead man! I am Mosby. Now call to the others that it is all right, to come on." And he did so; and five more of Uncle Sam's gallant defenders marched confidently up to the muzzles of as many revolvers and quietly surrendered.

With these prisoners and the information which he had gathered, he returned to us. He told us, as a piece of good news, and to encourage us for the attack, that the picket had been reinforced that day, so that there were two hundred Yankees there instead of one hundred, as we first thought, and he added, with a grim humour, "Now we'll get two horses apiece instead of one."

It was now getting along toward daybreak. You know the old adage, "*the darkest hour is just before dawn.*" We had a corresponding theory that men sleep soundest then and we usually made it a point to time our night attacks accordingly. Captain Chapman was put in charge of six or eight *carbineers* afoot and ordered to march straight down the pike until he came to something, after which his movements were left to his own discretion, to be guided by circumstances which the colonel proposed to help develop with the mounted men. I had a carbine and fell into Chapman's detail. After reaching the turnpike we did not go far before the exercises opened. Directly we saw some men in front of us and were ordered to halt. We responded with a volley and jumped out of the road among some bushes which covered a recent clearing.

The Yankees could not distinguish our numbers, and I am sure that, as in obedience to Chapman's orders to charge them, we rushed through those bushes, shooting and yelling like Modoc Indians, while our mounted men could be heard thundering down the pike, the enemy thought that a whole brigade was on them. At any rate, they promptly broke for bushes too, hardly firing back at us, and when our cavalry came up they found us sharpshooters in possession of the picket camp and running around among the tethered horses. Indeed, I fear that our impetuous captain rather over-did our part, or that the colonel failed to develop his circumstances with sufficient promptness for us to play to them. Instead of merely flushing the game for the mounted men to catch it, we drove so many of them out of reach into the darkness that only about sixteen of them were overhauled. I think, though, that we secured nearly every horse on that post, numbering about seventy.

We ascertained afterward that the picket had been divided, and the larger section, with the commissioned officers, had been camped as a reserve, some half a mile farther in, and we did not reach them at all. On this account the colonel's promise of two horses apiece did not materialise—but we got everything that was in sight.

It seems that there had been some rioting at this outpost the night before, and when Captain Auer heard the sounds of our attack he took for granted that it was another outbreak of his own men's hilarity, and while we were waiting on the road to gather ourselves together, here he came dashing up in a fine frenzy, demanding "what the blankety blank all this fuss means?"

"It means that Mosby has got you," a Ranger explained, as he emphasised his explanation with an appropriate movement of his revolver.

The captain was so shocked that it took him a moment or two to gather sufficient breath with which to whisper hoarsely, while the whites of his eyes expanded in the morning gloaming, "Well, this beats hell, don't it?"

I said the Yankees might have thought that Imboden's brigade was attacking them. In fact, they had some reason for thinking so. As we were rushing through the bushes Phil Lee thought to impress them by whooping out at intervals in his foghorn voice, "Hurrah for Imboden!" The ruse may have accomplished what he intended, but it brought on him a characteristic reprimand from Colonel Mosby, who was not without some jealousy for his own laurels. He told Phil that, like Peter, he had denied his master, and he had half a mind to send him to Imboden, of whom he seemed to think so much. But there was, like Peter's also, only a temporary fall from grace, and he never after had occasion to doubt Phil's loyalty.

Possibly a further effect of it was that the enemy attempted no pursuit of us, and we rode quietly back home with our captures. To facilitate this, however, we divided into two parties, one of which found a pretty deep but safe fording high up the river at Howellsville and the other got across somewhere lower down.

CHAPTER 5

In Fairfax County

About daybreak one morning in the summer of 1864, Bush Underwood aroused me from my slumbers, with an invitation to go with him on a scout about the neighbourhood of Georgetown. We had gone into camp near Thoroughfare Gap late the night before, after which I had been on picket for a couple of hours, so I felt very little like taking the hard service which I knew would attend the proposed expedition, but when I learned that the party had been partially made up of such spirits as Charley McDonough, Hugh Waters, Harry Sinnott and Bill Trammell, I recognised the compliment of the invitation and accepted it.

The objects of the expedition were, generally, to gather information, and especially to "confiscate" a certain very fine stallion belonging to a Union man near Lewinsville.

Underwood's description of this horse, together with the very recklessness of venturing so far within the enemy's lines, offered attractions irresistible to a Mosby man. Accordingly, about sunrise a half dozen of us set out across the country in the direction of Georgetown.

By noon we were within the limits of danger, and fearing that our further progress by daylight might bring us in contact with a patrol or scouting party of the enemy, or even a straggling trooper whose discovery of our presence would thwart our expedition, we retired to a body of pines to await nightfall.

After dark set in we resumed our march. Underwood had been raised in that part of Fairfax County, and it was his boast that he knew its every rabbit-path, as well as the political sentiments of all its inhabitants. And his unvarying success in scouting that section seemed to vindicate his claim. He was one of those cold-blooded, clear-headed, nervy fellows who never got "rattled." Perfectly fearless, he was at the same time cautious and patient, and seemed to have a genius for just that sort of business. Therefore we implicitly followed his lead, though we soon heard on every side the noises from Federal camps and knew that the least accident or inadvertence might at any moment bring hordes of the enemy down upon us.

I suppose it was nearly bedtime when we approached a house where Bush said he could get some information that he wanted. While the rest of us remained with his horse under the shadows of the neighbouring trees, he cautiously made his way to the rear of the dwelling. He soon returned with biscuits and sandwiches, which we proceeded "to put where they would do the most good," while he unloaded his budget of news.

He had learned that the prize horse (which, by the way, I believe to this *day was* a pure myth, conjured up by him to allure us) had been sent to Washington that afternoon. But he had ascertained the location of the various camps in the neighbourhood, with the names and numbers of the different regiments composing them. This was invaluable knowledge to us.

Furthermore, he informed us that there was a certain house near the Little Falls of the Potomac which a number of Yankee officers from a neighbouring camp were in the habit of visiting, the attraction being some very fascinating girls.

There was some debate among us as to whether it was exactly the fair thing to break up so interesting a party. But the chance of carrying back with us some Yankee shoulder straps, and possibly stars, not to speak of fine horses, overcame our scruples, and we determined to put in an appearance there during the evening, even at the risk of being regarded as intruders.

This house, however, was several miles away, and the road to it was not altogether as safe and open to travellers as it is today, (1907). Nor did we go very far before our adventures began. It was now considerably past midnight, and from the fact that we had been riding for some time within sound of the roar of the Little Falls I judged that we were nearing our destination.

We had been following our leader in perfect silence, and I confess that my meditations were not altogether cheerful. Here we were, a half-dozen foolish boys, forty miles from our comrades, surrounded on all sides by enemies—military and non-combatant—and liable at any moment to stir up a hornet's nest.

Should our leader and guide fall in a night skirmish, or by any chance become separated from us, the brightest prospect that awaited us would be to ride humbly into the nearest camp, and take our chances as being received and treated as prisoners of war.

It turned out that I was not the only one in that party whose resolution was being "*sicklied o'er by the pale cast of thought*" Presently Hugh Waters, who was riding by my side, leaned toward me and said, in tones of becoming seriousness, "Johnny, I have got a presentiment I feel that I am going to be killed tonight."

The fact is, I felt very much that way myself—and possibly I would have said it, if he had waited a little while. But he spoke first, and gave me the start on him. As much to hide my own weakness as to banter him, I answered,

"Oh, pshaw! that's all stuff. We'll be talking to pretty girls directly."

"Now, Johnnie, don't laugh at me. You know I am not afraid." (I wasn't so sure of that—judging him by myself.) "But I am serious; I know that I am not going to get home, and there are some things I want you to attend to for me." Then he proceeded to make his will and appointed me his executor. He divided out his few assets—"*the spoils of many a chase*"—among his relatives and friends, no doubt very judiciously. Finally he came to the mare he was riding. She was a superb animal, handsome as a picture, and distinguished among the boys for her speed and endurance.

"And Bess," he continued, patting her upon the neck, "I want you to try and carry her out with you and give her to Mollie L."

This last request aroused my interest.

"Mollie L.?" I asked; "why, what's your reason for that?"

"Well, I suppose I will have to tell you, as it won't make much difference now." And his voice became a shade more doleful. "Well, the truth is, I am in love with her—and—she's my sweetheart!"

"The mischief you say! You are not engaged to her?"

"Yes, I am, Johnnie, old fellow. You see I had to tell you, although I promised her not to."

"By George! I am engaged to her myself!" I answered, an incipient feeling of rivalry imparting some warmth to my tones, perhaps, in spite of the solemn business we had in hand.

Just at this interesting point our conversation was interrupted by a pistol shot, and Underwood, who had paced some distance ahead of us up the hill which we were ascending, came dashing back, lying flat on his horse. As we wheeled around our movements were expedited by some shots from a party of men who now appeared on the brow of the hill. They did not follow us very promptly, however, and after running a few hundred yards we pulled off into an old field and huddled behind a clump of bushes to await developments.

In a short while the squad of Federals, who, we supposed, were a patrol upon their rounds, passed leisurely along the road in front of us, and we picked up such scraps as these from their conversation:

"Where the devil did those fellows go?"

"They couldn't have been any of Mosby's men away down here."

"No, I guess they are a lot of Eighth Illinois boys out on a lark."

"Well, we turned the joke upon them anyhow."

It was no little relief to us that they took this view of the matter. Nevertheless, the questions submitted to the council of war which we held after they had gone, were still very serious ones.

It would not be very late in the next day when they found out their mistake, and we might expect the country to be scoured by scouting parties. Especially would the situation be aggravated if we persisted in our project of raiding the house on the river. Had ordinary discretion presided at our council, doubtless we would have set out for home and safety, forthwith. But the fool-hardiness of the venture prevented any one of us from proposing a backdown lest he be suspected of weakness—and we continued on our fatuous course.

Finally we reached the house we were seeking. Fortunately there were no dogs about the premises and we dismounted, and surrounded the dwelling without being discovered. Our knocking at the front door brought a head out of an upper window, and a female voice inquired who we were and what was our business.

"If there are any officers here, they are wanted at camp immediately," Bush replied.

"There are none here—nor soldiers either," was the answer. "But you can't come that over me. Bush Underwood. What in the world are you doing here?"

"Hello! that's Nannie Bell! What luck! Some of us boys are here, hungry as wolves. Come down and let us in."

Sure enough, she was an old acquaintance. But as we heard her steps descending the stairs, we took the precaution to cock our revolvers—for even ladies are not always to be trusted when there may be a sweetheart lost or saved. But she was "true blue"—or gray, rather—and, with the other ladies who soon joined us, gave us such comfort as the unreasonable hour of our call enabled them to offer. But they could not console us for the officers whom we failed to catch, and we soon rode away, decidedly crestfallen.

We were now decidedly of the opinion to strike Loudoun forthwith, content if we should reach there with whole hides and our stock of adventures—still further to be added to—instead of the booty we had hoped for.

We soon reached the shelter of the Big Pine Forest; and for hours threaded its obscure and devious bridle paths in single file, turning and twisting and doubling, it seemed to me, long after all idea of distance or direction had been lost.

About noon next day we came to a clearing in which stood the humble abode of one of Bush's friends. They were but poor folk, at best; and I doubt not that, with the precarious means of tilling their sterile soil and the frequent harassments and depredations to which they were subjected, Hard Times kept a pretty constant *"knocking at their cottage door."* But they gave us a hearty welcome and we had no reason to suspect that the larder was low. Often have I recalled with gratitude and something of regret the sweetly cooked and daintily served ham and eggs and richly browned cornbread which that day greeted our keen appetites.

One of the sons of the family stood watch for us on the neighbouring hill, and we ate, and baited our horses and rested in peace. After the refreshments, we took up our march toward the Dranesville Pike, which we approached through the woods, and very cautiously, for we were still within the Federal lines, and liable to run against a patrol or scouting party. Besides, we were not without the hopes of picking up some unwary passenger along that highway.

We reached the pike safely, and tying our horses back in the pines a short distance, "laid for our luck" along the wayside.

One squad of cavalry did indeed pass along within ten feet of us, but their numbers secured them undisturbed right of way. A few moments after, a solitary straggler came jauntily along, sitting cross-legged on his horse and inquiring at the top of his voice, "Who will care for mother now?"

Harry Sinnott stepped out from behind a bush and informed him that, if he had no objections, we would take care of him; and he might reasonably commit the old lady to a kind Providence—or words to that effect.

This matter-of-fact, not to say rude response, evidently shocked his sensibilities; and before he recovered himself he had been fully in-

Henry M. Withers
Company B

troduced to our party. We found him not unworthy game. His money, jewellery and arms were divided out among the rest of us; while his horse was assigned to Charley and Bush, in joint ownership. Neither one of them, however, cared to have the trouble and responsibility of getting the other one's half back to Loudoun; so while the others of us kept watch, they produced the inevitable "deck" and sat down there by the roadside and played out a game of "seven up" to determine which should own the whole of the nag. Charley won, a result which some of us had reason to regret before we reached home.

By dark we had gotten well beyond the picket lines and into a section of country with which we all were more or less familiar. Here the prisoner was paroled and turned loose, and McDonough took possession of his hard-earned asset. Here, too, Underwood and Trammell went off on some affair of their own, leaving the rest of us to make our way home.

We came upon the Little River turnpike about five miles below Aldie; and as our horses' feet struck the paved road we felt that we were indeed "almost home." But when we stopped at a house on the roadside to get a drink of water, we noticed considerable restraint, to say the least, in the manner of the good lady, who was generally rejoiced to see Mosby's men. A few inquiries developed the fact that she mistook us for Yankees, a large body of whom, she informed us, had gone up the road that afternoon.

This news brought a change over our spirits and put us again on the *qui vive*. The night was very dark and a high wind was blowing. This made marching upon a road upon which we were liable at any time to meet the enemy returning, decidedly dangerous, but we were dead homesick and determined to risk it.

Sinnott and I rode about a hundred yards in advance of Charley and Hugh with the led-horse; and in order that they might have a better chance to escape in case of trouble, we carried our revolvers in our hands, ready cocked, and it was understood that we should fire incontinently into anything we met.

We had ridden in this order more than a mile, and Sinnott and myself, riding closely side by side, had descended into a little vale, where the darkness could almost be felt. Suddenly our horses stopped. Straining our looks forward, we distinguished the forms of men and horses, just in front of us. Our horses and theirs had been stopped by touching noses.

Like a flash it came to me that they might be some of our own men, scouting; and instinctively I hailed them. But Sinnott, obedient to instructions, fired; and the response to my challenge was a groan, as the man opposite to him fell to the ground. It was no time now for the amenities of war; and the echo to the groan was the report of my pistol, and down went my *vis-à-vis*.

As we turned our horses pandemonium broke loose. The flashing of pistols threw a weird light on the scene, while the sounds of the arms and the shouts of men and clattering of horses' hoofs "*made night hideous.*" I fired back once or twice as I ran, but found that my shots only betrayed my whereabouts, and drew the enemy's upon me. So I addressed all my energies to getting away from there.

When I came up to Charley he was dismounted in the road; and my horse striking Hugh's just as he was turning, laid him and his rider sprawling by the wayside. That was the last I saw of any of my companions that night. As I subsequently learned, their experiences were as follows:

McDonough had been riding the captured horse to rest his own, and when the firing commenced he jumped down to change to his more reliable nag. Before he could mount the enemy was upon him. He had been outlawed by the Federal authorities for some desperate deed, and to him capture meant certain death. But with wonderful presence of mind he lay flat in the middle of the road, with pistol cocked and hand on trigger, ready to deliver that last shot which he always reserved for his own heart as the final alternative to capture. Poor fellow! before many months the awful emergency came, and he unfalteringly fired the fatal shot.

But that night he was spared, by the narrowest shave. The Yankees rode past him—one of them whose horse stumbled over him remarking that "there was one damned rebel they had killed." At the first opportunity he rolled out of their way and hied off into the darkness.

When Waters was dismounted in my unfortunate collision with him, he too crept out of the road, as the Federals came charging up, and lay quietly in the fence corner until they had gone by. Then he arose and made for the Bull Run mountains.

Their horses followed Sinnott down the pike and found a safe harbour in some citizen's close until they were reclaimed.

I turned off the pike, and, coming to some convenient thickets, spent the residue of the night there. With morning light I made my way back to Mosby's Confederacy.

In the course of the afternoon I cleaned up, donned my "best blockade goods" and rode over to Mollie L.'s to seek in her gracious presence refreshment from my hardships.

Imagine my surprise at finding Hugh Waters already there, ensconced in the best arm chair, playing invalid over some bruises and scratches which he had incurred in his fall of the night before. But so far from their being a source of discomfort to him, the scamp was supremely blest in the gentle ministration which they were evoking from "*Our Mutual Sweetheart.*"

He was evidently master of the situation; and "the subsequent proceedings interested me no more."

Chapter 6

The Point of Rocks Raid

Colonel John Scott, in his *Partisan Life with Mosby*, says that our attack on Point of Rocks, July 4, 1864, was intended as a diversion in favour of General Early in his operations in the Valley. I always had a suspicion that it was inspired by a grim sort of deference to "the day we celebrate." Certainly it was attended with all the usual accompaniments of a Fourth of July excursion, not excepting fireworks, confectionery and a sensational display of bunting. Special invitations, too, were issued to guests, and unusual attractions promised them; for our chief of staff, Joe Blackwell, and his chum. Bill Lake, of the Commissary, were along. They regarded themselves as belonging to a strictly non-combatant branch of our command, and had conscientious scruples against transgressing the limits of their sphere. Therefore, I opine that they were drawn with us by somewhat the same assurances of a picnic as gathered that historic army of civilians at the battlefield of Bull Run.

Point of Rocks is an important station on the Baltimore and Ohio Railroad, just across the Potomac from Loudoun County, and about twelve miles east of Harper's Ferry. It is named from the high promontory of solid rock in which a range of mountains terminates so close to the river's bank that the Chesapeake and Ohio Canal barely squeezes past it, and the railway, just alongside, has to cut through it. West of this tunnel for miles up the river steep and rocky bluffs bind the railroad track on the north. East of the tunnel lies the village, and on the mountain slope back of the town and overlooking it, was the Federal camp. The only access to them from the west was along the narrow towpath between the canal and the river, and from that a wooden framed bridge arched over the canal into the middle of the little town, some four hundred yards from the tunnel.

The river here is at least a quarter mile wide, but is split about midway by a narrow island which, beginning opposite the mountain's end, continues up the river about a mile. At the head of the island is a ford passable for horses at ordinary low water. This day the river was very low. But when Colonel Mosby and one or two companions undertook to cross there, on his usual preliminary scout, they discovered a Yankee picket on the island who promptly opened fire on them. The command was then out of sight, and I presume that the Yankees gave no special significance to his presence there, as it was by no means unusual for occasional Confederates to make their appearance in that vicinity. He returned to us on the Waterford road, and called for sharpshooters. An unusually large number responded. Carbines were not plentiful with us, as a general thing.

Directly after a fight we would be abundantly supplied, and our houses were well stocked with them. But they were unhandy things to carry and as most of our fighting was at short range, where the revolver was used, comparatively few of our men encumbered themselves with these guns. There were always some, however, who carried them for the sake of extra chances for adventure which the possession of them sometimes brought to us. That morning I think there were at least two dozen of us who dismounted and followed Lieutenant Ab Wrenn to the front, in the best of heart and anticipating high sport in sharpshooting across the river. Possibly, if we had known what awaited us, we would not have gone off with so much alacrity.

We made a rush across the river bottom and got places behind the big trees and fallen logs on the banks almost before the Yankees woke up to our presence. A few of them on the island hardly tarried to return our salutes to the holiday; and then, much to our surprise. Lieutenant Wrenn jumped into the river and called on us to follow. That was a feature of the entertainment that we had not costumed for, but not a man hesitated to take to water promptly.

In the meanwhile, our little mountain howitzer was run out on a river bluff behind us; and as we floundered through the water, shooting, yelling, stumbling over the round river stones and getting ducked overhead, rising and sputtering and firing again, the boom of our artillery proclaimed that the celebration was on. It seems that, somehow, the fuse to the first shell had been cut too short and it exploded in our rear; and as the pieces fell in the water behind us we realised something of the situation which has been described as *"between the devil and the deep sea"*; and we pressed, if possible, more vigorously toward the enemy as the lesser of the two evils.

But if our artillery excited us, it utterly demoralised them, and away they went. Some of them mounted their horses and sped down the river toward the Point of Rocks, others made their way over the canal lock and sought safety in the bushes on the river bluff beyond the railroad. These were joined by a party of excursionists from Washington who had steamed up the canal in a launch on a Fourth of July outing, and as the mixed lot of soldier and civilians scrambled up the steep hillside, they were indifferently targets for our sharpshooters. When a poor fellow, overtaken by a bullet, would roll back down the cliff, whether in blue or in summer jeans, it aroused the same sort of stir in the blood as that with which the ardent sportsman sees the flying game fall to his shot. This sounds savage, doesn't it? Well, it is human nature in war.

The mounted men had followed us closely and they got across the river before we landed, but they dashed off down the tow-path, leaving us to wait for our horses to be brought over to us, which were, somehow, unaccountably delayed. In the mean while, we proceeded to investigate the excursionists' boat which lay in the canal lock, and we found its contents worthy of the occasion. Those fellows were out for a good time. The choicest brands of liquors and cigars and various kinds of dainty foods were consoling us for our wetting, when a railroad train hove in sight from the direction of Harper's Ferry. We hurried from the boat and arranged ourselves alongside the track to receive it in due form. Just then another shot from our howitzer came whistling across the river. The engineer immediately reversed his engine.

We saw the train slowing up and rushed toward it in order to board it, but the engineer, who did not lose his head for a moment, succeeded in getting his train under way, and we were disgusted to see it move off before we got up to it. But you ought to have seen the passengers pile out of it while it hung on the turn, and take to the bushes on the bluff! A shot or two fired after them, purely in sport, however, seemed to paralyze some of them and they lost their footholds and rolled back down the hill. We did not disturb them further, and I suppose they all got away to tell their tales of hair-breadth escape.

At last my horse was brought over. As I was galloping down the tow-path I overtook Llewellyn, who had gone off afoot in despair of getting his horse at all, and was double-quicking it through the dust and the hot sunshine. "Take me up, and I'll give you half I get," he pleaded. Whether from pity or cupidity, you may judge as you please, I took him up behind me; and we got there "just in time to be too late." The fighting was over, the stores had been looted, and everything in sight had gone through the process of escheat and forfeiture. I did find a few pounds of candy, which I chucked into my haversack, and Llewellyn picked up a pair of lady's shoes which some overladen ranger had dropped. I did not have the heart to demand of him a division. But what the other fellows got is another story, which I will tell presently.

I have never understood why the taking of the Point of Rocks that day was such an easy job. It was manned by a company of cavalry and a regiment of infantry, and reinforcements were within easy reach. I do not count the cavalry, for they were the notorious Loudoun Rangers—a band of renegade Loudouners, under Captain Sam Means, for whom we ever bore a regard, ardent but misplaced in the sense that we could never get close enough to them to levy our attachment. This time they ran across the bridge over the canal, to which I have referred, paused long enough to tear up the flooring of it, so as to impede our pursuit, and then fled to parts unknown.

But something might have been expected of the infantry. When you recall that our only approach to them was over a narrow towpath on which we could ride only two abreast, that we were on the farther side of a rock-ribbed canal over which it was impossible for us to charge them, it is inscrutable that they did not get into that railroad tunnel and just shoot us down as fast as we showed ourselves. But the facts are that less than two hundred and fifty cavalry rode down on them in broad daylight, re-laid the flooring on the bridge before their eyes, crossed over it, and ran them as far as eye could reach, without loss or injury to a single man or horse. This sounds like a fairy tale, but it is literally true.

While our men were repairing the bridge, the infantry on the hill kept up a lively firing, but as they did not hit a thing, I presume they were simply burning powder to add to the hilariousness of the occasion. In the mean while, impetuous Harry Hatcher ran across on the sills of the bridge to the deserted "flag of our Union" which he saw drooping disconsolately on its staff as if in very shame for its cowardly defenders, and hauled it down and brought it back into worthier, if less reverential company. And then the boys got across. Some of them made for the camp on the hill, which was deserted when they reached it, and made bonfires there of such things as they could not bring away.

A few of them followed Major Richards out the Frederick City road in a fruitless chase after some fugitives who soon disappeared in the mountains. But the most of them stopped in the village, and after cutting the telegraph wires, proceeded to confiscate the contents of the stores and sutlers' shops. When I arrived on the scene, as already stated, this work had been consummated and the boys were hilarious. They had not had such a "glorious Fourth" since they popped fire-crackers with *pickaninnies* around the negro quarters.

The gang that recrossed the river that evening was a sight to behold. They were laden and garnished with, and otherwise affected by the assorted stocks usual to country stores. Bolts of cloths and calicoes were piled up behind and before them. Some of the latter, of gaudiest prints, served as sashes which streamed out from the shoulders or waists of the wearers; and yards upon yards of red and white bunting floated on the evening breeze. Boots and shoes, for both sexes, hung from the saddles and the horses' necks; and various kinds of tinware flashed back the sunlight from every conceivable point of contact with a cavalier.

The frequent presence of hoops and ladies' skirts and bonnets showed that the boys had not been unmindful of "the girls they left behind them." Hats for the fair sex, with impromptu trimmings of flashy ribbons, bedecked unkempt heads in fashions that were certainly striking as well as novel. I think that Dame Fashion—even she of Confederate lineage—would have fallen into a fit if she had beheld the liberties taken with her laws. As the command straightened out in the road and moved off toward Leesburg it looked for all the world like a parade of Fantastics. How far the captured groceries, of the wet variety, contributed to the grotesque appearance I feel a delicacy in saying. It might be assumed that my views were tinged with envy, as I sat and munched my poor candy and watched them.

Nor were we without spectators who manifested all kinds of interest in the passing show. Of course sounds of the carryings on across the river had roused the country-side, and the natives gathered in groups along our line of march. Some of these were content to watch the sight and gossip with the boys, others of a more practical cast of thought developed a disposition to find out what was in it for them, and induced some rangers to open a peripatetic retail business on the road. Money was scarce, but other currency was found. Even that austere historian, Colonel John Scott, records one instance of barter in which a mountain maiden secured a pair of shoes for a kiss. Certainly,

T. W. T. Richards
Captain Company G

ribbons and red sashes were noticeably scarcer when we went into bivouac in Mrs. Dawson's woods that night.

Next morning the men were relieved of all their impedimenta, for serious work. During the evening and night our enemies, who had been scattered to the four winds, got together and with strong reinforcements returned to the river at Point of Rocks and Noland's Ferry, a few miles lower down, and threatened to cross at each point. The prospect of losing their spoils for which they had so strained their consciences threw our "non-combatant branch" on to the verge of nervous prostration, and they cordially took charge of the work of impressing wagons and teams from the neighbourhood for hauling the captured goods back to a place of safety. They prosecuted it with such energy that a considerable wagon-train soon moved out toward the fastnesses of the Fauquier hills. This was quite a novel attachment to Mosby's men, their specialty being to attach themselves to the other fellow's wagon train.

Our sharpshooters again repaired to the river banks and proceeded to interest the enemy at long range. The day was spent in making such demonstration of force as should deter them from coming over. The presence of artillery with us, and so many dismounted men, may have suggested to them that we might be a detachment from Lee's army, and the colonel had us execute some manoeuvres which strongly fostered that illusion. Our visible numbers were multiplied by a shrewd stratagem through which the Yankees were made to see more than double. The road rises out of a deep hollow at the foot of Dr. Mason's meadow and passes up a high hill in full view of the Point of Rocks and a short mile south of the river. It then turns at right angles on the hill top and goes out of sight into the upper end of the same hollow. That the dust in it was fetlock deep goes without saying.

The command was marched over this hill, raising a cloud of dust through which it was dimly visible to the spectators across the river. As soon as the head of the column got out of their sight it would gallop down the hollow, through Dr. Mason's meadow and, falling in behind the rear, would march over the hill again. It was a kind of endless chain business by which regiment after regiment was paraded across the stage; and the amount of Confederate cavalry which was exhibited that day for the edification of those Yankees was limited only by the demands of the occasion. Of course our commander had to refrain from overdoing the thing, and see to it that the program was duly varied, lest the fake should be discovered. At any rate we did riding enough to keep the enemy on their own side of the river, and to make us sleep soundly that night in somebody's woods near Waterford. And the lights of the bivouac went out, and the curtain fell on the Point of Rocks raid.

CHAPTER 7

The Mount Zion Fight

While the command slept in the woods, and perhaps dreamed the Point of Rocks raid into the misty past, the pickets on the neighbouring hills guarded their slumbers, the scouts scoured the adjacent country for information which should determine our movements on the morrow, and Major Hibbs's famous Corn Detail secured the sinews of war. Though the men might go without rations, and perhaps fought all the more savagely when hungry, the horses had to be kept in prime condition, and, whatever happened, feed should be provided for them. We had no wagons to attend us, and the necessities of the case evolved "Major" Hibbs.

When a halt was made for the night he would summons his corps of favourites, consisting of "Ned Rector and several others," and set out in quest of corn. Sometimes they would be gone half the night, but his unerring instinct never failed to find a Union man's barn, and sooner or later he came in with bags of corn piled up behind and before the saddles. Nor was this as unpopular a service as it might appear, for it generally involved good feeding for the detail as well as for the horses, and not infrequently a distillery was included in the itinerary.

Pray don't make the mistake of assigning William Hibbs among the "non-combatants." Though his title was merely in courtesy to his quasi office of quartermaster, no braver man followed Mosby. Many years past military age, he rode side by side with his own sons, in the foremost ranks, and his poor maimed and scarred body attested his familiarity with hot battles. Childless and homeless, this loyal fellow finally died in the county almshouse. His fate sharply accentuates the difference in the results of the war to the Blue and the Gray. The former have the government, the offices, the pensions. Achilles won the victor's palm, because the gods made him invulnerable; but glory shines on Hector's grave!

Early the next morning our scouts, who had been in Leesburg, four or five miles away, brought important news. They reported that Major Forbes with his crack California battalion, had come up from Fairfax the evening before and was in that neighbourhood, looking for us; but I reckon he was looking with the same ardour with which the boy sought work—praying that he might not find it. Our presence in the immediate vicinity must have been known to the Union sympathisers there, of whom there were many, for some of our men had gone to that attractive burgh the night after the attack on Point of Rocks, to lay their trophies at the feet of their lady-loves.

Indeed, the firing on the river, which had been kept up with more or less regularity throughout the subsequent day, proclaimed that things were going on in which the gallant major might participate if he had a hankering for a fight. It is incredible that he did not know that we were only a few miles away, giving our undivided attention to his friends in our front, and that his opportunity was to come on us in the rear, and get us between the upper and nether millstones. But possibly he had some apprehensions of the experience of the fellow who caught the sleeping panther by the tail and had to call for "help to let the blamed thing go"—and his friends might not have crossed the river in time to meet the necessities of his case.

Upon receiving the report of the scouts Colonel Mosby ordered us up and we started out to carry Major Forbes's opportunity to him. But that gentleman seemed still inclined to elude glory; for when we came in sight of Leesburg we saw the Federals moving out in the direction of Aldie. There were about two hundred and fifty of them, finely mounted and equipped, and they had the reputation of being good fighters and well disciplined. Our own numbers had been reduced to less than two hundred by the departure of some of the men for their homes and we knew that in hunting a fight with these men we were not going on a picnic.

But when we reached Leesburg we heard such high boasts of how anxious they were to meet us, and what they would do for us if they could come up with us, that we were fired with ambition to overtake them. It was no light circumstance, either, that these taunts were communicated to us by the pretty girls of Leesburg, who lined the streets as we passed through the town and presented to us trays laden with most acceptable breakfasts. That was my first visit to the ancient town, and possibly the pleasant impression of its citizens I received that morning was somewhat responsible for the fact that I made it my home after the war and have lived there ever since. The immediate results were that the bright eyes and the breakfasts and the boasts put us in the best possible fighting trim, and we went after those Californians with the determination to wipe them off the face of the earth.

Colonel Mosby, however, was a wily as well as a daring fighter, and never let his valour get the better of his discretion—at least, not in the handling of his men. He always sought to secure for them every possible advantage for a fight, and his almost unvarying success in this was one of the marks of his genius. The loss of one of his trained partisans was a much more serious matter to him than the loss of many Federals was to their side and he could not afford to play a swapping game.

Somehow he learned that the Yankees were striking for Mount Zion, an old church on the Little River turnpike about two miles east of Aldie and some ten miles south of Leesburg. He assumed that they would take the most direct road there, the road which crosses Goose Creek at Ball's Mill, about six miles south of where we were. The natural advantages there for a surprise party are exceptional, so making a hurried detour we arrived there first and got into position to receive our expected visitors. Our mounted men were formed for a charge, behind the bluff around which the road winds after crossing the creek, and sharpshooters were hidden among the bushes along its crest, facing the enemy as they should cross the broad creek bottoms and enter the ford. I presume that it was intended for the *carbineers* to open on them as they crossed the creek, and while they were thereby disconcerted the cavalry would charge them. But whatever the plan was it miscarried, and after we had waited there some time, it was ascertained that the enemy had gone to Mount Zion by another route. We hurriedly moved away from there by an obscure road which came out on the pike about two miles south of Mount Zion.

Colonel Mosby was himself scouting vigorously; and when he came to us, marching cross country, we saw that he had changed horses and was mounted on his favourite sorrel mare. Whenever he appeared mounted on her, we knew there was business on hand, and I recollect the comments which went along the line when we learned that he had sent a special messenger after her for this occasion. He had located the Federals in an old field just south of the pike, in which they had halted to feed. To the west of them was a large brick dwelling and grounds. East of them, leaving the field and crossing the turnpike, was a body of woods about a hundred yards wide. The woods hid the

Yankees from our view when we came out on the pike on top of a hill nearly a mile below them. Their pickets in the woods doubtless discovered us at once. So, this was not to be a case of surprise, but a straight charge over an open road upon an enemy who was fully prepared for us. The only advantage of position was that we were between them and their home. This was a problematical one, because it was calculated to make them fight all the more desperately.

About a dozen *carbineers*, under Lieutenant Hatcher, went toward them in a sweeping gallop, while our artillery was being placed in position on the hill and the mounted men formed for the charge. The enemy's pickets in the woods fired some ineffectual shots at the sharpshooters, but we did not get within a hundred yards before they broke and ran back upon the main body. When we galloped into the woods which they had vacated, and scattered along the edge next to them, I saw a grand sight. A couple of hundred yards in front of us, upon the slope of the hill in the old field, the Californians were drawn up in two lines, one behind the other, facing us. Their alignment was as perfect as if on dress parade. Their officers were in position with their sabres drawn and the men sat on their horses with carbines ready. The shots which we fired at them from the woods seemed to me to be returned with absolute regularity at intervals along their line and threw bullets close enough to us to make it very interesting.

Then our cavalry came whooping up the pike. Just before they came up to us, the old howitzer boomed and sent a shell over their heads. I thought I could see the blue lines on the hill waver a little, but that was all. As the head of our column swept past us up the pike some of our sharpshooters dismounted and tore a gap in the fence at the corner of the field, and Lieutenant Wrenn, with a section of Company B, dashed through it and up the hill. I think this attack struck the Yankees while they were moving to adjust themselves to the charge which our first column was making upon what had been their left flank. Just then a fellow on a white horse was seen to break away from the column next to us and start across the field toward the south. By that time some of our boys on the fleetest horses had gotten up to them both in their front and on their flank. The volleys which had been intended for us as we should come up toward them in solid column, had been too long delayed; and as their saddles were being fast emptied by the deadly revolvers in the hands of the boys who knew no tactics, both columns, which had now become mixed up in one mass of blue, wavered and broke and followed the man on the white horse.

By the time I had remounted and come up, the fighting there was all over, and blue and gray together were sweeping across the fields toward Little River Church, where the road from Aldie passes to Sudley. At one of the cross fences which obstructed their flight Major Forbes made a desperate attempt to rally his men, but it was hopeless and brief, and as soon as the obstruction could be broken through the race began again. I was mortified to realise that this, too, was over before I got into it. The truth is that my horse was unaccountably dull, and in spite of the most vigorous spurring, I fell into the wake of the pursuit.

It was during this last rally that Major Forbes had a personal hand-to-hand set-to with Capt. Tom Richards and wounded him sorely, but had to succumb to the captain's staying powers and finally surrendered to him. All the way across the fields the fighting and capturing had been kept up, so that when the Sudley road was reached most of the enemy had been shot or captured. There were very few of them who road out on that highway that afternoon. When I reached Corner Hall, about two miles south of the church, I met the last of our men coming back, who informed me that not more than five or six of the Yankees had gotten away, and that Colonel Mosby and Johnnie Edmunds were after them. They, too, soon returned with the report that the fugitives had cleanly out-ridden them.

Notwithstanding that Major Forbes did not get a chance to deliver one of his deadly scientific volleys into our ranks, our victory was by no means a bloodless one. Eight of our men were wounded; four of whom, Henry Smallwood, Hugh Waters, Tom Lake and Frank Woolf, were lads of my own set, and my particular chums. Henry's death, which soon followed, was a great sorrow to me. He was a quiet, unostentatious little fellow, and absolutely reliable. The others recovered, and survived the war—through a special Providence.

Night fell before we gathered ourselves together. The mansion house, of which I have spoken, was turned into a hospital, and the occupants, the family of Mr. Samuel Skinner, were indefatigable in their ministrations to the wounded. It was necessary for us to remain there for some hours, and I was placed on picket. I was posted in the road below the house and on the edge of the battlefield. I have watched for the boys under many trying circumstances, for I think I never went on a raid that I did not have to serve on picket, but I never had as bad two hours as I had that night. The groans of the wounded men and horses, the pitiful calls for relief, the prayers, the heart-rending laments for loved ones were borne to me on the quiet summer night from the most distant parts of the battlefield, it seemed to me. To hear a poor fellow, within a few rods perhaps, calling for water, or for someone to move his dead horse off his broken leg, or to raise his head and let him die in peace, and yet not dare to leave my post and go to him, was an awful trial to a boy of warm sympathies. As I sat on my horse that night and listened to these sounds and thought of my young friends perhaps dying, up at the house, I realised what a modern soldier has so aptly formulated into the words, "*War is hell!*"

There was another incident of this fight which may seem trivial, but it was full of pathos to me. We finally halted for the night in a grass field some miles up the road, near Middleburg. Our horses were stripped and turned loose to graze on the luxuriant clover, and we sank on the soft sward, with our saddles for pillows. When I awoke in the early morning light I saw my horse standing at my feet with his head bending over me. His breast and forelegs were covered with clotted blood which had flowed from an ugly bullet wound. How long he had stood there in mute appeal for sympathy and relief, I do not know—perhaps all the night. But as I recalled how cruelly I had spurred him to the chase the evening before, how without a groan of protest he had responded the best he could, and how patiently he had stood with me, all unconscious of his suffering, on that lonely, miserable watch, I was not ashamed to throw my arms around his neck and weep out my grief and contrition. Poor Joe, that was our last ride to battle together!

CHAPTER 8

The Adamstown Raid

On the day General Early crossed the Potomac at Harper's Ferry in his memorable movement on Washington, Colonel Mosby sent a detachment of his command under Lieut. Joe Nelson over into Maryland to a point on the telegraph line, with instructions to cut communication and prevent or delay intelligence of Early's advance.

As we approached the Potomac through a defile scarce lighted by the early morning sun, I was aroused by a gruff voice calling, "Halloa, Old Stick-in-the-Mud!" I looked up and heard the ringing laugh of John Mobley, as he forged on toward the head of the column. He belonged to White's battalion, but for some months had been on detached service scouting about northern Loudoun and the adjacent country in Maryland. He was not more than twenty years old, but he was wonderfully shrewd and daring, and had made quite a reputation as a skilful scout and reckless fighter. His presence with us in the capacity of guide, and the heading of our line of march toward the river, assured us that we were about to "carry the war into Africa" again, and we braced ourselves for adventure.

By the way, I never saw the young scout after that day. Some of his performances aroused the bitter animosities of the Union citizens of that section, and soon after this two or three of them treacherously lured him into an ambuscade which they had arranged, and had him shot to death by a file of Federal infantry.

When we neared the river a call was made for *carbineers* to come to the front. I usually carried a carbine, notwithstanding the inconvenience, because I liked sharpshooting service. It may have been for the reason that it brought me some experiences which would not come to me otherwise, or it may have been that I preferred to do my fighting at long range. But my ardour for sharpshooting on the river, at least, had been decidedly modified in the Point of Rocks raid; so this morning when Cab Maddux asked to borrow my gun to go to the front, I had the discretion to humour his valour.

We found a small Yankee picket at Chick's Ford, where our detachment crossed; but they speedily gave us right of way, and I do not remember that our sharpshooters got a wetting.

I recall with distinctness the impression made upon me by the condition of the country along our line of march to Adamstown. Everything betokened peace and plenty. The crops were abundant, the stock fat and sleek, and the houses seemed the quiet abodes of thrift. How different from those which we had left in Fauquier and southern Loudoun! Indeed, the only signs of war were, now and then, some citizens hurrying away to the woods with a drove of fine horses. They evidently had an intuition of our affinity for such stock; though it was seldom quick enough to save them. Our boys usually succeeded in overhauling them and bringing back such horses as were fit for our service, and indeed many that were not.

We reached Adamstown early in the forenoon and found the store open, the shops running and the citizens enjoying an Arcadia of peace. Our sudden and totally unexpected incursion gave them their first taste of war; and if it was not altogether agreeable, you may be sure that we made it sufficiently pungent to them.

Our first care was to cut down a telegraph pole and snap the wire. After which we proceeded to provide for our families, and appropriated to our own use, with liberal hand and joyous hearts, "sundry goods, wares and merchandises," with which we found the shelves of the only store well laden. But in the very midst of our proceedings of "escheat and confiscation" we were ordered by Lieutenant Nelson to restore our prizes to their former owner. It seems that the storekeeper had taken that officer aside and convinced him by some arguments (of the *solidity* of which we have always been a little sceptical), that in spite of his surroundings he was an original, unadulterated secessionist and entitled to our protection and admiration. I cannot do justice to the feelings of disappointment and disgust with which we relinquished our booty. Much of it, however, was of such a character that it could not be restored, and many of the boys moved away with their heads as light as their hands, if their hearts were heavier.

From Adamstown we moved eastward and, skirting the Sugar Loaf Mountain, struck back for the river. Alongside this road we came to a country store over which the owner did not succeed in raising the

H. COLE JORDAN
SERGEANT, COMPANY D.

"secesh flag" in time to save himself. His stock consisted for the most part of "wet goods," which were clearly contraband of war; and the work of confiscation proceeded promptly and without interruption. Not altogether without interruption, either—for in the midst of our "taking stock" word came to us that the Yankees were after us in force and were also pressing toward the river to shut us off.

This started us away, and though our march from there to the river was not very orderly or dignified, it was by no means the retreat of a stampeded or demoralised body. The fact is the boys had been "confiscating" so freely at the country store that they had become more or less reckless. I never saw a time when Company A would not fight anything that got in front of it; but that evening I don't think the men cared much what got in front of them. They had no fancy for being surrounded and cut off in the enemy's country, but there was a hope pervading them that they would at least be overtaken at the river.

Indeed, so strong was the disposition to fight that some of them could not reserve it for the Yankees. For instance, Lieutenant Nelson and a private named Moon got into an altercation in which pistols were drawn and only the interference of friends prevented serious trouble. Again, as we were passing down the road to Monocacy, our old friend Bill Ellzey (peace to his ashes!) and a man named Toller came to such a high misunderstanding that, though our pursuers were then in sight, and in spite of all remonstrances, they deliberately got down in the road and hitched their horses and went at it fist and skull. We had to move on and leave them to fight it out; but their friends, the enemy, soon came up and separated them and sent them both off to Fort Delaware to cool off.

When we reached the river at the mouth of the Monocacy late in the afternoon, sure enough, some of the Yankees had anticipated us; and as we rode down on the tow-path a picket, which occupied a bluff a few hundred yards below us, opened fire on us at long range. The command was halted on the river road; and I recollect that near where I stopped there was a large pile of cord wood, sufficiently high to protect myself and horse, and I took advantage of the situation. Just then Lieutenant Nelson spurred his horse out from the column and galloped toward the Yankees, who were up on an almost perpendicular bluff and utterly inaccessible to him. I don't recollect that he called on any one to follow him. Indeed, I considered that he was only doing it for the moral (?) effect. But as the Yankees directed their fire at him and the bullets were knocking the dust up around him, I pulled my horse from behind the woodpile and started after him. At that moment, however, I received a very forcible intimation from a crack marksman on the hill that I was not wanted at the front. I felt a sharp tap on the side of my head, and the next thing I knew I was lying behind the wood pile again, with a handkerchief tied around my head.

In the meanwhile, Harry Hatcher and Major Hibbs, "with Ned Rector and several others," had gotten around in the rear of the pickets and, charging upon them unexpectedly, had killed or captured the whole party.

We then pushed on up the river to reach the ford at Noland's Ferry before another detachment of Yankees, who were coming down the river, should get there. We barely made it, too. I crossed over with the prisoners among the first. But the enemy came up in time to make it hot for our rear-guard. Cab Maddux, even in those days, made a rather attractive mark, but as the bullets were splashing the water around him, his characteristic solicitude for others was manifested. Seeing a comrade in arms struggling through the waves some distance off and not receiving that attention from the Federal soldiers which he thought due to his rank. Cab cried out at the top of his voice, "Hurry up. *Major* Hibbs! Come along, *Major!*"

The Yankees at once transferred their shower baths from Cab to the major, who showed his appreciation of the former's self-sacrifice by spluttering out to him that he was "*respectful* all at once."

Graft Carlisle had been assigned to take charge of the prisoners. He escorted them to the water and then, himself, returned to where the fire was hottest, which place, of course, was close to Lieutenant Nelson's side. As that officer caught sight of him he inquired with anxiety,

"Graft, where are your prisoners?"

"Gone over the river."

"Why are you not with them? I put you in charge of them."

"Why, I ordered another fellow to take my place."

"You can't do that!" yelled Nelson.

"Can't I?" answered Graft. "Well, I did do it."

And there the matter ended.

As Dr. Sowers was dressing my wound at a farmhouse on this side the river, Harry Hatcher came up and offered this consolation, "Never mind, Johnnie, old boy; I killed one of them Yankees for that."

Chapter 9

The Greenback Raid

I did not know for many years that the Greenback raid was, in one sense, the sequel to the Whitewood fight. This was a sharp little scrap which we had with the Eighth Illinois Cavalry one afternoon near the Plains.

This regiment was engaged in supervising the relaying of the tracks of the Manassas Gap Railroad. Or, more precisely, together with a considerable body of infantry, it was acting as guard for the workmen who were undertaking that job, to protect them and their work from interruptions on our part. Colonel Mosby determined to make them earn their wages, so to speak, and proceeded to interest them. Among many other entertainments provided for them, such as holding up their trains, tearing up their tracks and surprising their camp, he arranged this matinee.

He took about eighty of us out to their vicinity and casually exposed some decoys. The Federals caught sight of them and sent out their feelers. The vigilant eyes of these discovered others of us evidently trying to keep out of their sight. Then the regiment quickly mounted and came out. Of course, we hurried away when discovered, and their ardour increased. When we finally fled precipitately into the big body of timber known as Whitewood they were so close on our heels that they could not forbear from rushing on to bag their game. When they got well into the woods the fugitives suddenly regained their nerve and wheeled squarely about in the faces of their pursuers, while others of our men pressed on each of their flanks. This was a "number" on the program for which they had not arranged; and such of them as found it practicable to do so sought the protection of their humbler allies, the infantry, with a haste at least equal to the presumption with which they had left it.

But at one time things seemed pretty uncertain with us. The Eighth Illinois were no holiday soldiers, but by considerable odds the best fighters we ever tackled. Notwithstanding the surprise, they held us up for a space; and in the hand-to-hand fight Colonel Mosby, who was himself in our front rank and in the thickest of the *mêlée*, was thrown to the ground, his horse falling upon one of his legs. I am not sure but that the desperate rally of his men around him until he could remount really turned the balances. For, of course, we just had to stay by him, regardless of all consequences.

He told me in San Francisco in 1895 that he had been contemplating an attack on the Baltimore and Ohio Railroad trains in the Shenandoah Valley; he said that just about this time his scouts reported that the opportunities were favourable for making a successful one, and he determined to reward the boys who were in the Whitewood fight by putting them up against a train which would likely be laden with more valuable stores than were those they had been capturing on the Manassas branch. Accordingly, in a few days, after his injured limb braced up a little and he found that we could suspend operations at the Plains, we went over to the Valley.

We spent the greater part of the day in some high-rolling sport on the turnpike between Winchester and Martinsburg. The command was hidden in a piece of woods conveniently situated. From the elevations our scouts watched parties of Federals moving along the pike in squads of different sizes and on various missions. When one such came in sight a party from our camp would slip off around the hills to appear in their front; and when they ran back from them they would meet another of our parties which had been sent out in another direction to intercept them. With variations, this thing was kept up pretty much all day, most of the experiences being confined to the realm of comedy and marked by nothing more serious than lively horse-racing and the incidents usual to running fellows down and gathering them in. There were, however, some tragedies.

The party with which I was sent out struck a squad which not only showed fight, but which, when they found themselves hemmed up in the road, undertook a desperate race across country. One poor fellow foolishly made it necessary for us to shoot him. He must have lost his head, for there was no reason why he should not have surrendered. There was reason why two of his companions should have taken hopeless chances; for when overtaken they were found to be Jesse scouts, clad in Confederate uniforms. When I came back to the pike the wounded soldier lying there was still alive. I went to him to learn the extent of his hurt and to render assistance. He lay on his back, shot through the body, and insisted that he was dying. I did not think so, as there was not much bleeding, and tried to cheer him; but he talked of his home and his mother, and as he talked he suddenly rolled over, jerked his leg a time or two, and was gone. Of all the "passings" to which I was a party during the war, this is the only one that has really "left a haunt in my head." He was but a lad and had brought his death on himself so fatuously.

One of the Jesse scouts met his fate over in the field, the other was overtaken by a man who did not have the heart to kill him, as he ought to have done, for I am sure it must be much easier to die in hot blood. But he was carried back to camp and later in the day turned over to Ewell Attwell for execution. Ewell had a record for killing men in fight, but he told me that he just did not have the nerve to take that fellow out under the stars and all alone by themselves stand him up and shoot the life out of him. So he told him to turn his back and run for it and he would give him five steps start. How much that was worth to him in front of Attwell's revolver, God knows. Attwell swore to me that he himself did not know.

Late in the evening we moved away, and I recollect that the march that night was unusually brisk. We pulled up in a body of woods where we dismounted and left our horses with a detail, then marched a few hundred yards across a field and reached the railroad at a deep cut. Here we went to work on the track, and soon had one side of it so elevated on fence rails and old ties as to insure the upsetting of the engine when it should come to that point. Then we laid along the bank and waited for things to happen.

Some of the boys, perhaps most of them, soon fell asleep, but "*tired Nature's sweet restorer*" was not for me that night. The lights and sounds from a neighbouring camp first interested me, and then my imagination ran riot. Anticipations of what was certain to happen, and pictures of what might happen, in the next half hour, set my nerves tingling. It is not a pleasant thing to lie calmly under the stars and contemplate the usual contingencies of a straight fight. But the possible horrors of a railroad wreck, and the sufferings of women, children, and, not improbably, the presence of a carload of infantry, took such tangible shapes in my meditations as to give me a very bad half hour.

Presently I heard the train coming and I hurried around waking up the boys. I then went back to my place and watched and listened to the thumping of my heart. Nearer and louder came the sounds and quicker beat my pulses. Directly the headlight of the engine shot around a curve not far off, and as the engine rushed almost under me, it seemed, my heart well-nigh choked me. And then there was a tremendous thump and the shriek of the steam and the sound of a single shot and then—"the deluge." "Board her, boys!" rang out the colonel's crisp, steady tones. That brought me back to sense and braced me. The conductor of the train seemed to take in the situation more promptly than any of us, and never for a moment lost his nerve. He jumped off between his train and us, swinging a lighted lantern, and cried out that he surrendered the train. Down the bank we rushed.

As I ran up the steps on the platform of a coach a tall Ranger was standing with his pistol poked through the door ajar, calling on somebody to surrender. Being short and slim, I slipped under his arm and jumped in. On the first seat sat a soldier with a lady beside him, who, as I stopped, assured me that her "husband was a sick man." Just behind them sat a gentleman, across whose portliness stretched a gold watch chain. He must have noticed that it fascinated my gaze, for he promptly presented it to me, without detaching from it a beautiful gold watch. Of course I could not accept such munificence without some inquiry into the condition of his finances. The generous old man responded to this with the offer of his pocket-book, but I had barely noticed its plump appearance, when a long lank arm reached over my shoulder and appropriated what my modesty might have declined. By this time the boys were crowding into the car. As I moved down the aisle I felt a gentle touch on my arm and a sweet voice asked if I would "protect them." Of course I would, and took my seat between as pretty a pair of cherubs as ever made a fool of a soldier boy. And I stayed there, too, until the looting of the car was completed.

After the looting the cars were to be burnt, but they had to be emptied of certain valuables. First, of course, came the ladies, who were disposed as comfortably as practicable with their baggage which was gathered from the car. You may be sure that my fair *protégés* received every needed attention, not only from myself but from other gallants whom their beauty attracted. I believe they were the *belles* of the occasion; and I am sure that they really enjoyed the affair, and doubtless had many stories to relate of their flirtations that night with Mosby's "Guerrillas."

The occupants of one car were immigrants who could not understand even enough English to learn how to get out of a fire. They sat

J. West Aldridge
Company D

immovable under every inducement to "change base." Finally, when the situation was reported to the colonel, his eye fell on a big bundle of newspapers which had been intercepted, and he ordered that they be set afire and thrown into the car. This gave rise to the only comical feature of the occasion. When the fire brands fell into the aisle, the dumb creatures didn't stand on the order of their going, but went tumbling heels over head out of the windows.

We ourselves barely escaped a stampede. Cab Maddux had been left with the horse detail back in the woods. Now Cab was nothing if not enterprising, and as he saw the lights and heard the sounds, he just couldn't stand it. So here he came, rushing across the field. When he came up, it was with some cock and bull story about the Yankees coming. Nothing can be more demoralizing to a cavalryman than to be attacked away from his horse, and for a moment or two the situation was more than threatening. The colonel, however, promptly got control of affairs, and when he satisfied himself that it was a false alarm, maybe Cab didn't get a roasting. It wound up with a threat of that direst of all punishments to a Mosby man—to be sent back to the regular service.

But why was it called the Greenback Raid? Well, I'll declare, I well-nigh left Hamlet out of the play. Before the cars were set afire such things as appeared valuable were taken out. As an officer whom West Aldridge had ordered out stepped upon the ground, bearing an innocent looking satchel, Charley Dear courteously relieved him of his baggage. As he parted with it, he charged Charley to be careful with it, as it contained greenbacks. "Greenbacks, greenbacks!" shouted Charley as he made his way toward the colonel. An investigation revealed a great roll of uncut sheets of the "long green," and Charley's eyes were not the only ones that assumed the dimensions of saucers at the ravishing sight.

About this time West Aldridge came up with a similar fairy-tale, and substantial exhibits to bring it into the realm of fact. In his final clean-up of a car he noticed a large dark object on the floor between two seats, covered with a handsome gum blanket. There was no response to the investigating kick that he gave it, but the lifting of the blanket revealed a Yankee officer, crouching and clinging to a forlorn hope that he might be overlooked. So tenaciously did he embrace it that West's call on him to come along was unheeded until it was emphasized by the click of his revolver in his ear; and then as Major Ruggles rose to his feet and yielded to his fate, he managed to drop his *poncho* into the place where he had hidden. He moved off with great reluctance, as one who had left his heart behind him. These peculiarities of behaviour recurred to West's mind after he had turned over his prisoner at the car door, and impelled him to return and get that precious *poncho*. I think he must have been afraid of snakes, for he investigated it again with his foot before picking it up, and found it to be a heavy tin box. As he bore it away it suggested treasure to his excited imagination. The first thing was his horse, and then he sought Colonel Mosby.

"What have you got?" a voice inquired as he was making his way around the crowd.

"Gold; a safe of gold!" he gasped, and his eyes glittered wildly in the star light.

"Come here, boy," and the voice was low and stern and metallic. "You don't have to find Mosby, or tell anybody about this. Let's you and I strike for Loudoun with the stuff." That suggestion brought West to his equipoise. I would not have liked to be the object of the contempt that flashed from his eyes, nor to be the one to whom he hissed back, "And be a thief?" The man to whom he said it was one of the *desperadoes* of the command, but he only answered, "Well, you are a damned fool!" and stood out of his way as he went on toward Colonel Mosby.

Before this find was published and while the fire and smoke from the burning train were going up toward the abode of the Recording Angel (and I wonder how he wrote up that night's transaction), Major Ruggles remarked in taunting tones, as he stood on the bank among the boys, that he had contributed upward of two hundred thousand dollars to that fire. "Look here, Major," West replied, and he pulled back the gum and tapped the box with a caressing hand. The major's countenance fell.

When the contents of the tin box and the satchel were added together they amounted to the handsome sum of over one hundred and sixty thousand dollars. I had as well add here that the next day at Bloomfield they were impartially divided out among the boys who were on that raid, so that each one received about $2,200 in crisp new greenbacks, in uncut sheets of various denominations. My old haversack never bore such contents before; and to tell the truth, my eyes have never fallen upon such a sight since. Some of our prisoners informed us that even a larger amount of money than this, belonging to another paymaster, was missed by us and consumed with the burnt train. Possibly this was true and probably it was said to make us feel bad.

The only man who did not participate in this division was Colonel Mosby himself. No sort of solicitations from his men could induce him to take a share. His emphatic response was that he was fighting for glory, not for spoils. I have always wondered what he took us for? But so sensitive on this point was he, that he would not even permit Mrs. Mosby to accept a purse of gold which the boys subsequently made up and tendered her.

After the train had gotten well afire, we gathered up ourselves and the things which we had saved from the wreck, and took our departure; some of us not without regard for the *"girls we left behind us."*

When about daybreak we reached the neighbourhood of Kabletown we learned that Captain Blazer with his band of picked scouts were encamped in a piece of woods not far from the line of our retreat. We had it in for him, because of his recent treatment of Company A, and thought to return his compliment in an early morning call, and induce him to go home with us. Before the sun rose we dashed into his camp; but it was only to find empty beds and the fires still burning by which his men had commenced cooking their breakfasts. The wily old chap had caught wind of us on the breezes that attend the spring of the day and had given us the go-by.

Among the prisoners whom we brought from the train was a fine looking lieutenant. He was a German and a professional soldier who had seen service in one of the Continental armies. In an interview with Colonel Mosby he took pains to impress upon him that he had no sentiment whatever in our war, but had joined the Federal service only for the sake of experience and to perfect himself in American military tactics.

While he was reposing under the shade of a tree near Bloomfield the next morning, a Ranger stood before him and expressed admiration of his handsome cavalry boots, and ended with demanding a trade. This was duly effected. In a few minutes another came up and went through a similar proceeding with reference to his hat. When the third man, in a decided condition of negligee as to breeches, opened negotiations for his bran-new trousers, the lieutenant thought the limit had been reached and demanded to see Colonel Mosby before undressing. He was promptly carried to that officer, and indignantly stated his grievance with some pretty strong remarks about the customs of civilized warfare being abused.

"Did you not tell me that you came over here to learn American tactics?" drawled the colonel.

"Yes, yes," he stammered; "but who ever heard of such treatment of prisoners?"

"Well, those are our tactics," said the colonel, and the incident was closed.

I always thought that the colonel arranged this lesson for the foreign gentleman who was seeking experience.

CHAPTER 10

The Blazer Fight

While Colonel Mosby was occupying as much of the attention of Sheridan as he could and absorbing that of General Augur, in the fall of 1864, there was another Federal officer engaged in attracting the attention of Colonel Mosby and all his men—indeed, he had a special contract not only to interest the colonel, but to take him and all his belongings, dead or alive, and that officer was Captain Richard Blazer. This brave man was a West Virginian, who had gone into the Northern army, and had so distinguished himself that he was specially chosen for the task of driving away or destroying Mosby and his command. However rough he was on the members of the Forty-Third Battalion of Virginia Cavalry, Mr. John Scott says:

> His kindness to citizens was proverbial, and everywhere within the range of his activities the citizens were ready to bear honourable testimony to his character.

How effective was his work let his own report show; but, with all allowance for self-praise, he was certainly a thorn in Mosby's side.

Headquarters Independent Scouts,
Middletown, Va., Oct. 24, 1864.

Sir: I have the honour of submitting the following report of the operations of my command since the 18th of August:

On the 18th, learning that a party of Mosby's guerrillas were in the vicinity of Myerstown, I proceeded to that place and overtook them near the Shenandoah River, and, after a chase of three miles, I drove them across the river, capturing one prisoner. The army having fallen back to Halltown on the 25th, according to your orders, I went into Loudoun County, and after operating for several days I killed five of Mosby's gang and captured three prisoners. The army having again advanced to Berryville, on the night of the 3rd of September I learned that Mosby, with a considerable force, was at Snickersville. Early on the morning of the 4th I crossed the river at Backus' Ford and moved up the river to where I could get up the mountain through the woods.

I struck the pike east of the top of the mountain, and moved on their camp. Finding that he had left during the night in the direction of Charlestown, I determined to follow. I recrossed the mountain through Lewis Gap, and, by a forced march, I overtook them about 2 p.m. at Myers' Ford, and, after a spirited fight for several minutes, I completely routed them, with a loss on his part of thirteen killed, six wounded, five prisoners and seventeen horses. My loss was one killed and six wounded. Since that I have had several small affairs with them, in which I have always defeated them, except twice.

On the 20th Lieutenant Ewing, with five men, was attacked on the Berryville pike, near the Opequon, by a superior force, and all captured except himself. On the 23rd Sergeant Fuller, of the Fifth Virginia Infantry, with ten men, was attacked near Summit Point by fifty or sixty guerrillas. He fought them until he was overpowered and four of his men were killed, one wounded and the rest all captured but three, who made their escape.

Having learned that a man by the name of Marshall was recruiting a company in the vicinity of Ashby's Gap, and that they were to organise on the 25th, I proceeded to their reported rendezvous, near White Post, and completely surprised them, getting Marshall and four of his men, and capturing all his papers. In another affair below Front Royal I left eight of his murderers to keep company with some that (were) left by General Custer; these, with a number of others that I have picked up through the country, make an aggregate, in killed, forty-four; wounded, twelve, and prisoners, including two captured in the advance to Cedar Creek the first time, twelve. My entire loss is five men killed, seven wounded and eight prisoners.

    I am, sir, very respectfully,
          Your obedient servant,
              (Signed)   R. Blazer
          Captain Commanding Independent Scouts
      Assistant Adjutant-General, Army of West Virginia.

After this report was filed, indeed, shortly prior to the occurrence of which I am about to give an account, Captain Blazer had come upon Company A of Mosby's battalion while bivouacked in a glen of the Blue Ridge, and completely surprised and routed them, killing some of their best men, capturing more and shooting down and capturing their commanding officer, Lieutenant Nelson, who to this day carries in his hip the leaden souvenir of the occasion.

Company A was now burning for its revenge. Things had come to such a pass that that section of the country was not large enough to hold the rival clans, and it became a military necessity that Blazer should be wiped out. So Colonel Mosby dispatched Major A. E. Richards, with his squadron, consisting of Companies A and B, upon the mission.

We crossed the mountain and the Shenandoah River one afternoon in a terrible rain, and spent the night, without fires or shelter, in Castleman's big woods, a few miles northeast of Berryville. Early the next morning we moved out in quest of our game. But the vigilant Blazer had due notice of our approach, and, as we afterward learned, pretty accurate information as to our numbers. He broke camp, mounted his men and promptly took up the gage of battle. The parties were about equally matched as to numbers. Each recognised that the decisive hour had come, and was none the less eager for the fray. But each also appreciated the immense advantage of "getting the bulge," as our Harry Hatcher called it, on the other. And now began manoeuvring for position. We actually followed each other around in a circle, the commands being kept in the ravines and under the river bluffs, while the hostile scouts frequently caught sight of each other from neighbouring hills.

While this game of hide and seek was going on, two of our scouts—Charley McDonough and John Puryear, rode up a hill and found themselves within a short distance of several other soldiers in Confederate uniforms approaching them. They took for granted that they were some of our scouts, though they did not recognise the individuals. McDonough, however, was outlawed by the Federal authorities, with a price upon his head, for some desperate deeds previously committed by him, and this made him cautious of making new acquaintances. Declaring that he wouldn't allow men whom he didn't know to ride up on him, he quietly withdrew, while Puryear, with some impatient expression at Charley's timidity, awaited the strangers, who, when they came up, proved sure enough to be Jesse scouts, a class of Federal scouts wearing Confederate uniforms, in which disguise they succeeded in "taking in" many an unwary Johnnie Reb.

Puryear was a brave youth, who bore a heart always ready for a soldier's fate, and he bowed to the inevitable with the best grace he could. But an experience awaited him of which he, poor fellow, little dreamed. When he was carried by his captors back to Lieutenant Cole, the second in command to Blazer, who had charge of the scouts, that officer of course questioned him as to the whereabouts of our command, and equally, of course, he refused to give any information. Lieutenant Cole should not have expected it from him. But I suppose he was a man who looked upon war as a barbarous business, anyhow, and considered barbarous means justifiable for military success. At any rate, he insisted upon Puryear's betraying his comrades, and threats of instant death failing to move the loyal-hearted lad, he proceeded apparently to put his threats into execution. A rope was placed around the prisoner's neck and he was suspended from a tree until nearly unconscious, and then lowered and again questioned. Once, even twice, was this repeated. But the boy still refused to answer, and the brutal torture was stayed. Possibly the exigencies of the hour were more responsible for it than any spirit of relenting on the part of Lieutenant Cole.

In the meanwhile. Major Richards had found his place and opportunity, and made his dispositions.

Our scouts had reported Blazer's command as moving southward up the Charlestown road, which at Myers's shop intersects a road running thence eastward to the Shenandoah River. Major Richards at once moved us past this shop down the river road as if in a great hurry. Of this he took care that Blazer should be duly informed by a citizen upon his arrival at the cross-roads. Marching perhaps a quarter of a mile down this road, he reached a narrow strip of woods, not more than a hundred yards wide, which borders the road on the south and runs parallel with it a considerable distance. Just back of the woods was an open field, which sloped rather abruptly from the woods into a deep valley and then rises again toward the south, in full view of the road at this time of the year. Along the top of this back hill, on the southern boundary of the field, ran an old rail fence. From this fence to the road the distance was perhaps three hundred yards.

Now, passing through these woods, Major Richards left a few men scattered here and there in them, as though they were scouts. Just beyond them to the south, under the brow of the hill. Company B was

JOHN R. TILLETT
COMPANY H

drawn up in line of battle, facing the road, so disposed that the enemy would not see them until one or the other should reach the hill top. Still farther to the south, down in the vale, Company A was halted in line of march. And so we waited.

As we expected, when Blazer reached Myers's shop he was informed that we had just left there in something of a hurry. On he pushed after us, at double quick. When he reached the woods on the river road, and was moving past them, his attention was attracted by our decoys, which had been left there. A few shots passed between them, when he halted his men and faced them in line toward us, and was about to deploy skirmishers into the woods. At this crucial moment Company A moved hurriedly out of the valley into his view, upon the southern slope of the old field, toward the back fence, through which some of our men were seen tearing gaps for dear life. The impression was at once made upon him that we had taken fright, and were in full retreat. Here was his chance. The gods were propitious; the man should not be wanting. Ordering a charge, on he brought his men pell-mell through the woods after us.

This was what Richards had calculated on. Company B sprang to the charge, and, to Blazer's utter surprise, met him with a yell and a volley at the top of the hill. His men were of the true metal, however, and stood the surprise and the shock like heroes. The two lines closed up, and for more than a minute (and that's an age for such business) stood horse to horse, emptying their revolvers into each other's faces. At this point murderous work was done on both sides.

But as Company B made its charge Company A halted in its retreat, and, at the word from Hatcher, faced about on the instant, dashed back at full speed, rushed up the hill into the woods, and struck Blazer's still struggling and astonished men on the left flank. Not even a halt was made, and we carried the enemy in hopeless, reckless rout back through the woods into the road, and on past Myers's shop to—well, I don't know where. The truth is, that all except five or six, who were unusually well mounted or got off in good time, were overtaken and captured.

Captain Blazer stood his ground among the last desperate fighters, and only when he saw that the day was hopelessly lost and his veterans had fallen thick around him, did he betake himself to flight. He was well mounted and made a race as gallant as was his fight. More than a mile up the road, and away ahead of the main body, he was overtaken by Syd. Ferguson, a burly young Ranger. Pursuer and pursued had emptied their pistols, and Blazer paid no heed to the youth's calls on him to halt until Ferguson finally, running beside him, knocked him prone in the road with the butt of his revolver.

While we were rushing pell-mell up the road, Rangers and Federals running side by side, behind and before, dashing mud into each other's faces, I nearly participated in a peculiar class of tragedy to which some of our best men at times fell victims. I came up with a great burly fellow, who was forging ahead. He paid no attention to my calls to surrender, and spurring closer, I rammed the muzzle of my revolver against his broad back. The psychological influence of it was prompt, for before I could pull the trigger he turned his head and John Foster's big gray eyes rolled at me. I nearly fell from my horse as I realised how near I had come to killing one of my chums. Of all the sensations of that day—and the day was full of them—I believe that was my heaviest jolt.

He wore one of those new Confederate uniforms which, saturated with rain and bespattered with mud, was undistinguishable from Union blue, and out of his mask of red clay no features but his eyes were recognisable. When he told this story to his little wife, long years afterward, I could not clearly make out whether the look which she turned on me was mostly of gratitude to Providence for its interposition, or—of contempt for my being such a fool as not to know her boy under all circumstances.

As the rout passed Myers's shop I saw a Federal officer strike out from the main body of flying men, evidently to seek his own salvation. My horse, which was strong and fleet, made after him, and in less than a hundred yards' run I was alongside him. On my call to surrender he halted and raised both hands. I saw that his pistols were in his holster, and leaned over to unbuckle his belt and secure them. As I was bent over my attention was attracted by the sound of a horse's feet, and I raised my head to see Puryear rein up behind us. His face was distorted with anger or excitement, and he was pointing a cocked pistol at the officer's head.

Puryear was, of course, released from his captivity as soon as Blazer's column broke. I learned afterward that he at once fell upon his guard and wrested his revolver from him and fell into the chase. Lieutenant Cole became the single object of his pursuit, and, his eye once falling upon him, he had followed him like a Nemesis throughout the whole desperate race until he came up with him in my possession.

I raised my hand and cried, "Don't shoot this man; he has surrendered!"

Puryear answered, with an oath, "The rascal tried to hang me this morning." I knew that he had been in the enemy's hands, and asked the prisoner if what he charged were true. There was a moment's hesitation, and no response; then the crack of a pistol, and Lieutenant Cole fell against my side and rolled to the ground between his horse and mine. I dismounted and took his belt, with a pair of revolvers, from around him. Let me pay this tribute to his memory—both pistols were empty. I believe I failed to state that when I overtook him he was bleeding profusely from a wound in the breast, which he had received in the fight. As I moved away he rolled his dying eyes toward me with a look I shall never forget, and I would gladly have tarried to give him such comfort as I could. But this was no time for sympathy, and I hurried back to the road.

A soldier who shortly afterward went to him and got his watch and a small sum of money from his person told me that he was dead when he found him.

Perhaps somebody will be interested in the following sequel, which came to my knowledge a quarter of a century after the events narrated above.

I was sitting by my fireside last winter discussing this fight with a friend whose family resided near the scene and were eye-witnesses to much that I have written. He told me that his father had assisted in burying the Federal dead, and took special charge of the remains of Lieutenant Cole, with whom he had had a pleasant acquaintance. A few days after the fight—possibly the next day—a detachment of the First Pennsylvania Cavalry rode up to his house and asked if he knew where the lieutenant's body was buried. When he told them that he himself had buried it he was asked if the body showed any signs of having been rifled. The questioners were very anxious about this, because, they said, he had a large sum of money in a belt around him. This information, of course, made Mr. Chamberlayne, the citizen, very nervous, also, for if the money should not be found his own position might be made not altogether a happy one. So he carried the party to the grave without delay, and the body was exhumed.

Greatly to his relief the belt, with the money, was found intact. His comrades said the amount was $1,800, but I can scarcely imagine the circumstances that would induce him to carry so much money about him in his precarious kind of life. However, soldiers were curious people. The sum was considerable, at any rate. How like kicking himself, when he reads this, will the man feel who got his watch and purse! I cannot myself say that I do not regret that I did not carry my own researches in that direction further.

Perhaps that dying look expressed a wish to communicate the presence of the treasure to me, who at least made an effort to save his life.

How the news of this fight reached the enemy is told officially by General Stevenson:

> Headquarters Military District of Harper's Ferry,
> Harper's Ferry, Nov. 19, 1864.
>
> Lieutenant-Colonel J. W. Forsyth, Chief-of-Staff,
> Middle Military Division, in the field.
>
> Colonel: Two of Captain Blazer's men came in this morning, Privates Harris and Johnson. They report that Mosby, with 300 men, attacked Blazer near Kabletown yesterday about 11 o'clock. They say that the entire command, with the exception of themselves, was either captured or killed.
>
> I have ordered out Major Congdon, with 300 Twelfth Pennsylvania Cavalry, to Kabletown, to bury dead and take care of wounded, if any, and report all facts he can learn. Shall immediately furnish report as soon as received.
>
> Respectfully,
>
> John D. Stevenson,
> Brigadier-General.

Captain Blazer was sent to Libby Prison, where, in a card printed in the *Richmond Enquirer* in 1864, he said he was well treated. He survived the war, but fell a victim to yellow fever at Gallipolis, Ohio, about the end of October, 1878,

CHAPTER 11

The Fight at Dulany's

But things did not always go our way. The fight at Dulany's illustrated how simple and apparently conclusive combinations sometimes do not work.

One morning a detachment of nearly two hundred of the Eighth Illinois cavalry went out from the Plains on a scout toward Upperville. Captain Frankland got together about a hundred of our men and fell on their trail. As they approached Upperville in the afternoon we came up with them, having gotten between them and their camp, and Frankland proceeded to make his arrangements for another "Dranesville affair."

The turnpike from Winchester to Alexandria—the great highway of Mosby's Confederacy—passing through Upperville runs practically east and west. About a mile east of Upperville, at No. 6, the road from Rectortown comes out on the pike. Westward from this point for perhaps a half mile a narrow strip of woods ran along the south side of the pike, back of which the open fields stretched to Henry Dulany's mansion, which sat on rising ground nearly another half mile away.

We were out on the Rectortown road in the neighbourhood of Dulany's when we learned that the enemy was approaching No. 6, up the turnpike. The news bringing the assurance that matters were now coming to a crisis was received with great jubilation. I never saw our boys keener for a fight, or knew them to go into one in better spirits. And this, notwithstanding the usual incident which occurred when we came to form the battle array down under a hill east of Dulany's house. It presents a characteristic which I shall pause to set forth.

We had no special regulation as to the location in the ranks of individual men—whether on the march, on parade, or in formation for battle. The men just fell in, at all times, just where the opening was convenient. I noticed that when on the march, especially when we passed farmhouses and villages where *"bright eyes were sparkling for us,"* the front ranks were always filled by the fancy fellows who wore the waving plumes and the gay gilt. I noticed, too, that when the formations for fight were being made up these same gentry always had something about their trappings to adjust, or some other personal matter to look to, which detained them while the practical utility men got into their vacant places. Therefore we seldom had a chance to *"follow these plumes of Navarre amid the battle's smoke."* In this way it happened that when we turned into Dulany's field and moved toward the Federal's flank, I had gotten pushed into the first set of fours beside Lieutenant Ab Wrenn, who was leading the column.

As I stated before, the boys were almost hilarious, laughing and jesting; and I recollect that Will Anderson, riding in the second file, was singing an extemporaneous parody on the *"Vacant Chair,"* in which he substituted Yankee saddles for chairs, and multiplied them indefinitely. Whatever may have been the excellencies of his poesy in other respects, it certainly was not like that of the Seers of old, inspired prophecy; for it was not many minutes before he was singing a different song and the others were feeling the force of the old adage, "He laughs best who laughs last."

When our party turned into the field another detachment kept on down the No. 6 road toward the turnpike. I suppose their mission was to strike the enemy at another point at the same time we attacked them, and it seems that another party was held in reserve, possibly for cutting off the escape of fugitives. They were never called on for that purpose at least, and I do not know what became of them.

We rode across the field toward the Dulany house at a brisk trot, keeping behind a swell of ground which stretched from the house eastward and hid the enemy from our view. Then we raised the hill diagonally, and I caught my first sight of the men whom we were hunting. It seems that somehow they had gotten knowledge of our presence and had advanced a considerable distance south of the woods and were moving toward us in three platoons. They must have been within three hundred yards of us then. When we appeared they seemed to adopt converging lines, still moving toward us in a walk, so that when we came up to them in front of Dulany's mansion the three bodies had practically consolidated and our little squadron of less than fifty men was "up against the whole show."

As we trotted down the hill, I noticed an ominous silence behind us. I recollect a feeling of astonishment that we had gotten so close without the customary rush and yell. I believe that no firing had been done by either party up to that moment. Instead of the call to the wild rush, I saw Lieutenant Wrenn draw back his horse. He had seen what I now turned my head and looked upon with a sickening shock—everything behind the two front files was swerving around in front of the house toward the barn-yard gate at the west. They had recognised the helplessness of the situation and promptly proceeded to arrange *"to fight again another day."*

Just then the Illinoisans opened fire on us with Spencer rifles, and three men were knocked out of our first two files. George Turberville at my left side caught it in the thigh; the man beyond him to the left was killed, and George Gulick, just behind me, was struck plumb in the forehead. Dazed and unable to take in the catastrophe, we five fools sat there until another volley swept through us and brought down two more of our number. Then, half crazy, we rode down in front of the line of smoking carbines and emptied a revolver apiece. We were then close enough to distinguish the buttons on their coats. After that came chaos.

When I reached the barnyard gate some of our men were going through it, all mixed up with the Yankees, some of whom had rushed up. Others pressed after us through the barnyard, down a narrow lane which crossed a branch at the foot of the hill; but they did not follow us into the field at the end of the lane, into which our men retreated. Indeed, I think very few, if any, of them got as far as the end of the lane. They evidently did not have sufficient confidence in their position as masters of the situation to feel like taking any liberties with it.

Out in the old field our men were quickly rallied by some officer whom I cannot recall, and moved back to the gate of the lane. Here they were met by an irritating fire from the long-range guns of the Yankees up on the hill in the barnyard and around the mansion-house. The hiss of the bullets and their pattering on the fence made our men restless, and there was a determination not to stay there; but the sentiment was divided as to the direction in which to go. Some of them just could not realise that we were whipped. Cab Maddux and another one of those fellows who "didn't have sense enough to know danger when they saw it" dashed back up the lane, and got as far as the barnyard again before they discovered that the path of glory was all their own. Its loneliness impelled them to desert it by the quickest possible route. A heavier hail of bullets just then had determined

A. E. RICHARDS
CAPTAIN COMPANY B; PROMOTED MAJOR
FIRST SQUADRON

the rest of our detachment to depart; but they moved off across the field in good order—or, at least in full possession of themselves—and unpursued.

I had been separated from them; and when I returned to the gate, under fire from a squad that sought to cut me off, I found no comrade in sight, except Charley Hawling's horse, which was quietly cropping grass. In the first rush down the lane Charley's horse fell sprawling and delivered his rider into the road, laid out, apparently dead. He was one of the devoted eight, and as we left him I felt some sense of the irony of the fate that brought him untouched through the fires of that hell, to such a comparatively inglorious end. He lives, however, to tell the tale of how some Yankees roused him to consciousness and carried him back toward the barnyard, where he saw two lines of their fellows drawn up. When they came to the gate Charley thought it too narrow for him and his three captors to pass through it abreast, so he held back to give them precedence.

The backward movement seemed to accord with his feelings and was adopted by him with such vigour and promptness that he was some distance down the hill again before they got their guns to working; but when they did so, it was to such effect as to make the road too hot for him and lift him over the fence into the bottom of a spring branch in one of the out-lots of Dulany's grounds. When the firing ceased he arose and made for a convenient hen house, into the top of which he ensconced himself and remained there until the Federals departed.

I do not think that many Yankees followed us south of Dulany's house. I know that there were none south of the house fifteen minutes after we rallied, except a few with long-range guns moving about the back yard. The fact is, that Lieutenant Grogan was entertaining them on the eastern side. It was thought that the fight failed because Grogan did not come to time and strike them simultaneously with us. He came to time, all right, but was the victim of bad scouting. We selected our ground and then failed to know it, and that ignorance was fatal to us. I never learned the secret of the disaster until I got it from the lips of Lieut. Font Beattie this blessed August, 1906. He says that when Grogan's men charged they ran up against a wide and deep ditch, trimmed with a ragged rail fence.

It was absolutely impassable; and in following it in search of a crossing place, they were led away from the Yankees; and not until they reached the place where the Upperville road crossed it, could they resume their line of approach. In the meanwhile, the Federals had given us our medicine, and were then ready to administer to Grogan; which they proceeded to do with promptness and dispatch.

The rising ground intervened between Grogan's party and ours, so that we could see nothing of his movements. Doubtless if we had done so, we would have consummated our threatened dash back up the lane and relieved the pressure on him; and there might have been a different tale to tell of that afternoon. But—

Of all fool words of tongue or pen,
The idlest tell what might have been.

The cold, sad record is, we were whipped in detail; and the Eighth Illinois did it. And I will add that they were worthy of their laurels.

Among those of our men who were shot in front of the Dulany house was Joe Bryan. His chum, Charley Dear, saw him down at the front reeling on his horse—perhaps, heard a call from him—and worked his way some distance through the storm to him. Charley's idea was a rescue, and he called to Joe to fly. But the youth, without even down on his cheek, braced his lank, callow form to its height and, Charley says, in a fine frenzy shouted, "A Bryan never flies from a foe!"

"This Bryan is—an irresponsible." Well, that's a liberally polite translation of what his more practical friend did say as he threw his arm about him and bore him bodily away.

As the evening shadows lengthened, bare-headed, depressed and alone, except for Hawling's horse, whose disreputable appearance added nothing to relieve the situation, I rode over the Goose Creek hills and left Dulany's field to history.

The MS. of the foregoing was submitted to Mr. E. A. Worrell of Company C, Eighth Illinois Cavalry, and a Past Commander of the Post of Survivors of that regiment, with whom the author has formed a very pleasant acquaintance. He writes under date of August 21, 1906:

> I read it at our Regimental reunion at Minneapolis on the 14th, during the National Encampment of the G. A. R. Our boys were so taken with it that they had a number of copies of it struck off to take home with them. I was in Company C and was with Corporal Prut in advance of our advance guard. As we came up the hill about opposite the Dulany mansion on the pike, two of our boys were coming up the hill from toward

Upperville. They and we stopped. Prut said, 'You take the one on the dark horse and I will take the other.' His man fell dead from his horse. Mine wheeled and ran, the loose horse following him. I gave them a chase and came near being captured myself, as the Johnnies got between me and our advance guard and flankers. Soon after this we were engaged in the prettiest fight I ever saw. My company was in front of your line, that formed on the level pasture field after coming out of the timber north of the mansion.

From a paper by Sergeant W. A. McHenry, Company C, Eighth Illinois, read at the same reunion, I make the following extracts:

Of all the organisations in the Confederate Army I think the Eighth Illinois remembers most vividly Colonel Mosby. And I have often wondered what kind of a man he was that he could give us such warm receptions. I can assure you that when we were ordered into his field of operations there were no stragglers—it was just as dangerous in rear as in front. Our communications were cut and there was no other alternative than to fight our way to our destination and return. In the fall of 1864 we were encamped at Rectortown for a short time, from which we took side excursions to the various receptions.

One was with Captain Lincoln in command of six companies of our regiment. You will remember we went to Middleburg, thence up the pike to Upperville. We had no more than left Middleburg when it became apparent that we needed skirmishers in rear and flanks as well as in front. And those in rear felt like keeping as far in front as possible so that the zip zap might not reach them. It was not long before it was dangerous to get too far to the front, as you could see Mosby's gallant chargers getting ready to wipe up the dust with us. However, it was willed to be otherwise.

I take the following from Dr. Hard's history of the regiment: Lieutenant Clapp with Company K in advance held their ground against great odds as long as they could, and finally fell back, giving away to the right and left to let Lieutenant Corbet charge the enemy with his squadron, consisting of Companies C and B. Meanwhile, about one hundred and ten men charged the advance in impetuous style, but the gallant and steady bearing of Captain Wing's squadron, Companies G and H, saved our men from any damage. Captain Wing and Lieutenant De-Lancy, of Companies G and H, both reserved the fire of their commands until the enemy came up, and then poured in a well-concentrated volley.

Just then Captain Berry came up with his Company L, and with a well-directed volley sent the enemy flying, and joined Captain Wing in the headlong pursuit after the Confederates. It soon became a general scramble to pick up prisoners. After the forces became scattered, a number of the enemy tried to escape through a lane in the field at a large house, but our forces were upon them before they could get the gate open and they were captured. Thinking that we had gained honour enough for one day, we wended our way toward camp at Rectortown across the fields. . . .

I have mentioned these few receptions that Colonel Mosby and his men gave us because they are familiar to me. Other comrades might give many more and I presume that Colonel Mosby and his men might give us accounts of meeting us at other times when it would not sound so well on our side. But I am willing to risk that they will say that we never showed the white feather in their front and we can say with equal truth that we considered that to meet Mosby and his men at close range meant certain death. . . . . We are very sorry that Colonel Mosby could not be here with us. It had been arranged to give him a warm reception, not, however, that kind that he gave us forty-one years ago in Virginia, but a soldier's welcome.

CHAPTER 12

Drawing Lots For Life

On August 17, 1864, General Sheridan reported to General Grant:

> Mosby has annoyed me and captured a few wagons. We hanged one and shot six of his men yesterday.

And again on August 19 he reported:

> Guerrillas give me great annoyance, but I am quietly disposing of numbers of them.

And again on August 22:

> We have disposed of quite a number of Mosby's men.

On October 29, 1864, Colonel Mosby reported to General Lee:

> During my absence from my command the enemy captured six of my men near Front Royal. These were immediately hanged by order, and in the presence of General Custer. They also hanged another lately in Rappahannock. It is my purpose to hang an equal number of Custer's men whenever I capture them.

This dispatch was endorsed by General Lee as follows:

> I have directed Colonel Mosby through his adjutant (who delivered the dispatch to him) to hang an equal number of Custer's men in retaliation for those executed by him.

Which instructions were "cordially approved" by the Secretary of War.

The foregoing is from the Records of the Rebellion. They are the cold recitals of history. I submit below some of the "reading between the lines," some of the actual human experience of passion, pathos and suffering which made the history of those days.

One morning in the summer of 1864 a detachment from Mosby's command attacked a body of Federals at Front Royal, Virginia. Through some unaccountable mistake of our scouts, what we took for a foraging party turned out—after we had gotten into them—to be a heavy column of cavalry and artillery. In cutting our way out of the desperate situation, a Federal officer was run down by the wayside; and in that delirium, the delirium born of tasting of blood which often catches men on such occasions, some of the Rangers fired shots at the prostrate man as they passed him, some of which took effect. He survived, however—at least long enough to give his comrades some account of the affair, which was made an excuse for what it now appears had already been determined upon as a policy toward us.

General Custer had six of our men, who were captured at that time, executed under circumstances which, as they were narrated to us, seemed unnecessarily cruel. They were led through the streets of Front Royal with ropes around their necks—one poor fellow, named Long, led before the very eyes of his mother pleading for mercy for her boy—and hanged like dogs upon a hill upon the outskirts of the village. Upon one of their bodies left swinging by the roadside was this placard:

> This shall be the fate of all of Mosby's men.

This was practically an unfurling of the black flag against our command; and, as a matter of fact, was followed by the summary execution of several others of our comrades who happened to fall into the power of General Custer; notably, the execution of young Ab. Willis—an account of which is thus given by an eyewitness:

> After capturing him they selected a spot where stood a tall, slender white-oak sapling. Man after man ascended to the top, until their weight bore it to the ground, where they held it firm while they pinioned his arms behind him and placed a halter around his neck. Then making the halter fast to the extreme end of the sapling, at a given signal they simultaneously relinquished their hold, when he could be seen swinging back and forth, until the sapling had spent its force, his lifeless body dangling in the branches close to its trunk.

When cut down he had a placard on his breast saying:

Hung in retaliation for a Union soldier *said* to have been killed by one of Mosby's men.

For the protection of his men, as well as for the vindication of his position as an officer of the Confederate Army, it became necessary for Colonel Mosby to resort to that last recourse of war, the *lex talionis*.

Many Federal soldiers were captured by us during the weeks that followed, and with the exception of some who happened to fall into the hands of relatives or special friends of the murdered men, under circumstances that precluded interference by our officers, they were all sent back to the Confederate authorities as prisoners of war. Colonel Mosby deferred his contemplated reprisal until a sufficient number from *Custer's own command* should be captured to vindicate upon them our honour and dignity without making Colonel Mosby chargeable with wanton cruelty.

After a while we returned from a raid into the Shenandoah Valley with twenty-six of Custer's men; and it was determined to select six from among them to placate the *Manes* of our dead comrades—and this was to be done by lot.

Accordingly, one bright morning, at Rectortown the prisoners were drawn up in line, heavily guarded, and informed of the ordeal that awaited them. God grant that His sun may never shine upon another such scene!

As the adjutant read the order, reciting the sad facts that led up to it, and declaring the dreadful climax that faced us, his solemn tones were more than once interrupted by emotion. The poor fellows had been putting the best face they could upon the prospect of a long imprisonment, and were chatting and jesting with some heart. I leave the reader to imagine the awful change that passed along the devoted line as they realised the import of the adjutant's words.

Our own men, too, were scarcely less affected. The prisoners had been in our company a day or two, and, as was always the case after the first embarrassment of capture had passed, quite pleasant relations had been established between them and us. We had ridden together, laughed and talked, and divided our rations and tobacco with them; and indeed between some of them and us quite a feeling of comradeship existed. The precipitation of the present state of affairs was a shock to all of us.

I saw the eyes of more than one Ranger fill with tears, and dear old Harry Hatcher—the man who had led Company A in most of its desperate charges and whom Colonel Mosby has with his own hand written down in history as "*the bravest of the brave*"—actually wept like a child.

There were twenty-six little slips of paper placed in a hat, upon six of which were numbers. The hat was then to be passed along the line of the prisoners and from it each was to draw a slip. The men who should draw the *numbered* ones were doomed.

My station was at the farthest end of the line from that at which the grim Ranger with the hat started upon his ominous errand. As each man stretched his hand and drew his lot, one could read one of the most pathetic chapters in human experience. The hard-featured, bronzed old veterans reached for the fateful slips with an appearance of stolid indifference which did not change whether a blank or a number was withdrawn. The bright-faced, hopeful young men, to whom life was sweet, met the test with expressions of keen appreciation of its import, which changed to glad relief, dull despair, or manly resignation as they eagerly looked at their tickets, while some, alas,—and not all youths,—had scarcely nerve to stand the strain, and broke down utterly when their blood-shot eyes caught sight of the fatal numbers.

I was specially interested in three of them who stood near me. Two of them were drummer-boys—mere lads—whom it seemed hard indeed to subject to such a death. In fact, an appeal was made to Colonel Mosby in their behalf, but he did not feel that it would be just to the others to discriminate. Perhaps he thought that there could be no gradation in such a savage phase of war. Perhaps he recalled the pink and white faces of his own little lads who had been executed at Front Royal. The third was a handsome young lieutenant of artillery whose name was Brewster, I think. He was a gentleman, intelligent, refined, courteous; and had won the goodwill of all of us. One feature of his case which particularly interested us was that he met that morning for the first time since the beginning of the war, his brother, who was a major in the commissary department, and had a few days before been captured out of a different command on this side of the mountains. You can understand that there was one heart beside his own that beat more rapidly as the hat approached him, and held fast its throbbing while he tried his fate; and, believe me, there were many who shared his brother's joy as the pure white scrap of paper was exposed.

But what of the little drummer-boys?

One of them stood dazed throughout it all. The other broke out in piteous lamentations which even yet sometimes ring in my ears. Now he would bewail, in heart-rending tones, his poor old mother whose only support he said he was, and who was awaiting in her far-away cottage the coming home that would never be; now he would call in most pitiful terms upon the great and good God who sat beyond the bright skies. As the hat drew near his cries became more piteous, his prayers more importunate, more hysterical.

It has reached him; he sobs. He lifts his eyes to heaven. "O God, spare me!" He stretches forth his hand—"Precious Jesus, pity me!" He reaches into the hat—"Merciful God!" He withdraws it; looks— "Damn it, ain't I lucky!" he cries, as he leaps up, strikes his feet together, and fillips the paper to the ground.

I cannot describe the revulsion of feeling that shocked us all.

But our rising indignation was cut short by infinite pity as his poor little companion drew from the hat the last fatal number, and fell to the ground in a heap as if a bullet had gone to his vitals.

This last result seemed horrible. He was scarcely in his teens. Surely such a sacrifice to the God of War must be averted. Could men, brave men, consent to this?

Wait! While our officers were consulting and importuning the colonel, a whispered conference was going on among the prisoners who had escaped the draft. And now, out of the very arms of his brother, who had just received him back from death as it were, the artillery officer stepped forward and said that, at his instance, his fellows had agreed to submit to another draft for the selection of a substitute for the lad, if we would consent.

Inasmuch as the proposition was volunteered by them, Colonel Mosby acceded, and preparations were forthwith made for the second ordeal. Again the hat passed down the line of heroes (for did not this sacrifice vindicate their claim to be such?) until—the irony of fate!— it reached the young lieutenant, who this time drew the marked slip.

I believe he stood it better than the rest of us. He simply asked opportunity to write a farewell letter to his wife and that it and his watch and ring should be sent through the lines to her. I think I never saw Colonel Mosby more affected than when he gave him the assurance that they should be sent at the first opportunity.

And then the arrangements were made for departure, the last farewells were said; and the doomed little band were marched away toward the mountains by their executioners.

How they were taken back to the Valley, and, in the solemn hours

A. E. RICHARDS
CITY ATTORNEY OF LOUISVILLE, KENTUCKY

of the night, from the limb of a great oak that until recently still stood beside the highway beyond Berryville, had their brave lives choked and shot out of them, is a matter of history which I need not repeat.

Did I say "they." There was at least one exception. This, too, is recorded in the pages of history, else one might charge my imagination with a strain after poetic justice.

As the sad party was crossing the Blue Ridge it met Captain Mountjoy of Company D returning from the Valley with another batch of prisoners from Custer's cavalry. In the course of the interview between the parties Lieutenant Brewster recognised a Masonic emblem upon the person of Captain Mountjoy, and gave him the "signal of distress" of that fraternity. To this our captain promptly responded, and took the responsibility of substituting one of his own captives in the place of his brother Mason, whom he brought on back with him.

It is needless to say that the rest of us applauded his action and greeted the lieutenant with sincere rejoicing. Colonel Mosby, however, reprimanded his favourite officer most severely for interfering with the decrees of fate, declaring his "command was no Masonic lodge." But I believe in my heart that it was only for the sake of discipline, and that his secret satisfaction was as great as ours.

Then, too, one of the condemned men made a desperate "strike for liberty" as his would-be executioner approached him to perform the "last sad offices" upon him, and succeeded in escaping in the darkness. I never learned whether this was the "substitute" or not; but let us believe it was, and that the "Fates" thus vindicated themselves from human interference.

Chapter 13

A Lively Ride Before Breakfast

Hugh Waters and I lived at his mother's home, about one mile south of Middleburg, a home just on the far edge of a large body of timber, which extended more than half way to the village. On the east side of her farm, and within a quarter of a mile of the house, ran the road from the Plains to Middleburg; and about the same distance to the west was the road from Salem (now Marshall) to Middleburg.

During the winter of 1864-5 there was a heavy fall of snow, which laid on the ground for some weeks and became covered with a thick crust. One cold night Hugh and I camped out in a rock-brake on his mother's farm, within a hundred yards of the Plains road; but the rocky cliff, at the foot of which we made our bed and tied our horses, and the clump of trees about it hid us from sight from the road. Indeed, we relied on the cold weather to keep our enemies at home, and the warning which we would get from the sounds of their travelling over the snow if they should have the enterprise to turn out.

We slept the sleep of unconscious innocence. The next morning about sunrise we were awakened by Mrs. Waters's negro man, Edmund, with the information that a large body of Yankees had marched along the Plains road a short while before, had called at the house to pay their respects to us and gone on toward Middleburg. It is needless to say that we made a very hasty toilet and got away from there in short order. We left Edmund to take charge of our bedding and hurried off toward Middleburg to take observations.

When we reached the Salem road we met Lieut. Font Beattie, who also had been induced to rise early by a party scouting uncomfortably near his quarters. He assumed responsibility for our movements, and led us on toward Middleburg in pursuit of information and, incidentally, adventure. Well, we succeeded in finding both.

We followed the road to the top of a hill on the edge of the town and saw the streets filled with blue-coated cavalry. At the same time the wearers of the blue coats saw us, and hastened to exchange greetings with us. We felt, however, that salutes at a distance were all that the occasion required of us, and retired with some precipitancy in the direction whence we came. The Yankees insisted on closer associations and pressed their attentions with great ardour.

We were making good our courteous purpose to leave them in possession of that neighbourhood, and were getting out on the Salem road in fine shape, when we rose on a little hill about a half mile out. And there, coming toward us, and not more than two hundred yards away, was a road full of Yankee cavalry! On each side of us was an abominable stone fence, of the sort, you know, which very few horses will jump. As we pulled up, the enemy in front commenced firing. It did look like a hopeless situation.

But Beattie was not the man to give up as long as there was daylight between him and the toils. A short distance behind us we had passed a gap in the stone fence which would let us into a field and to the big woods beyond it; and our leader turned us back to it, just as some of the Salem party sprang up the road toward us. The pursuers from Middleburg were scarcely within good range as the last one of us jumped through the gap, but a good shot "gave pause" to the foremost of them. Somehow, both parties of the Yankees found ways through the fence too; and in a moment the situation was this—we three running by a straight line for the woods, and Yankees to the left oblique, and Yankees to the right oblique, making after us with absolute assurance of running us down. If we should make the woods, they were barren of foliage and almost as open as the field. But just within them was a hill, and over it—well, the Yankees didn't know what. And neither did we, for that matter; but the religion of a Mosby man was never to throw up his hands as long as he could stick to his horse, for he trusted much to that "chapter of accidents" which is in every book of fate. It contained deliverance for us that morning.

The snow was at least six inches deep and, as I stated, was covered with a thick crust, and it greatly affected the speed of all parties. I was riding a Yankee horse, quite recently "acquired." I was soon dismayed to find that he was falling behind my companions; and, what was worse, he did not seem to care if he was. The shooting and yelling and my vigorous application of the spur made no impression on him. Whether it was actual leg-weariness, or sheer brute stubbornness, or the aroused affinity for his old companions, I do not know. But the cold fact is that when Beattie and Waters rode into the woods, my horse had slowed down into a walk and was a considerable distance behind them.

The pursuers were then scarcely a hundred yards from me, and were calling to me in jeering tones, between shots, "Come out of that overcoat, Johnnie!" and other like pleasant salutations. The truth was that I had on a splendid new overcoat—one of the fruits of the Greenback raid—and their remarks about it made me feel sick. I verily believe that it was my salvation at that moment, though. The heartless fellows were close enough to see that it was an unusually fine one, glistening with brass buttons and some other garish trimming, and they evidently took me for an officer. Now, do not lose sight of that, for I think it was the key to what followed.

As my companions were riding away over the hill in the woods, and I realised that my horse had flunked on me, in my desperation I involuntarily called out to them to stop and take me up. They wheeled and commenced firing.

The Yankees doubtless heard me call to them to stop, without distinguishing what I said about taking me up. They saw my horse drop into a quiet, dignified pace, and did not understand that it was not due to my management of him. So, attributing to the "officer" a most magnificent nerve, they assumed that I was now rallying my men from the ambush into which we had decoyed them. The manly response of Beattie and Waters clinched the matter. And I pledge you my word of honour that the whole Federal party pulled up within almost touching distance of me and let me march in a quiet walk over the hill. I soon came up with my friends and we rode away unpursued.

CHAPTER 14

The Hamilton Fight

One of the results of the great Burning Raid made by the Federals was the destruction of our stores of provender. As will be readily understood, our horses had to be kept in tip-top condition, and to secure supplies was a prime necessity.

Near the centre of Loudoun County was, and still is for that matter, a rich section known as the Quaker settlement, occupied by Quakers, and even in war times successfully farmed by that thrifty sect. They were of course non-combatants, but they were, with few exceptions, loyal to the United States Government; indeed, I may say, that with most of them their loyalty amounted to offensive partisanship. Their barns and store-houses were full, and this was so obviously a provision of Providence for our necessities that Colonel Mosby could not hesitate to appropriate it.

A detachment of something like a hundred and fifty of our men were sent up into this Egypt to impress wagons and haul the golden grain away to our homes in southern Loudoun and Fauquier. Those were merry days of the ingathering of our crops. The spring was early and the weather fine, and the harvesting progressed most satisfactorily. Through the days the boys rode from farm to farm, and their happy songs lilted over the hills. I think those staid old Quakers must have had their patience tried by the incessant plaints about Katie Wells and Gentle Annie, which the fresh spring breezes bore to their unaccustomed ears.

But there were other things which vexed their righteous souls more than this, I doubt not, and even more than the loss of their corn. The men were billeted, in squads of five or six, around among the farmhouses, and they had to be fed on Union victuals. But I must do our entertainers the justice to testify that they suffered with great grace, and if they kept back anything better than they set before us they were pretty high old livers when all to themselves at home. I think the motherly instincts of the good housewives stirred with a sweet comfort as they saw the boys enjoy their pies and jams; and I am sure that the eyes of the demure maidens flashed quite naturally as they served apples, nearly as rosy as their cheeks, to the soldier boys, who did not fail to give some expression of their appreciation.

While all on the surface was so lovely, we knew that these same gentle folk were in close touch with the Federal forces across the Potomac, and that the "grapevine telegraph" kept their friends constantly advised of the situation. We knew, too, that their devotion to peace would not deter them from any kind of cooperation with their said friends which would secure our early retirement to the quiet rest of prison life, or even the more perfect peace which prevails where the wicked cease from troubling—them. So, in anticipation of some such movement, every morning the men were rendezvoused at Hamilton. If the reports from our scouts and pickets were favourable, they were dispersed to pursue the duties of their new vocation.

One morning they were not disbanded; the expected was about to happen. Hamilton is a small village situated about the centre of the Quaker district on the turnpike from Snicker's Gap, in the Blue Ridge Mountains, to Washington. Harper's Ferry, which was then occupied by the Federals, lies less than twenty miles off toward the north. The road from that point into Loudoun passes for twelve miles through a narrow valley which is bounded by the Blue Ridge on the west, and absolutely shut off from the rest of the county on the east by a steep and rugged range called the Short Hill. There is no practicable passage over it between the Potomac and its southern end, where nestles the little village of Hillsborough.

Through this valley a Federal force could come without any risk of discovery until they should emerge into "God's country" at the mountain village, thence broad highways led into middle Loudoun. One highway, scarcely six miles long, stretched over high hills and through deep dales to Hamilton; and another to Purcellville on the turnpike, a couple of miles west of Hamilton. This morning our scouts reported that a squad of them had found a force of Federals at Hillsborough the previous afternoon, and that the Yankees had chased them several miles and then returned between the Hills; that the force appeared to consist of a considerable wagon train escorted by a regiment of cavalry, and that it was then moving out toward Purcellville.

A wagon train with a cavalry escort was just in our line of business, and the men fell all into a flutter. But Colonel Mosby was a classical scholar, and the thing looked so inviting on its face that it reminded him of the "*Greeks bearing gifts*." So the command was moved back to Lincoln, a mile or so south of the pike, while scouts were sent out to take observations.

Sure enough, they found the wagon train moving quietly down the road toward Hamilton, with its escort of cavalry in close attendance. These latter seemed very jealous of our too near approach, and opened fire at long range upon our party of scouts, and chased them back a short distance toward Lincoln. But the sharp eyes of our men had discovered that the innocent looking wagons were modern reproductions of the Trojan horse, and every one of them was loaded up with infantry. Upon their reporting to Colonel Mosby, he sent them back to the pike to move along their flank and keep him advised of their movements. I wish to put on record the names of that scouting party, for they did good service that day—keeping in touch with the Federals' left flank all the way from Purcellville down, and getting touched up pretty lively themselves whenever they stuck their heads over the hills or emerged from the skirting woods. They were Bob Eastham, Jim Burgess, Towny Vandevanter, Will Vandevanter, John Adams, and just before their final service were joined by Manning and Jim Wiltshire, the latter of whom took charge of them and brought on the collision.

The road out of Hamilton takes a very eccentric course toward Lincoln. Leaving the turnpike about the middle of the former village it runs southeasterly, past open lots and farmhouses and then through woods, for perhaps a half mile; then turns abruptly westward past William Tavenner's field for about two hundred yards, when it turns again at a right angle, over a hill and passing another body of woods, breaks away southwesterly toward Lincoln. Hills and dales and abrupt turns mark its whole course.

The body of woods last mentioned drops away from the road into a little dell; and into this our men were moving. In the meanwhile, Wiltshire's scouting party kept in sight of the Federals until the head of the column was well into Hamilton. Then it advanced through the hollows and behind the woods on the Lincoln road toward the village until it came in front of the Yankee cavalry which had turned out into the Lincoln road. Our scouts were then near the outskirts of the village some distance north of William Tavenner's. The infantry were

HARRY T. SINNOTT
COMPANY B

unloading and deploying into the open lot south of the town. These sights made Wiltshire's boys uneasy, and they manifested a disposition to "report again to Colonel Mosby." But the leader had already received full instructions and he held them to their position in the road, even after the Yankee cavalry had opened fire upon them and broken into a charge. They had gotten within pistol range before our boys got word to "go," and the racing began.

In making the sharp turn around William Tavenner's orchard, John Adams's horse ran against a tree and threw him. Before he could get up the Yankees were on him. Over the hill our decoys came, the Yankees close behind them, past the woods in which we lay. Many of the fleetest chasers had gotten past us when we rushed out of the woods into the road, which was now crowded with them in hot pursuit of our boys. It seems to me that they might have expected something of the kind; but the fact is that they were so surprised that they made no show of a fight, but turned and rushed back with all the energy they had. This is proved by the fact that but one of our men, Captain Manning, was scratched by them at that point. John Chew and Binford were shot a half mile closer in toward the village, and young Keith was killed by the infantry's fire on the outskirts of the town.

Captain Glascock was in command of our men. In the arrangement for the onset he had placed his own command, Company D, in position, and the section of A which was attached to him was moving back deeper into the woods when Wiltshire's party came dashing past. The sight of the Yankees close after them raised a question in our minds, and when Glascock ordered D to charge, A righted about in their tracks and rushed out on the road, tail end foremost. But either end could have properly been marked "extra hazardous." The roadway at once became congested, and some of us broke through the fence to cross the triangle of Tavenner's orchard and catch the fleeing foe on their flank. But Colonel Mosby was in the Tavenner yard and stopped us from further pursuit in that direction, because "the woods in front were full of infantry." But he did not succeed in calling off our men who had followed around the road.

They pursued the flying foe back beyond the first body of woods, until they saw the long blue line of infantry rise up from behind the hedge fence that skirted one of the village lots. As the volley rang out, our boys swayed off into the woods by the roadside, but left Keith lying dead in the road from a Minie ball which had entered his eye. When the smoke cleared away the infantry, too, were seen to be running back to the town full tilt. The citizens of Hamilton swear that they were so demoralized that they broke ranks, and some of them threw their guns away and took refuge in the cellars of the houses.

Jim Sinclair insists that he rode through the town, collected "tribute" from a Yankee soldier in the middle of the street, and rode out by another road. I think that it is admitted history in that neighbourhood that some of the Yankee cavalry spent that night on the other side of the Potomac.

We had the whole party badly whipped, but didn't know it. The War Records show that there were not less than 1,100 of them, and our numbers in the fight did not reach one hundred and thirty. Two of our men were killed, and two wounded, one of whom fell into the hands of the enemy. They had fifteen killed and seventeen captured. We could never learn how many of them were wounded, but the citizens of Hamilton say that they were not less than fifty, for several houses were appropriated for hospital purposes, and their surgeons were busy all night.

The next day this precious wagon train was paraded through Loudoun by Upperville and Middleburg and back to the Snickersville pike, where reinforcements met it. We followed it closely with anxious attention, and offering every possible inducement to that regiment of six hundred cavalry, but not once could we induce it out of the range of the infantry's guns.

We thought to ride into their flank as they crossed Goose Creek over the narrow bridge in the pike below Upperville; but their ingenuity was equal to their fears. For when we dashed upon them they had already unloaded their infantry and deployed it over the creek bluffs, so that the cavalry might cross under the cover of their Minie rifles.

Finally, as the shades of evening lengthened, we charged upon their rear at Middleburg, but achieved nothing except the glory of galloping through the streets under the admiring gaze of our sweethearts. And this was my last ride down to battle with Mosby.

CHAPTER 15

A Pair Of Scouts

Most of Mosby's men were fairly good scouts. Their constant dependence upon their observation and alertness, and the experience of the methods of the enemy, made them all more or less reliable in that line. Many of them were experts, and could run a picket or secure a countersign, or pierce to the recesses of a Yankee camp without it. But when it came to high art, Bush Underwood and John Russell were without rivals. Indeed, they did not rival each other.

Their respective spheres of operation were upon the extreme eastern and western boundaries of Mosby's Confederacy; one among the Federal camps in Fairfax and about Alexandria and Washington; the other among the moving columns and wagon-trains which traversed the lower valley of the Shenandoah.

Underwood was reared under the sombre pines of Fairfax, and he knew their forest recesses "*as seamen know the sea*." He was of a pronounced Anglo-Saxon type—almost an Albino—with an Indian's cast of features. He was cold blooded, calculating, patient; fearless, yet wary; shrewd and watchful, but dogged in pursuing his ends. He seemed to have an "instinct" for a Yankee camp or picket, and the Federal flag waved over no precincts south of the Potomac which were sacred from his invasion by night, if not by day. I have watched by his side within a few hundred yards of the Chain Bridge over the Potomac. He slept his allotted hours away as peacefully as if his mother kept vigil over him in upper Loudoun; every minute of these same hours is accentuated in my memory with the vigour of a nervous chill.

He never got rattled; but would adjust himself to an emergency, to take it in and do just the right thing, with a promptness that was instinctive. He and Jim Sinclair sat at breakfast at the Pot House. Through the open door they saw a squad of Federal cavalry ride up to the yard gate, scarcely thirty feet away. Out of the back door, down the garden path, to the stable they flew. As the Yankees got around to the stable-yard gate, they jumped the fence, without bits in their horses' mouths, and scurried across the fields under the stimulus of a fire at pretty close range. When they got out of sight and straightened themselves up, they started out to do some hunting on their own account. The column out of which their visitors had come was moving along the highway toward Middleburg. They would cross Goose Creek at Benton's ford; and to this point, where something interesting was liable to be offered them, Bush and Jim pushed.

As they warily approached the ford from the woods, around an abrupt bluff which skirted the road, they saw the van-guard, which had already crossed, disappear around a bend on the Middleburg side of the creek. But within ten yards of them two Yankee officers sat upon their horses, which were still slaking their thirst.

"Surrender! and come here quick," Bush called in those cold, deadly tones of his.

The Yankees looked up into the muzzles of a pair of revolvers; then they threw their anxious gaze back down the road along which their followers were even then due. Bush understood the look and appreciated all that it meant.

"At the word 'three' we fire. One—two—" Well, you ought to have seen those horses scramble up the bank—and within full sight and inside of a hundred yards of their approaching friends. Before these latter could take in the situation, the officers were around the bluff and over the hills and safely away on a trip to Richmond, under an escort which gave them distinguished attention.

Lieutenant Russell was an Irish boy, scarcely eighteen years old, who had been reared among the environs of Berryville. In the idle hours spent in hunting and fishing he had acquired a familiarity with the immediate neighbourhood, and a general knowledge of the country. It was an open country; and if the Yankees once caught sight of you, it was a run to the home base for one party or the other—in their case it being the nearest camp, and in ours the east bank of the Shenandoah. There was no cover for the sleuth; it was only the "bold, bad man" who could hope for glory in scouting that field.

John had had no advantages of education, but he was gifted with great shrewdness and nerve, and an instinctive knowledge of men. He had the Celtic *genius* which, either discarding all intermediate processes of reasoning or working them out in his sub-consciousness, simply saw conclusions and went for them, as a matter of course. For instance, if Berryville were in the possession of the Yankees and he wished to enter the town, the only reasoning thing that he would do would be to locate the pickets, so to know where *not* to go; and his next act of consciousness would be to wake up at the point that he wanted to reach. If one should ask him how he came there, he could never tell. I have pumped him assiduously for details of such movements, he has travailed in soul to give forth to me; and yet nothing definite and tangible has ever come of our joint efforts.

One evening Companies C and E, under Lieutenant Colonel Wm. H. Chapman, crossed the Shenandoah and bivouacked in Champ Shepherd's woods about three miles east of Berryville. Chapman learned that Sheridan had occupied Berryville that day, and that Torbert's cavalry was somewhere south of there. General Kershaw's force of Confederates had approached the town from the direction of Winchester, and his advance posts were located within speaking distance of Sheridan's pickets. The situation was promising and Chapman was entirely willing to add something to its gaiety. He sent Russell and a couple of companions into Berryville for details.

The first definite information that I can get locates John's scouting party in Doctor Neill's stable-yard, about in the centre of the town, after all honest men had gone to bed. From the stable-yard a narrow, rocky lane about two hundred yards long led to the Millwood pike, which opened into the main street of the town (or the Winchester pike), less than two hundred yards more north of the lane. From the front of Neill's house, which is now widely known as the hospitable residence of Hon. Marshall McCormick, a beautiful lawn swept down to the main street. Leaving his companions with his horse behind a convenient outhouse to await his signal, Russell crept up to the rear of Dr. Neill's house and gave the tap on the chamber window which answered for the doctor's night call.

"Who is that?" whispered the doctor, after raising the window with what seemed to John to be an unusual degree of caution.

"It's me—Russell. What's the news?" answered John, with less regard to carefulness than the doctor thought appropriate to the occasion.

"Hus-s-h! Go away from here!" the doctor faltered back. "There is a Yankee picket in front of my house and the reserve is resting on my front porch."

But the insistent visitor stayed, risking a collapse on the doctor's part, until he learned that Sheridan had moved his troops back a mile on the Charles Town pike, and that Kershaw's advance guard was camped in Boxwell's woods on the hill to the left of the town, and just then he heard a horseman ride up the lane into the stable-yard and call "Halloa!" This new arrival was to the relief of the doctor, but it introduced a new feature into the situation which called for John's prompt investigation and he went straight to meet it. It was so dark that only the outlines of the horseman could be made out, but John took for granted that he was a Yankee and assumed that he concluded the same about himself. Our friend, of course, held "the drop on him."

"Well, what can I do for you?" he asked in his most blarneyish tones, and with a touch of Irish brogue which prevented his speech from betraying him.

"I have lost my way and want to find the Millwood pike." He had just left the Millwood pike to turn into that lane. But John did not think it advisable to tell him so—not yet awhile.

"Why, what in the world do you want to find the Millwood pike this time of night for? You had better put up here with the rest of us."

"No, I must hurry on. I have dispatches for General Torbert, who is somewhere between Millwood and White Post, and it is important that he should get them. My four comrades are waiting for me down the hill here."

"Oh, that's another matter," graciously answered John. "A couple of friends and myself are here pie-rooting around, and we will be glad to show you to the pike." And he gave the whistle that brought the other boys out with his horse.

They moved off down the lane a piece, when a new thought seemed to come to Russell. He had ridden in front of the Yankee, and turning his horse so as to come close along side of the courier, he said:

"Say, pardner, let me see those dispatches."

"Of course I can't," answered the Yankee.

"Oh, yes, you can," was insisted, and enforced with the argument of the ready revolver. Of course there was nothing to do but to hand over the precious papers.

The escort waiting down at the road were quietly advised of the situation and promptly responded to John's invitation to a midnight ride to Chapman's camp. The dispatches proved to be of such importance that Colonel Chapman himself immediately set out for Kershaw's camp with them. It was reported that they advised Torbert of the location of Kershaw's wagon-train, and that Fitz Lee, who should escort it, had gotten separated from it for a few hours, and instructed the dashing Federal cavalry leader how to cut it off and capture it.

The departure of Colonel Chapman left his brother Sam, the fighting parson, in command of our squadron. With that knowledge the boys "felt a presentiment" that something was going to happen. And they were not disappointed.

The next morning Captain Chapman moved the command toward the storm-centre. Keeping under cover of the hills between which bold streams ran to the river, he neared the Millwood pike about a mile south of Berryville. When he emerged from a little valley about a couple of hundred yards from it, they saw it blue with Federal cavalry, moving from the direction of Millwood. It looked as though there was a regiment of them.

The Reverend Chapman considered that Mosby's men were organised for fighting purposes; that whenever Providence presented an opportunity for a fight it was his simple duty to embrace it and trust the Lord for consequences. So he incontinently pitched into what was in front of him. His impetuous and unexpected charge sent the Yankees a-flying. Most of them broke across country toward Winchester. Our men followed them nearly a mile, and captured seventy-five or eighty of them, besides quite a number who were shot and left on the fields. We lost four of our own best men, however, Jarman and Iden were killed outright, and Lieutenant Frank Fox and Clay Adams were mortally wounded. Others were slightly hurt.

Captain Sam himself was a relentless pursuer. When last seen approaching Gold's woods four Yankees were in front of him. He returned eventually with four *horses*.

In the meanwhile, the command of our men devolved on Lieutenants Russell and Font Beattie. The emergency was now one which called for a high order of talent. Sheridan's forces were less than two miles away to the north. The party which we had attacked was evidently Torbert's advance returning from Millwood at the south; and the river—our blessed home base—was not less than four miles away. The nearest practicable crossing was Shepard's ford, and for that point Russell struck out.

But Torbert's main body had been stirred up by the sounds of the fight, and had no doubt been advised of the situation by the fugitives who had escaped from it. And so the trip of our boys to the river was

W. L. Dunn, M.D.
Surgeon Forty-third Battalion Virginia Cavalry

soon made interesting by the close attendance on them of Torbert's cavalry. Over the neighbouring hills regiments and regiments of it were seen moving also toward the river. Every now and then some of their skirmishers would dash up near enough to burn some powder at us, but the range was too long, or their nerves were unstrung, so that the shots served only to excite our men. They recognised that the Yankees were manoeuvring to get to the river first in overwhelming numbers and just quietly gather them in. They looked to Russell as their Moses; but, like the children of Israel, too, were much disposed to murmur at him for leading them into the hopeless situation.

This pushed the poor boy to his limit. Exhausting his Irish suavity in soothing and nerving the boys, he at the same time had his combative side on the strain to beat those Yankees to the river and keep them from closing in on him. The interval between the lines was scarcely three hundred yards when we rose the river bluff in Burchell's field a half mile above the ford. But the Yankee advance had already touched the river road, and was coming down toward Lanham's blacksmith shop, situated on the bank. And now Captain Sam's Providence intervened.

Horace Deahl and Cy. McCormick, of the Sixth Virginia Cavalry, were at this blacksmith shop, having their horses shod. Deahl happened to be mounted when the blue file of the van-guard showed itself approaching the shop, and being somewhat of the sentiments of the boy at the circus who "killed snakes wherever he saw them," jumped right at them. Perhaps the temerity of the act took them by surprise, or suggested that he had good backing, and they gave way before him. When they saw him dash by them and fly up the river road alone they hastened back to the shop. Poor Cy. had mounted and started in the other direction when he ran up against one of those detestable gates which even yet obstruct that river road. His efforts to open it from horseback were futile and he dismounted and took to the bushes. But his career as a bushman was soon brought to an end by his attentive friends, the enemy.

All this took precious moments, during which our boys were dashing down the road to Shepard's ford; and when the Yankees came up, our rear-guard was joyfully pulling for the shore. We escaped without the loss of a man and brought out nearly a hundred prisoners and horses. So John's character as a successful Moses was re-established for all time.

Chapter 16
My Boy Frank

Frank and I were foster-brothers in the sense that we drew our earliest sustenance from the same abundant fount. In the division of my father's estate, which took place while we both still wore short skirts, he was allotted to me for my very own property. We continued to be playmates, sharing our childish joys, as well as other things which came to us, not excepting sorrows growing out of occasional switchings at the hands of our respective maternals for escapades into which he loyally followed me. It will be hard for many of the present generation to understand that while as we grew in years, our intimacy was perfect, the relation of master and slave was strictly maintained. Perhaps the key note to the situation was struck by the wit who defined a perfect alliance as being one in which *"one party loves and the other consents to be loved."*

In early youth Frank and I were separated; he to remain with his mother at my grandfather's home in Clarke County, and I to spend the years of my tutelage at Warrenton, in Fauquier. Our friendship was put in repair every summer during the vacations which I spent at the patriarchal headquarters.

In the fall of 1863 my mother thought that she detected some symptoms about me which made her uneasy, and which she thought could be best dealt with by my stern old grandfather. Accordingly I was sent to his home.

It would be beside my story to tell of the quiet pleasures of that winter at the old homestead—all the dearer to memory now, because they are the last that it bears of the dead and gone Virginia plantation life. Not less than two dozen of the negroes remained there; the crops of the year had been abundant and were harvested without interference; and the threshings and corn-huskings made honest work for the days, while the notes of the fiddle and the banjo which floated from the "quarters" at night softened the hours around the glowing fires "up at the house."

But with the quickening of spring the impulse to hie away to the army mastered me. I had not spent many nights under the hay-stack when I rode in to breakfast one morning and found Frank waiting for me. He had literally run away from the freedom which was his any day that he chose to claim it within the Federal lines, to the joys of being a slave to his young master. But his heart was in his service, and, like his master, he still regards the days when he was an honorary member of Mosby's command as the happiest of his life.

His employment consisted mostly in following me around, when at home, and attending to the horses; and especially in keeping the spare horses out of the way of Yankee raiders. This latter service brought him some adventures. The Yankees could seldom get very close to our vicinity without some notice of their approach; and then Frank's duty would be to rush the horses to the neighbouring mountains. Some times this notice would precede their coming by the briefest intervals; and more than once Frank crossed the creek, which seemed to be the accepted danger line, under the fire of his pursuers. Rather an anomalous kind of "run-away nigger," was it not?

In some way—I never discovered how—he came into the possession of a pistol. He wore it around on extra occasions, in holster to belt, just like a sure-enough soldier, and no doubt he felt himself to be one. But we all of course regarded it as a very harmless amusement and only chaffed him about the promptness with which he would not use it when he should get a chance.

One day the Yankees were running him and some white boys, who also were trying to save horses, pretty close. One Yankee ran a long way ahead of the others—that sometimes happened when there seemed to be no danger in the pursued. Whether Frank was really impeded by his led-horse or oppressed with a sense of the possession of that pistol, he fell behind; and when he pulled out of the creek his pursuer was entering it on the other side. The boy turned and cocked his revolver.

"You'd better go back, mister; 'cause you'll fall in de water when I shoot."

The Yankee promptly pulled back, in the light of this unexpected development, and cried:

"You're a damned fool, boy!"

"Yes, I knows I is. An' dat's what makes me goin' to shoot."

That closed the incident, and each pursued his respective course.

★★★★★★

The Reverend Frank Hall, of Cedarville, Virginia, is now, (1907), a gray-headed old grandfather. He insists that he is indebted to his early associations with me for the fact that he entered the ministry; but he respectfully refrains from saying whether my influence wooed him into the paths of peace, or he was moved to enter them by my "horrible example."

We keep up our friendship of boyhood's days. He comes now and then from his home in a distant county to visit me. And what I do feel a pride in is that my white friends of his neighbourhood tell me that Frank and his children and grandchildren are, by long odds, the most respectable and reliable family of coloured people in that community.

CHAPTER 17

Eulogy of Rev. Sydnor G. Ferguson a Typical Mosby Man
(Read at the Reunion at Berryville, Va., 1904.)

Comrades: In the sweetest songs there are minor chords of sadness. Amid the joys of these reunions we are reminded that

To the Past go more dead faces,
Every year;
Come no new ones in their places,
Every year.

There can be no recruits to our brotherhood. It has been long since the last initiation was had under the blue light of burning powder and to the weird music of the battle's roar; and the ceremony can never be repeated. The years will not be many until two or three of us, perhaps, will meet and part—and Mosby's Command will be a thing of history.

Since we gathered a year ago, a representative of the very best type of our peculiar soldiery—Rev. Sydnor G. Ferguson—has passed away from us to the world of spirits. He was among the youngest, strongest, and most vigorous of us; and we reasonably hoped that it would be he who should perform the final offices of his religion for John S. Mosby Camp. But, as the sun rose on the morning of March 7, 1904, without a moment's warning, the last roll-call came to him, and promptly, calmly, manfully—as in the old days—he answered, "Here."

I do not know what excellences of a soldier Syd Ferguson did not possess. He was only a boy—eighteen years old—but he filled a man's place up full. He was brave without being rash, modest and retiring, but always ready; and his courage was of that high order which could quietly wait in the thick of dangers until the moment for action came and then would go the limit of duty. He was too sensible to be indifferent to danger, and too honest to affect bravado; but with a thorough consciousness of all that it meant, he would ride unflinchingly up to the very face of death. But I need not recall the characteristics nor recount the deeds which won him a foremost place in your esteem, my comrades—yourselves worthy judges of soldierly qualities. No more can be said for him, in this regard, than that you admired and loved him.

I had the privilege of a close intimacy with him after the war was over. Together we took up again the broken threads of studies which had been interrupted by grimmer duties; and under peaceful academic shades at Upperville, Virginia, the ties which had been welded in the fierce heat of war were riveted into an attachment which I believe will hold beyond the grave. Our paths of life then drifted far apart, and it was at rare intervals that we met. But you and I followed with glowing eyes his strong and steadily upward course in his chosen walk, and whenever we heard of the courage and consecration and success with which he fought the powers of evil, as he had fought other foes by our side, our pulses quickened and our bosoms swelled with pride, as we claimed, "He was a Mosby man."

And he was ever loyal to us. During the last few years of his life he and I got side by side again, and I know that his great heart beat for his old comrades in arms with a pathetic yearning. We filled a place in his life second only to that which his immediate family occupied. He thought much of us, he spoke much about us, and he gave to us freely of the rich "coin of His realm"—he prayed much for us. His ambition was to maintain a position of influence among us from which he might be made a blessing to us. His hope was that, as we passed down the western slope of life together and the hardness, bred of manhood's struggles and antagonisms, softened under the rays of the setting sun, the associations of early days would reassert their strength to draw his comrades with him into the paths of peace wherein he trod.

Perhaps his most notable pulpit performances of late years have been his annual sermons to old soldiers, inspired by a deep sense of the value of his religion and an intense desire that its blessings should be shared by those to whom his soul was bound by the ties of youth and common experiences of hardship and dangers. Possibly, our tender memories of him will prove more potent toward the accomplishment of his hopes than was even his bodily presence among us.

I do not know of any of all our number who more brilliantly than he has illustrated the truth that the same qualities of intelligence, nerve, and force of character which were essential to distinction in our ranks, insured influence in civil life. The world and the church have acknowledged Sydnor G. Ferguson as one of the best of them. Let us hold him in proud and loving remembrance as one of the best of us.

ALSO FROM LEONAUR
AVAILABLE IN SOFTCOVER OR HARDCOVER WITH DUST JACKET

AN APACHE CAMPAIGN IN THE SIERRA MADRE by John G. Bourke—An Account of the Expedition in Pursuit of the Chiricahua Apaches in Arizona, 1883.

BILLY DIXON & ADOBE WALLS by Billy Dixon and Edward Campbell Little—Scout, Plainsman & Buffalo Hunter, *Life and Adventures of "Billy" Dixon* by Billy Dixon and *The Battle of Adobe Walls* by Edward Campbell Little (*Pearson's Magazine*).

WITH THE CALIFORNIA COLUMN by George H. Petis—Against Confederates and Hostile Indians During the American Civil War on the South Western Frontier, *The California Column, Frontier Service During the Rebellion* and *Kit Carson's Fight With the Comanche and Kiowa Indians*.

THRILLING DAYS IN ARMY LIFE by George Alexander Forsyth—Experiences of the Beecher's Island Battle 1868, the Apache Campaign of 1882, and the American Civil War.

THE NEZ PERCÉ CAMPAIGN, 1877 by G. O. Shields & Edmond Stephen Meany—Two Accounts of Chief Joseph and the Defeat of the Nez Percé, *The Battle of Big Hole* by G. O. Shields and *Chief Joseph, the Nez Percé* by Edmond Stephen Meany.

CAPTAIN JEFF OF THE TEXAS RANGERS by W. J. Maltby—Fighting Comanche & Kiowa Indians on the South Western Frontier 1863-1874.

SHERIDAN'S TROOPERS ON THE BORDERS by De Benneville Randolph Keim—The Winter Campaign of the U. S. Army Against the Indian Tribes of the Southern Plains, 1868-9.

GERONIMO by Geronimo—The Life of the Famous Apache Warrior in His Own Words.

WILD LIFE IN THE FAR WEST by James Hobbs—The Adventures of a Hunter, Trapper, Guide, Prospector and Soldier.

THE OLD SANTA FE TRAIL by Henry Inman—The Story of a Great Highway.

LIFE IN THE FAR WEST by George F. Ruxton—The Experiences of a British Officer in America and Mexico During the 1840's.

ADVENTURES IN MEXICO AND THE ROCKY MOUNTAINS by George F. Ruxton—Experiences of Mexico and the South West During the 1840's.

AVAILABLE ONLINE AT **www.leonaur.com**
AND FROM ALL GOOD BOOK STORES

ALSO FROM LEONAUR
AVAILABLE IN SOFTCOVER OR HARDCOVER WITH DUST JACKET

LIFE IN THE ARMY OF NORTHERN VIRGINIA by *Carlton McCarthy*—The Observations of a Confederate Artilleryman of Cutshaw's Battalion During the American Civil War 1861-1865.

HISTORY OF THE CAVALRY OF THE ARMY OF THE POTOMAC by *Charles D. Rhodes*—Including Pope's Army of Virginia and the Cavalry Operations in West Virginia During the American Civil War.

CAMP-FIRE AND COTTON-FIELD by *Thomas W. Knox*—A New York Herald Correspondent's View of the American Civil War.

SERGEANT STILLWELL by *Leander Stillwell*—The Experiences of a Union Army Soldier of the 61st Illinois Infantry During the American Civil War.

STONEWALL'S CANNONEER by *Edward A. Moore*—Experiences with the Rockbridge Artillery, Confederate Army of Northern Virginia, During the American Civil War.

THE SIXTH CORPS by *George Stevens*—The Army of the Potomac, Union Army, During the American Civil War.

THE RAILROAD RAIDERS by *William Pittenger*—An Ohio Volunteers Recollections of the Andrews Raid to Disrupt the Confederate Railroad in Georgia During the American Civil War.

CITIZEN SOLDIER by *John Beatty*—An Account of the American Civil War by a Union Infantry Officer of Ohio Volunteers Who Became a Brigadier General.

COX: PERSONAL RECOLLECTIONS OF THE CIVIL WAR--VOLUME 1 by *Jacob Dolson Cox*—West Virginia, Kanawha Valley, Gauley Bridge, Cotton Mountain, South Mountain, Antietam, the Morgan Raid & the East Tennessee Campaign.

COX: PERSONAL RECOLLECTIONS OF THE CIVIL WAR--VOLUME 2 by *Jacob Dolson Cox*—Siege of Knoxville, East Tennessee, Atlanta Campaign, the Nashville Campaign & the North Carolina Campaign.

KERSHAW'S BRIGADE VOLUME 1 by *D. Augustus Dickert*—Manassas, Seven Pines, Sharpsburg (Antietam), Fredricksburg, Chancellorsville, Gettysburg, Chickamauga, Chattanooga, Fort Sanders & Bean Station.

KERSHAW'S BRIGADE VOLUME 2 by *D. Augustus Dickert*—At the wilderness, Cold Harbour, Petersburg, The Shenandoah Valley and Cedar Creek..

AVAILABLE ONLINE AT **www.leonaur.com**
AND FROM ALL GOOD BOOK STORES

www.ingramcontent.com/pod-product-compliance
Lightning Source LLC
Chambersburg PA
CBHW030229170426
43201CB00006B/153